THE QUESTION OF NATIONAL DEFENSE

Other publications by the same author:

WIRTSCHAFTSPROGNOSE
THE LIMITS OF ECONOMICS
THEORY OF GAMES AND ECONOMIC BEHAVIOR
  (with John von Neumann)
ON THE ACCURACY OF ECONOMIC
  OBSERVATIONS
ECONOMIC ACTIVITY ANALYSIS
INTERNATIONAL FINANCIAL TRANSACTIONS
  AND BUSINESS CYCLES

The Question of
National Defense

OSKAR MORGENSTERN

RANDOM HOUSE　　NEW YORK

To DOROTHY, CARL and KARIN

Preface

It requires a certain audacity to write on the question of national defense in view of the complexity and confusion of the situation. But the justification is that with some effort it is possible to look through the haze and to arrive at a clear formulation of some essentials. Some of these confirm the efforts now under way in the Defense Department, some suggest a different emphasis and still others argue for a basic reorientation. The fundamental principles which emerge show the overriding need to make our retaliatory deterrent force "invulnerable" by the choice of properly mixed systems, as is explained in Chapter 4, entitled "The Oceanic System." They also demonstrate that far greater efforts have to be made—and can be made—to protect this nation in a great diversity of ways in this, her most critical period.

Once some clarity has been brought into the picture and some basic thoughts have been formulated, the reader may feel that my conclusions are obvious. It is not my intention to try to be original; rather, I endeavor to find the truth. If it appears obvious once it has been stated properly, so much the better. But a collection of simple, true statements taken together need itself no longer be obvious. The great Danish physicist Niels Bohr once observed that there are two kinds of true statements: those which everyone agrees are true, and those, called "deep truths," whose opposites are also "deep truths." The reader will judge for himself whether this distinction is applicable to thoughts about the problems of defense and into which category my findings or those of others belong.

Besides estimating the position and strength of this country it is necessary to judge the state and development of the enemy, Russia. Here I have been guided by the fact that if the enemy's strength is overrated we are merely wasting treasure and effort, but if we underestimate him, we are forsaking our lives and the life of our country.

This book is based on a long and profound involvement with defense problems, ranging from the mathematical theory of strategy to the observation of the logistics of supply, encompassing also frequent studies of diverse weapons systems and their installations here and abroad. I have also over the years benefited from many discussions with friends in the scientific community, in government laboratories and industry. I owe special thanks to countless officers in the military services who were always ready to discuss and argue with me; though we sometimes differed, we always shared the conviction that no effort is too great to discover the direction in which our defense must develop. All these men shall remain nameless. They might not like to be associated with some of my views and judgments, and even the customary disclaimer that only the author is responsible for the content of his book might not offer them a sufficient safeguard.

Oskar Morgenstern

Princeton, N.J.

Contents

Preface   vii

1   *Prologue*   3

2   *The Threat*   9
The Fundamental Facts of the Day
The Threat
The Supreme Threat
The Cost of the Threat
Provocation
The Principle of the Imposed,
    Involuntary Reaction
Offensive and Defensive Weapons

3   *The Shield: Deterrent and Retaliatory Forces*   **27**
Stalemate or Parity
Deterrence
Retaliation
Defense and Retaliation
Retaliation Weapons
Defense of the Retaliatory Force
Mixed Systems
Methods for Decreasing the Vulnerability
    of the Retaliatory Force
Hardening Draws Fire
Early Warning
Superiority of Offensive Power Versus
    "Invulnerable" Forces

Alarms, Errors and Attacks
Geese and Meteors
The Mythical Major
Invulnerable Retaliatory Forces
    on Both Sides
A Stopgap Device

4 *The Oceanic System: The Invulnerable Force*   80
Hardening the Zone of Interior
The New Extent of Sea Power
The Early End of Known Fixed Bases
Mobile Dispersion of the Strategic Force
Political Consequences of the Oceanic System
Other Systems of Mobile Dispersal: Space
A Second Stopgap Device

5 *Attrition, Shelters and Recovery*   104
Long War or Short War?
Attrition Strategy
Attrition in Limited War
Shelters
Shelter Time
Shelter Cost
Evacuation
Recovery after Attack
Active Storage: The Sub-Economy
Recovery
Shelter Construction as a Provocation

6 *Limitation of War*   134
Is the Question Absurd?
Not a Precise Notion
Limitation of Aims
Historical Experiences
Thermonuclear Stalemate and Limited War
Weapons Systems for Limited War
The Spectrum of Nuclear Weapons

Logistics
"Police" Actions and Conventional Weapons
Negotiated Limited War

7 *Technology and Strategy: The War of
    the Laboratories* 159
The Locus of the Current War
Technological Change and Strategic Experience
Weapons Intelligence
Basic Scientific Research and
    Weapons Development
The No-Sayers
The Universities: Mainstay of Our Future
    Power?
The True Boss of Government Research

8 *Economic Power and Burden* 191
American and Russian Power
The Limit to the Burden
The "Military Worth"
Strategic Requirements
Lead Time and Productivity
The Vulnerability of the Integrated Economy
Economic Warfare
Long-Run Prospects

9 *The Security Process: Information,
    Intelligence and Secrecy* 224
What Facts Are Given?
The Dilemma of Public Information
Russian Information Policy
The Great Information Giveaway
"We Have . . ."
Intelligence
Programing for Intelligence
Secrecy for Security
Indiscretion and Betrayal

Scientists and Secrecy
Spies
Telling Our Strength: The Stockpile

10   *Negotiations and Diplomacy in
        Nuclear Parity*   261
     Wanted: A Science of Politics
     Brass Hats and Striped Pants
     Negotiations with the Enemy
     Negotiating during Nuclear Hostilities
     Techniques of the Political War
     Standard Illusions
     The End of the Struggle

11   *Epilogue*   292
     The Conventional End
     The Fascination of War

     Appendix: A Note on the Literature   297

     Index   299

THE QUESTION OF NATIONAL DEFENSE

1 Prologue

The occasions when a great nation in times of peace has had to face the possibility of sudden and total disaster have been few. Yet such is the case for the United States today; and if disaster comes for this country, it will also come for many others. This is, of course, the consequence of a deep antagonism between the Western world and the Communistic bloc, coupled with an explosive development in weaponry. In the very near future it will be possible for every point on earth to be threatened from any other point on earth—threatened with absolutely total destruction and, if it so pleases the attacker, made uninhabitable for centuries to come. Even now the entire area of the United States can come under such attack, though it would be delivered with weapons that are already obsolescent, having been superseded by others of more advanced nature and embodying new effects.

The means to cope with this situation, to neutralize this

danger are of a complexity never before encountered by statesmen and soldiers. The problems raised are harder than the
most difficult problems ever solved in science. They are much
less understood, not clearly described, not sharply defined. No
specific science exists that is designed to cope with them, and
the great, accumulated experience of the military has for the
most part become obsolete. Politically and diplomatically new
phenomena also have arisen which do not fit into any of the
well-known patterns of behavior. New threats have become
possible and are likely to be employed, to which any and every
response is fraught with extreme danger. There is no longer
much room for common sense, because there is little here that
was ever common in earlier human experience. One cannot
approach large nuclear weapons on a common-sense basis,
neither their employment nor their avoidance.

In this time of peril we find distressing confusion wherever
we look: one day we are assured that this country is so strong
that no one will dare to attack it; the next day we are told that
we are in mortal danger. Some of our military and political
leaders tell us that the plans and provisions to cope with hostile
intents are entirely satisfactory; others, equally competent and
also highly placed, deny this vigorously. The system of defense has become so complicated and involved that even some of
those who make it their profession to study it become confused
and cannot evaluate our strength in the light of the capabilities
of the enemy. The power to participate in any detail in the
processes of political and military decision vanishes to practically zero for the ordinary citizen, a serious matter for the
survival of a living and meaningful democracy. The complicated nature of the defense organization also gives rise to the
familiar belief that anything so complicated must certainly
have been thought out carefully, a view that is nurtured by
whoever is in charge of the establishment.

All this reflects the fact that the discussion and analysis of national defense are beset with immense difficulties if they attempt
to rise above the political strife of the day, the rivalries among

the services and the pursuit of special interests by the diverse armament industries. In the absence of firm guidance from established science and valid experience it is little wonder that terms are frequently employed that have the appearance of authority while behind them there is exactly nothing. "Sound military decision" and "calculated risk" are some of these phrases. The first expression is entirely empty and the second never indicates what the risk is, how it is to be measured and what the alleged calculation actually consists of. Yet they are encountered all the time, indicating perhaps a craving for precise thought and the feeling that it should be possible to arrive at generally acceptable, objective conclusions. Indeed, precision would be most welcome. We do need guidance. It can come only from combining experience with a highly developed, proven system of thought. Loose thinking is seldom permissible. It should be avoided like the plague in the discussion of our strategic-military problems since the answers we need affect our survival, individually and as a nation.

We could be farther ahead if a greater, more persistent effort had been made to develop a body of thought, a method with which to approach the novel problems which lie in a new dimension of human existence.

To illustrate: there is simply no comparison between the mental effort spent in making the first atomic bomb and the brief, superficial survey made for its use—in fact, whether it should have been used at all, when, where, under what precise conditions. In the few committee meetings held at the time no effort was made to go deeply into the matter, let alone to develop sophisticated scientific methods with which to determine a solution. Not that it could have been done easily: our ability to cope with social, political and strategic problems cannot even remotely be compared with our ever-increasing understanding and mastery of the physical world. Since the end of World War II efforts have been made to evolve some advanced military strategy doctrine; but in all fairness to the institutions set up for this purpose there has apparently been little tangible progress in that direction. Yet it is here where hard thinking would pay off most handsomely, rather than in refining and perfecting still another engineering system marginally useful in weaponry.

In the initial phases of dealing with new and difficult areas, many undefined concepts and notions such as the above-mentioned "calculated risk," "sound military decision," etc., are unavoidable and indeed necessary. But after many years and decades of use they should have assumed a more concrete meaning. Their survival in the language and literature is an indication of the lack of rigorous thinking in the field of military and national strategy. The use of a seemingly precise terminology, the talk about "calculation" when nothing is being calculated, is no way to overcome the vagueness of the approach.

Neither the public discussion surrounding the secret Gaither Report of 1957, nor the public Rockefeller Report of 1958—to name only two recent statements about the American strategic problems—shows an appreciation of the chief points that shall be made in the following pages. Thus there is a justification to set them forth.

Our discussion refers exclusively to facts that are in the public domain, for which there is good reason to assume that they are correctly stated. From these facts deductions are made. We hope that they are correct; at any rate they can be inspected and accepted or rejected. There immediately arises the curious dilemma that without discussing those facts which are classified as military and atomic secrets it is impossible to know whether it is of vital importance one way or the other that these secret facts are not included here. Yet, if our security policy makes the sense that is claimed for it, the difference should be large. We cannot settle this point while remaining within our limitation of dealing only with published information. Thus one might ask: Why should the public bother to draw any conclusions whatever from the limited information at its disposal? One answer is, of course, that even on the basis of public facts alone one arrives at some alternatives so important that the government and the military men will have to demonstrate to the public why proposed courses should not be followed.

It is generally underestimated how much one can deduce from publicly available information. The fundamental observation is, unfortunately, that incomplete, ineffective use has been made of this information, except by a very few people who were denounced as pessimists or warmongers. For example, the growing economic and military strength of Russia and her great strides in applied science and technology were for years clearly before everyone's eyes. Yet all this was consistently derided; the challenge this development offered to the United States was not seen and the proper response was not forthcoming. Now that the appearance of the Russian Intercontinental Ballistic Missile (henceforth ICBM) and of the large artificial earth satellites has shattered at least some complacency, there is a tendency to go to the other extreme and assume that the United States cannot find and maintain an adequate position in this new world.

The misinterpretation of available facts is, of course, a common human characteristic. If it were different, we would have no need for science. We would not have stumbled for thousands of years through explanation after explanation of the same celestial phenomena until finally Newton gave a description of the laws of gravity. And so it goes on everywhere. Why should it be different in this enormously complex field of politico-military-technological life, where aims and means are so poorly described and the unexpected turns of events continuously add new facets to an already bewildering picture? The study of nature is interesting, exciting and important, but there were never connected with it such dangers for all mankind as have become apparent during the last few years. So it is not surprising that the discussion of military technology and the politico-strategic situations which the new discoveries have produced deeply affects our emotions. It is very difficult to control them when these problems arise.

One of the worst effects of emotions is that they often make us blind to some facts, so long as these are uncomfortable for our argument, our feelings, our ideals. Pointing out such circumstances is an unkind act. In our polite society frank speech is discouraged. But when this attitude relates to questions involving the very survival of the nation and of each individual, it is singularly unfitting to remain evasive. Now it is not only possible, but in fact the duty of everyone, to state precisely what his knowledge and conscience compel him to say. If this country and with it so many others are threatened, as is indeed the case, any other course would be despicable. But it requires an uncommon effort to say exactly what one thinks—if only because it is so difficult to determine what one's thought actually is or ought to be.

Only complete candor and frankness, sparing no feelings, deep respect for the facts however unpleasant and uncomfortable, great efforts to know them where they are not readily available, and drawing conclusions guided only by rigorous logic can bring the discussion of our defense problems forward. In other words, a coldly scientific attitude and procedure are demanded.

In this spirit we shall first look at the threat to which the country is exposed.

2 The Threat

"We shall bury you."—KHRUSHCHEV

The Fundamental Facts of the Day

These are the facts that stare us in the face, facts we shall not be able to get away from in our lives and which we shall deal with in the following pages:

(1) *Nobody has shelters:* there is no place to hide in safety should a large, thermonuclear war break out. There is no place for anyone to go, not for the masses, not for the common man, either in the United States, or in Russia, or in Europe: nowhere. Only the heads of government and the top military commanders are relatively safe—provided they can reach their deep shelters within half an hour or within two to three minutes, depending on the type of attack. Both the governments and military leaders have always been in safer spots than the common man—since time immemorial. They are trying to preserve this position.

(2) The individual weapons against cities and population masses are thousands of times more powerful than they were

only ten years ago, and millions of times more powerful than
twenty years ago. One single bomb can harbor a force greater
than all the explosives used by all belligerents in World War II
or even greater than all the energy ever used in any form in all
previous wars of mankind put together. Yet this force is concentrated in a device which can be transported in a conventional aircraft of which there exist thousands. And in the world
as a whole there are dozens, probably hundreds, if not thousands, of such bombs. If that number of bombs does not exist
but is wanted, they can be manufactured without difficulty by
at least three countries: the United States, Russia and Great
Britain. Soon France will join this group. Soon it will be possible for this force to be lifted by missiles or be put in orbit
around the earth, the former to be sent to any spot on earth,
the second to be brought back over any region to devastate it.

(3) Defense against these weapons is practically nonexistent; indeed it is now impossible. It exists only in the fertile imagination of some men, not in physical reality.

(4) Two hostile parties face each other today, each claim-
ing to be powerful enough to "destroy" the other (in a sense
which convinces the other that he is destroyed if the event
should happen). For destroying his enemy the attacker has to
pay a price. Destruction means in this context the killing of at
least tens of millions of people, though we shall discuss more
subtle ways of doing away with a nation. There exists no third
force with power to stabilize or neutralize the conflict.

(5) Each party professes its peaceful intentions, but the
other party does not believe in them. Rather each party recog-
nizes the deadly and growing capabilities of the other. The inherent peaceful intentions and wishes of the broad masses of
the people are disconnected and remain ineffective.

(6) This situation has developed persistently since the end
of World War II, and in it the position of the United States has
steadily deteriorated and is continuing to do so at increased
speed.

(7) Wars are made by governments and not by the people.

It is clear that this is not the description of a *stable* world. Let the word "stability" here mean that the given situation has no innate tendency to deteriorate, in a common-sense meaning of the word, as, for example, to a mere shooting war of large dimensions. Nor is the situation preserved if one of the two opposing parties deviates significantly from its present behavior, as, for example, when one party develops a new highly efficient weapon of attack or a profoundly powerful new method of defense.

At this point we must ask ourselves whether we should be satisfied in making the present situation stable by the introduction of some new devices. Stability as such is not necessarily desirable, but it is clearly more desirable when it can be achieved at a low level of effort and arms efficiency than at a high one. If stability can be obtained with the existing weapons technology and the given distribution of power among the contestants, perhaps by the introduction of new strategic concepts, we would certainly prefer it over the present instability. We know, of course, that other conditions, such as universal disarmament, are even more to be preferred but remain unattainable. We have, as yet, discovered no way to reach them, and we have hardly made any intellectual effort worth mentioning in trying to find new methods for effective disarmament. Consequently, one must study the possibility of first making the present situation secure against deterioration.

The Threat

Unless its intentions are offensive, in which case a country will arm as a matter of course, even a peaceful country will arm if it sees itself exposed to a threat from another nation. We are in this latter position; hence, our large defense effort. The following interrelated steps are involved:

(1) To recognize the existence of a *threat* to us, by virtue of the intentions of the enemy supported by his military and economic power. This threat may be real or imagined; it may be falsely interpreted, i.e., appear larger or smaller than it

"really" is, in other words, as it would appear to a fully informed observer at the moment, or as later historical research
may disclose.

(2) To determine the nature and imminence of the threat.
The nature of the threat may assume many forms. It lies in the
very existence of nuclear weapons in hostile hands. It is shaped
by weapons technology and by the strategic capabilities of the
enemy.

(3) To design the optimum strategy to meet, and, if possible, to supersede, this threat, and to consider only strategies
which are feasible economically and technologically.

(4) To find and develop in time weapons suitable for the
strategic concept chosen and to produce and deploy these
weapons systems in proper quantities, as demanded by the
optimal strategy. To invent new weapons and introduce them
at least as fast as the opponent introduces new devices.

(5) To initiate the public policies which will support the
required measures: i.e., economic-fiscal support, psychological
measures, etc.

In this way the threat to us will be countered by a threat to
the other party. This is our response. Clearly they may not
interpret it correctly, they may under- or overestimate it. The
two threats may compensate for each other, but, over
time, such a situation will hardly remain stable because of
changes in intentions and changes in technology. There will
also be random disturbances which may give an advantage to
one or the other side in a manner not contemplated by either
one.

To determine the threat made by the opponent more
specifically, it is necessary for us to attempt the discovery of
the following:

(a) *The fundamental interests* of both parties, in order to
see where the sources of conflict lie. These must not be stated
interests, but basic interests, shorn of all adorning verbiage.
It has to be discovered what is vital to each for survival and
whether that vital thing is within technical reach of the oppo-

nent's power through use of weapons or other means of pressure or destruction.

(b) *Intelligence* of the enemy's capabilities, i.e., his weapons, their character, quantities, deployment, rates of changes in production and location, etc.

It will always be difficult to satisfy both conditions completely; in some respects it will be impossible. There arises also the situation, as at present, where technology alone gives each opponent such power that whatever his fundamental interests are—and they may be peaceful—the mere possession of this overwhelming power constitutes a potential *supreme threat*. Under these circumstances the other party is left no choice whatever, assuming it wishes to survive and maintain its identity: it has to acquire the same power in order to compensate. And it has to do this in the shortest possible time interval lest the first party interfere in this process of equalization or neutralization. It can do so by preventive war. No major country is in this situation now, but the world has sometimes been through this stage. For example, the United States could have made preventive war up to perhaps 1948 or 1950. This country did not choose to do so, either for moral reasons or because the military did not seem to require it.

Weapon development sometimes favors defense, sometimes offense. We shall see later that at present the offense has a clear edge, and that therefore the strength of a party will be primarily measured by the amount of offensive weapons possessed. Should one side discover and subsequently construct impregnable defenses, thereby blunting the existing threat by an opponent, a situation will develop similar to the above one which invites preventive action before the impregnable defensive state has been reached.

While the mere possession of overwhelming power (now specifically thermonuclear power) *eo ipso* poses a threat, it will naturally be the greater, the more the basic interests of the various parties differ. This is particularly the case when, in addition to the short-run and long-run material interests such as in raw materials, access to the sea, etc., each party adheres firmly to some fundamental but different moral-political principle. Islam, for example, had for a long time committed Mohammedan nations to spread the faith by fire and sword to unbelievers. Similarly with other principles. If a principle does not demand an active intervention it may still differ so much from the opponent's principles that it intensifies the opposition and produces the tendency to turn open conflict into military action.

The Supreme Threat

The supreme threat is the one which involves the complete subjection or destruction of the enemy country. This can take two forms:

(a) Country A can subject and absorb Country B completely as an independent political unit. This may or may not be accompanied by a change in the mode of living of the population of B, which is otherwise allowed to remain alive.

(b) Country A can completely, i.e., physically, destroy Country B. This means the razing of its cities, the killing of most or all of the people, the devastation of its lands to make it uninhabitable.

For both there are many precedents in history. The *first* case was recently exemplified by the absorption in 1938 of Austria into Nazi Germany; even the name of the country could not be used any more within Germany. There are countless other instances spread over the whole course of recorded history. The *second* case also finds many illustrations; they become more numerous the farther we go back in the history of warfare. Even the most highly civilized peoples of their times, such as the ancient Greeks and Romans, when they had the power to do so, often destroyed their opponents in this final manner. One must not think only of the barbarous hordes of the Mongols.

We should qualify "complete destruction" for the present times. The upper bound of such destruction, according to the above definition, is the annihilation of virtually all life in a country, the destruction of its cities and of any power to revive.

We shall ignore, at least for the time being, that there is a still higher bound, namely, that all life may be extinguished on earth, at least all human or all higher animal life. This would result from the spread of deadly, radioactive fall-out. It could be incidental to a great thermonuclear war or it could be planned by a suicidal-maniac group. There is no question whatever that the technical feasibility for such an event is now already[1] in the hands of at least three countries and that within a few years many more will command it, unless drastic, far-reaching action, which may never be entirely foolproof, is taken. It would not even be necessary to have a large armament industry for a country to accomplish this. It suffices to possess reactors for peaceful civilian uses (and who will not have them in a decade?), which can easily be converted into producers of special, deadly radiation that could be spread over the entire earth. Who can foresee what blackmail from what sources the world may have to suffer!

As a rule the destruction of a country will mean the destruction of its *will* to resist and its *power* to resist. It is possible, as we saw, sometimes to achieve the former without fighting. But now we are concerned with the aspect of power, assuming the will to use it is unbroken.

Consider the supreme threat: "Country A can destroy Country B." This has at least the following different meanings:

(1) The existing, ready, military force of A can destroy the existing, ready, military force of B.

(2) Country A can act as in (1) but also in addition can destroy B's population, industry and any recuperative ability.

The difference between (1) and (2) is that Country A may

---

[1] This is not completely novel, as is usually thought to be the case: For decades already, almost any "civilized" nation could have wiped out most of the world's population by trivially simple and cheap devices involving bacteriological agents only.

have so much power left over—in case (2)—that B can never rise again, being either exposed to the continuing threat or having already suffered the corresponding physical damage.

The novelty, for more recent times, in regard to this power of destruction, lies in the *readiness of the force,* in the fact that *existing* power can accomplish that much at a moment's notice and that therefore mobilization, the raising and training of armies, building of bases, etc., by the attacked country matter as little as for the attacker. It is true that a large-scale attack by one country upon another requires preparations even in the missile age. In its early stages some of these might be discovered. But the need for preparations decreases steadily and rapidly. The moment is inexorably coming when no perceptible preparations at all will be needed, when truly all that will be needed is the throwing of some switches for solid fuel missiles poised in deep shelters or transported by submerged submarines.

Since nobody can conceivably stop this technological advance, and since there is no diminution in the fundamental conflict between the West and the Communistic world, an organization has to be found to prevent at least the accidental release of the stored, ready energies of destruction.

The Cost of the Threat

Our military leaders inform us as follows: "The United States can destroy the Soviet Union many times over, and soon the opposite will be possible." There are at least two meanings to such a statement:

(a) "Country A can attack B and can penetrate with so much of its existing force through B's defenses that B is destroyed." This happens presumably in one blow or in an almost continuous, sustained operation of not great duration. This means destruction of type (2) above, which is clearly not the same as (b) below.

(b) "Country B, when attacked by A, although 'destroyed' has some power left over and of this remaining force can get so much through A's defenses that A is destroyed in the same sense as B." This might be called the big "thermonuclear exchange."

Items (a) and (b) both describe a threat by A to B: In each case a cost is connected with the execution of the threat, other than the conventional one of the economic-industrial cost of constructing and maintaining the threat-force. In case (a) this is the cost of losing part of the force in the operation itself. This is the conventional military cost of staging an attack. Clearly the destruction of B, though feasible, may not be worth this cost, and in that sense, though not physically fully effective, the defenses B can put up are adequate to deter the aggressor. The last ten years have shown that this kind of deterrence becomes less and less effective, and it is reasonable to predict that this tendency will develop further. New technology under development and more already on the horizon will make this kind of deterrence vanish altogether as a suitable means of preventing an attack. The "real" cost lies therefore in the *other* damage *suffered by the attacker himself:* death and destruction of the homeland, devastation of cities and farms—utter ruin. This cost can run from zero to infinity, the latter standing for the total loss of everything. This cost has to be added to the no longer very interesting standard cost of attrition of his attacking forces. However large the latter may be, there exists a point where the indirect "real" costs become so high that one can neglect the attrition costs altogether (which might conceivably even go to zero). This point has been passed in the relations between the United States and Russia. The values of the destroyed attacking forces amount in either case to nothing compared with the value of the homeland destruction.

While this much is clear, there is an unknown of first magnitude in the picture: What degree of damage to its own country would either the United States or Russia accept if each could be assured that the respective opponent could be completely eliminated? This is a subtle question which needs to be explored but only after many other points have been clarified. But there exist problems in science which, while quite legitimate, have no known answer. In some cases it can even be proven that a solution is *in principle* impossible. This happens, for example, even in some parts of mathematics where questions can be sharply formulated. But here, where we deal with far more vital matters, the problems are fuzzy and their treatment is correspondingly vague and uncertain.

It is, however, possible to make the following observations:

If the cost of the threat to the threatening party is very much smaller than the cost to the threatened party, there is a great possibility of compromise by the payment of compensations to the former. Even though the threatened party has to give up something, both sides gain: the first by receiving the compensation, the latter by avoiding the damage resulting from the execution of the threat. This is not a nice situation to have, but clearly it is frequently encountered—in business, politics or war.

If the threat is very costly, i.e., if there is virtual stalemate, so that the loss of one party presupposes the loss of the other, there is little chance of lasting adjustment. These conditions are highly unstable. It is then unwise to make explicit threats at all. It is bad enough to occupy a position in which these threat conditions hold. But this is the case in a thermonuclear stalemate.

If there are more than two parties in this game new complexities arise. It suffices to point out the following: Even if Russia were able to destroy the United States at a cost to herself she deems acceptable, there may exist a third power, say China, whose undamaged position then approaches or exceeds that of Russia, though before the destruction of the United States she was a negligible factor. In that sense the third power, though weak in itself, can exercise a restraining influence by affecting the evaluation of the costs of the threat.

If large numbers of nuclear weapons of high yield, together with the capability to deliver them anywhere, are in the hands of more than the two major parties, further complications arise than those normally considered. But this condition may not be fulfilled for several decades and we shall therefore not attempt to deal with it.

Provocation

At this very moment of writing there exists a threat made by the Soviet Union against the United States. It is countered by our defensive forces and by a threat we are able to exercise against Russia. There is a temporary balance since obviously we are not in a shooting war. But the threats may change: we may have a *provocation.* Any marked positive deviation by either party from the present state can be viewed by the other as an invitation to act in regard to this change. This is not at all tied to the present technology but is as old as warfare. Any mobilization by the neighbor poses a new threat. Frequently mobilization was used as a means of exercising political pressure and often succeeded in bringing about the desired effect without the need of actually going to war. In earlier times such variations were visible; they could easily be discovered by the usual methods of intelligence. As long as mass armies, with numbers running into millions, had to be called up and moved to a border, there could be no secrecy.

The point is that mobilization, even though it changed only the state of *readiness,* brought about a *discrete* change in the balance of ready power. For that reason a mobilization was always found to be alarming, in the nature of a pressure, a provocation. The same is true also of redeployment of forces, concentration of existing troops on a border, the amassing of a fleet (such as the British fleet build-up, however futile, in the Mediterranean before the Abyssinian war in order to check Mussolini).

When mobilizations are still in order and the technology of warfare is held at that level, *surprise attacks* are unlikely to play a decisive role. In 1914, for example, no country could have attempted to make a surprise dash across its border with its existing forces, hoping thereby to achieve a decision in its favor. The force would soon have spent itself without accomplishing anything of value against a sufficiently large neighbor. But in 1941 Japan, with a new technology available, could make a major surprise attack at Pearl Harbor, even though with the same negative results. Now, in 1959, either Russia or the United States could—with a much higher chance of success—try, with forces in being, to knock out the other completely. In the near future (of a few years) there will be certainty. This is our technical development told in another language.

At the present state of technology, where a striking power may exist such that what is in virtual readiness is identical with the finally needed decisive power, a strategic mobilization for the big thermonuclear exchange is no longer meaningful or possible. The other tactical operations of changes in deployment, concentration of forces, etc., still remain of some importance, but the nearer we come to the time of, say, fixed emplacement of missiles, the less important will these matters become.

However, since weapons technology is rapidly changing, it is in that area where today's possible provocations must be sought. Instead of mobilizing—and thereby gaining an advantage in power—a country will develop and produce a new weapon and thereby cause the discrete change in relative power compared with that of the opponent.

While mobilizations, concentrations of fleets, etc., are immediately widely known—and sometimes there is a desire to have them known—changes in weapons technology may go on in secret. Russia certainly does not tell us about her steps, while we stupidly advertise even plans and projects and talk freely of "having" new devices when, in fact, they often exist only in the minds of their proponents.

A provocation, whether deliberate or not, need not always be fully effective. This noneffective state is reached under either of two conditions: *First,* when one opponent, already overwhelmingly more powerful than the other, increases his strength still further and no combination against this new strength can be found, e.g., by formation of alliances. Such cases have obtained frequently in history. They were very uncomfortable to neighbors but they did not alter the original threat conditions fundamentally. *Second,* when both parties are at approximate parity and each one is, under these circumstances, able to destroy the other at any rate, though at a definite cost to himself. This is a novel possibility exclusively due to modern nuclear weapons and the new techniques of rapid, almost instantaneous delivery.

The discrete increase in strength of A may mean either of two things: A may be able to "destroy" B more fully, more certainly, or A may introduce defensive measures such that B can no longer retaliate as effectively against A's attack, can therefore no longer really "destroy" A. If A already has the power for full and complete destruction of B, an increase in that power is as meaningless as in the first case above. But an increase in defensive power is a significant change in the situation and must be recognized and evaluated as such. We shall see later (cf. p. 130 ff.) that this is particularly the case with respect to the construction of certain types of shelters.

So far we have considered only that both antagonists make great efforts to get ahead in their armament race. In particular we envisaged only that a disparity might be due solely to the inequality in effort. But there is also the possibility of exhaustion on the part of one of them, due to costs, fatigue, lessening of determination and will power. The consequences of such behavior are quite clearly not the same as when the disparity appears while each is straining to the utmost to get ahead of the other. On the contrary, now the temporarily weaker will not feel induced to attack the one who is about to become stronger because of the default of the former. Rather the reverse is the case. The stronger may feel that it is to his advantage to exploit the situation lest the first have a change of heart. This asymmetry is important, though well known. The lesson is that when both efforts are high neither can slacken without promptly inviting disaster. Unilateral action to reduce the arms race is impossible and not compatible with the desire for national survival.

In the light of these distinctions the question of preventive action has to be asked. Such action is clearly tied to time intervals, i.e., to the time it takes for one party to carry out a provocative step. Furthermore the element of surprise, and, partly connected with it, the unconventional use of existing weapons, assume significance.

The Principle of the Imposed, Involuntary Reaction

The possession of the initiative in military operations is frequently of great advantage. This is not necessarily so, because a particular initiative may be of little value and the opponent may be prepared for all types of actions taken against him. Indeed, he should be so prepared if he understands strategic principles well. This applies in the domain of existing weapons, forces, equipment and is often viewed in connection with tactical situations, which we may regard as short-run problems.

There exists, however, once more the phenomenon of change, especially in the peacetime struggle for supremacy, which would make war unnecessary by assuring absolute dominance.

The involuntary reaction imposed upon the opponent can then become an important instrument in this peacetime contest. For example, if Country A builds a large fleet of tanks it forces the opponent B to make a sufficiently large investment in anti-tank weapons. Or if, as at present, Russia has built about 500 submarines, the United States is required to develop, produce and position anti-submarine devices.

It is good policy to choose that weapon whose anti-weapon imposes the greatest possible strain on the production facilities and military efforts of the opponent.

One must therefore look for those regions in the opponent's make-up which would cause him the greatest trouble. There are quite often such possibilities, but they have been sadly neglected by the United States. As a rule, Russia has determined our armaments production by imposing plans of merely involuntary reaction upon us. Our greater wealth would have permitted us frequently to choose such weapons systems which would have imposed a great strain upon Russia. Although it is already late in the race, there are still ample opportunities for us to pursue this policy.

Instead of looking for the anti-weapon when one side introduces a new weapon or, more frequently, decides on quantity production of a known one, the other side can strive to develop an entirely new procedure of warfare so that the weapon in question is made obsolete, rather than combated. This is more difficult. It always involves a step forward in technological development and is never easy to take. But this too has happened in history. Applied to our example, it would mean the invention of a weapon used *instead* of tanks, rather than against them, making the tank as well as the anti-tank weapon obsolete. Thus the manner of that particular phase of warfare would change. Fighter planes, valuable against most bombers, become pointless against modern missiles. The latter are different in kind; they are an answer to the fighters other than improved defensive armament of the bombers against fighter planes.

This principle could be further illustrated, but there is no need to develop the point at length here, since a great amount of detail would be necessary which cannot be accommodated at this juncture. Our strategic plans and proposed weapons systems should be viewed in the light of this principle. As a rule this is not done. These somewhat remoter but nevertheless profoundly important effects of our armament schemes and production schedules are not studied, because of the lack of integration between the Department of Defense and other agencies, which is in turn due to a lack of appreciation of the possibilities that exist in this area.

Offensive and Defensive Weapons

There are three kinds of weapons: weapons for offensive use, weapons for defensive use, and dual-purpose weapons. Most fall in the last category; the others have gradually evolved over time. To illustrate: Bow and arrow, sword and shield can be used for either purpose; and if we come down to the present day we find the same situation—battleships, destroyers, tanks, cannons or airplanes always have offensive and defensive uses. But together with the development of weapons technology has gone some specialization. For example, fortresses, and stones and boiling pitch dropped from their walls are for defense; scaling ladders and rams are for attack of fortresses and for nothing else. Some arms are designed *primarily* for one or the other use but can be adapted, sometimes by unexpected, clever use only, for the opposite purpose.

Now, however, there arrives the age when the two principal categories split fundamentally. In our age of specialization this is not surprising. But the consequences are formidable and the tendencies which this development expresses are of the highest importance. The significance lies in the *commitment* made in the acquisition of one or the other type. In other times a general-purpose weapon or force, being useful for defense as well as offense, was cheaper. Merely to possess larger quantities offered an insurance against surprising needs for one rather than the other use and their handling was greatly simplified.

Consider on the other side the Intercontinental Ballistic Missile (ICBM), the Strategic Air Command (SAC) and Polaris, as the underwater-fired fleet ballistic missile is called. All are *offensive* weapons; they cannot be defensively used against any attack, not even as destructive elements against enemy bases, because of the time factor involved: i.e., since we may assume the state of possessing ICBM's in such numbers that their entire rapid dispatch is equivalent with our principal effort, the enemy can be assumed to have been finished thereby. This and this alone is the purpose of ICBM's, not for us defensively to destroy his bases *after he has attacked,* or while the attack is in progress, to weaken his attack. This would work only during a long drawn-out operation.

Anti-ICBM's—would that they existed and were harmless to ourselves!—would be, in the same manner, perhaps even more clearly, a specialized weapon, good for nothing else but defense.

The point is not to state whether one or the other type is good, but merely to show the consequences in greater costs, greater complication and greater difficulty of operation.

In this tendency resides a great and subtle danger which is best described by reference to similar experience elsewhere: Every system which is highly specialized is in an increasing danger of extinction. Such systems become less mobile, less useful, less adaptable. They require for their survival very precise circumstances, and when these change, sometimes very slightly, their end is at hand. There are two tree-dwelling species of bear in Australia; they differ mostly by virtue of the fact that each is dependent for its food on the leaves of a different species of tree; they cannot interchange the trees, and nothing else will do for food: a most precarious, thin basis of existence! Compare the hog with them—it can eat practically anything. A possible future anti-ICBM can be made obsolete by a new offensive weapon (e.g., a satellite carrying a large nuclear charge) and with it all the investment in its production, installation, training of crews, etc., is gone. Ironically, the new weapon may not even be new, it may merely be an unconventional use of another, already existing one! It may even be simple. It may, for example, be a bacteriological, non-lethal device!

It would, of course, be wonderful if the art of warfare should specialize to such a degree that war became hopelessly complicated and could not be conducted by either side. The complications certainly are mounting fast, indeed to a degree the uninitiated layman can hardly fathom. Unfortunately the military and their scientists in both camps think they can still cope with the difficulty—save one: the terror of the weapons.

To sum up: The specialization increases. Both defense and offense have made great strides forward since the last world war. The offensive weapons of that time would stand no chance against the defense that could be mounted against them now. But these same defensive forces are left hopelessly behind in the progress that the highly specialized offensive weapons systems have made.

In this light the reader should judge the hollow assertions that we possess adequate "defenses" capable of blunting decisively any attack that can be mounted against the United States.

3 The Shield: Deterrent and Retaliatory Forces

Stalemate or Parity

A stalemate is defined as the condition in which one side can do damage to the other only under conditions such that the damage he suffers himself is at least equal to, or only slightly exceeded by, the damage rendered; and this has to be true simultaneously for *both* sides. The strength of the two antagonists cancels out.

A stalemate can occur at any level of armament. The interesting cases are those at high level and—in particular—in regard to nuclear weapons. The reason is that any high-level stalemate is apt to be less stable, and a nuclear one least stable, because of the ease with which the weapons can be used and because of the rapid progress of new nuclear weapons, a process that has not yet come to end. A stalemate will not be disturbed if each side equally adds to, or subtracts from, its strength. Thus there is a static and dynamic view of stalemate; it can exist, for example, when only the given weapons are considered, but equal changes in their quantities occur. The true dynamic change is, however, one of performance, caused by technological improvement. (We may neglect the case where the composition of the armament in possession of the two sides changes and delicate questions of the worth of one weapons system in terms of another weapons system appear.)

A nuclear stalemate at the highest level is the condition of "nuclear plenty," where each side has the assurance that it can destroy the other even though the price for accomplishing this will be its own destruction.

A stalemate as such is not absolutely undesirable, but neither does it offer a guarantee that no action will be taken by either side. Stalemate refers to the equipment in the hands of both sides and to the known forms of its uses. There is, therefore, a great inducement to think of new, unconventional uses or strategies in order to give the tools on hand a new meaning, thereby to create superiority. One of the most important is surprise. We deal with it later.

A stalemate need not cover *all* forces of two protagonists. There may be a stalemate at sea, in the air, in a particular theater of war. The consequences of a partial stalemate are for each side to try to find other areas where the conflict can be carried out more advantageously with different means and techniques. An important consequence is that in the case of the present conflict between the United States and Russia—because of its world-wide nature—the tendency toward localized or "limited" war in distant countries increases. This, too, will receive more attention (cf. p. 142).

Deterrence

A deterrent force aims to prevent an enemy attack. It is fully effective if the enemy who would like to attack in order to obtain a certain objective abstains from doing so. In that sense, the entire military power of a country can function as a deterrent. The fact that the United States has not been attacked (directly) by Russia since the end of World War II is due either to the possibility that Russia did not want to attack us (even if our deterrent force had been much smaller or perhaps even zero) or to the strength of our deterrent force, presumably in particular to our nuclear capability. We can forget about the first possibility; we would have been attacked had we been much weaker.

The *simplest form* of fully effective deterrence is for a country to have *direct deterrence,* i.e., to have defenses such that the enemy cannot overcome them. If a country is not itself bent on attack and conquest, it would need no other force. It is doubtful that such a situation has ever existed between major countries or countries of nearly equal size. Clearly Mexico or Cuba are deterred from attacking the United States—if they ever needed to be—by our defensive capabilities; we need not in addition deter them by our power of destroying them. But this is not interesting. It is not easy to determine how large our defenses have to be to deter Russia, and it is not certain that such defenses can be created.

Deterrence may never be feasible. This can be due to the fact that the enemy is enormously strong: Mexico or Cuba (to return to our example) could not produce a defensive force which the United States could not overcome. Or it can be due to the fact that the technology of attack has developed so that —whatever the quantity relations and sizes of countries involved—it is *technically* impossible to have a fully effective defense. It is conceivable, for example, that Cuba might discover a superweapon with which she could destroy the whole of the United States. No defensive effort on our part could then stop an attack from that country. The historical experience is, however, that military men charged with defense usually overestimate its possibilities. (This is particularly the case now when optimistic statements about the possibility of defense of the United States from attack by airplanes or even missiles are considered while at the same time we are told that most of our Strategic Air Command could get through the comparable Russian air defenses.)

The problem of how strong defense ought to be would be easier to settle if one had to deal with only one weapons system used for attack. But there are in these times many, each of different strength and each greatly variable in deployment. This complicates matters enormously and the proper lessons must be drawn (cf. p. 40 ff.). Since a fully effective passive defense is only a hypothetical border case, with the probability of its ever occurring definitely having reached zero, one must look for other forms of protection from attack. Thus the ideas of retaliation and counterattack are introduced.

Counterattack is a device as old as any warfare. It consists of using one's own offensive attack forces (which may be highly specialized for this purpose) in order to weaken the enemy's attack, take away his initiative, force him to divert energy from his own attack to his defenses. All this is routine and need not occupy us for any length. Suffice it to say that a country's defensive strength is to be measured not only by the direct defense it can put up but also by the counterattack it can mount simultaneously.

Retaliation

Retaliation is something rather more comprehensive. Its idea is that if the enemy attacks, quite apart from the opposition one can put up by direct defense and counterattack, he will be punished where it hurts him most and possibly in a manner which is most distasteful to him. One purpose is to make the possible success of the initial attack worthless to the enemy; the other—farther-reaching—aim is, of course, to discourage him altogether from starting a conflict. In this manner the possibility of subsequent punitive retaliation works as a deterrent.

"Retaliation" used in this latter sense is only a more dignified word for the generally detested "blackmail." It assumes that the enemy will have acted *first,* so that there is a moral justification for threatening or doing the nasty things one proposes to do such as the destruction of his defenseless noncombatant population. One may have no choice in the matter, but the moral embellishment is supposed to help. The idea of retaliation is, of course, also as old as humanity, and a basic principle in more than one religion. But it has never played as prominent a role in warfare as today. In fact, it is now in an almost central position in the scheme of things as far as the two principal antagonists are concerned. Weapons development has given warfare the paradoxical turn that it is not the attack on the *military* power and installations where the massive danger for the peoples of the world lies. Rather it is the fact that one's own government may start a conflict, or let itself be driven into one, with the fearful consequence of mass killings and utter ruin of country and nation because of the retaliatory action by the enemy.

There were periods in world history when the military fought the military with little involvement of the people though these were affected by the outcome of such struggles in such matters as the forced change of religion, submission to a different prince, or other subsidiary matter. But they lived on. As long as soldiers fought soldiers, one could conceivably leave the business of fighting and war to them—though it was hardly ever done. But now warfare includes far more than simply the confrontation of military forces as such. Yet adequate means have not yet been developed by which a nation brings its entire weight—political and economic as well as military—to bear against its enemy in modern warfare.

Retaliation can also be vengeance pure and simple. In that case it may come late, long after the conflict or the deed by the enemy. Vengeance is not part of the operation itself in which retaliation proper figures with the purpose of preventing an attack or, if prevention did not work, of making it impossible for the attacker to exploit his gains. The attacker is to be punished and the threat of this punishment is to hang over him. Thus the vengeance aspect of retaliation is not what figures principally in attempting to understand the functions of a retaliatory force.

A retaliatory force is similar to a police force. The ideal police would prevent crime before it happens, or at least decisively interfere with its execution. If it cannot do this, the police will find the criminal and bring him to justice. We are protected by the police though they are not in our house. This is the meaning of the saying that crime will not pay; it is not that years after the crime some relative of the victim will come and heap vengeance on the murderer. This may happen too, but it is not in the scheme of things as far as the design of an efficient police force is concerned. The existence of the police is to act as a deterrent. In addition, the safe containing the treasure is made so strong that the robber will have great trouble in cracking it. Both precautions together should make it unlikely that a crime will even be attempted.

It is sometimes argued that the death penalty is not a good deterrent against murder because many murders occur nevertheless. Therefore one might argue that the deterrent against aggression on this country might not work either. But the parallel is faulty: The murderer has a good chance not to be found, or when found to escape, not to be convicted, or, if convicted, to receive mild punishment, to be granted clemency, etc. All this is different from the present military situation. There the alternative to *not* seeing the deterrence is a very high probability of obliteration. The point is to make this probability "equal to one," that is, to make obliteration certain and automatic.

If every potential murderer were sure that the very moment he commits the murder he too is killed, few murders would occur.

Defense and Retaliation

The *size of the required retaliatory force* is determined by the state of our own defensive force and by the enemy's strength, which the retaliatory force has to overcome in order to make itself felt in a manner and with a power so as to be effective. Potential retaliation as an active (not merely punitive) component in the military picture is meaningful only if it has a deterrence function.

A retaliatory force has to get through the enemy's defenses. Otherwise it does not exist. The entire force will not be able to penetrate. Thus its size is determined by the expected attrition and by the power it needs to have after attrition in order to inflict a damage upon the enemy that we believe he would consider forbiddingly large. The damage to be inflicted upon the enemy is thus not necessarily related to the damage his attack can inflict upon us: The latter may be much larger, or it may be insignificant.

It may be larger if we have very valuable (to us!) installations compared with which he may have nothing. The barbarian Vandals and Goths destroyed precious Rome; a child with a knife could destroy the Mona Lisa. A small and poor country could blow up New York or Washington with a hydrogen bomb clandestinely brought there. Nothing held the Vandals back, the Mona Lisa is guarded, and no small country will plant hydrogen bombs in the United States, suspecting that this would mean its end (but would it—would we even know which country did this?). If the damage is small, we might retaliate in a minor way, measure for measure, but the guess is that there would be no small damage if the United States were directly attacked. The reason for this is simple and the principle is old: If you plan to attack the king, you have to kill him. Thus we can rule out the small attack on the homeland; the Japanese learned what it meant to stage the attack on Pearl Harbor and not to be able to follow through. They did not kill the king. This lesson will not be forgotten by any potential aggressor for a long time to come.

Retaliation is an operation different from counterattack. This has important consequences. The strength of the counterattack has to be geared to that of the actual or potential attack. Consider an actively aggressive enemy submarine force. Against it we have to put up a defense, some of which may be direct defense such as dropping depth charges, formation of convoys, etc. Other defense may be counterattack against their submarine bases, the shipyards where they are produced, etc. Similarly with active aggression by airplanes, ground operations and whatever else might be involved. The point here is that the counterattack has to be specific, to be pinpointed to particular targets related to the nature of the attack. In strength or weight it has to correspond to the strength and weight of the enemy's effort. *Not so with the retaliatory force.* Retaliation will seek other targets than defensive counterattack. It needs other weapons, other procedures, other timing. It *may* need less power than an effective counterattack might require. It may be cheaper. But it does not follow that retaliation should be employed at all, or be employed immediately. These are different considerations.

If the circumstances are such that retaliation needs less power, or less specific power, and if a retaliatory force is actually on hand—and in particular if the enemy does not possess a retaliatory force of his own—then the temptation to use it is very great. It has been so used, for example, in colonial conflicts. There the colonizing power, lacking specific equipment, knowledge and trained men, found itself sometimes hampered in fighting against the natives in the jungle on the terms of the jungle. What could be easier than to send some planes to destroy the villages of the natives with all inhabitants so as to exercise a pressure that would cause the fighters to give in? Meanwhile the European capital of the colonial power was safe from counter-retaliation by the natives. Even in 1957/58 events of a similar nature occurred in the Yemen and between France and Tunisia.

If counterattack and retaliation seek the *same target,* then there is clearly no distinction between the two. But if an attack is made on targets *other* than the sources of power of the enemy (even if these sources be widely defined), then this attack is retaliatory in nature. It is important to understand this separation of targets: the retaliation targets are not necessarily the primary military installations of the enemy. These are sought only if they happen to be located together with the retaliatory target. In other words, with retaliation one attacks where it hurts, but not necessarily where it hurts the immediate power of the enemy. One hurts what is most precious to him, hoping that this will cause him to abstain from further attack, or, preferably, one merely threatens to hurt him. The moral undertone in all this should be observed: If we initially destroy the enemy's capital, we are barbarous murderers, but if we attack it *in retaliation, even though his attack may have been directed against one of our military installations,* we feel justified in producing exactly the same damage and horror. Now we believe that this is the way to stop him, or to punish him if he can no longer be stopped. And we may be forced to do this, even if repugnant to us, because the source of the enemy's aggressive strength and its placement may be completely out of our reach for a direct countermeasure.

In retaliation then lies the only "defense." It is, of course, no defense at all because it does not ward off or blunt an attack already in progress by specifically interfering with it. Retaliation may upset the progress of an attack indirectly: if the enemy sees his population killed, although this may not substantially lower his immediate power or even affect it at all, he may abstain from further action and be induced to make peace. The speeds of his attack and of our retaliation may, however, be so great that the enemy cannot recall his force. This will certainly be the case if his attack is in the form of massive salvos of ballistic missiles. There is a catch to this hope and expectation: our retaliation may cause him to add to his military attack (with all its side effects suffered at any rate by our people) his own retaliation power—if he has additional strength or a separate force left. So there clearly is the possibility that a big mutual exchange takes place—in these times in the form of large hydrogen weapons.

Retaliation Weapons

Present technology has produced the curious result that the weapons needed to attack (or counterattack) an enemy's military force are frequently different from the weapons that serve best as retaliation weapons. Sometimes there is an overlap; but the tendency seems to be to produce more and more differentiation. It is also notable that the main effort in the development of new weapons appears to go toward the retaliation weapons of mass destruction. The other effort is toward small weapons, but this is not an absolute contradiction of the above statement. Smallness in weapons should rather be viewed as smallness in *warheads;* i.e., it is now incomparably easier than it was only a few years ago to pack the same punch, the same "yield," in technical parlance, into a very much smaller volume. This allows the development of high-yield retaliatory weapons in the megaton range (i.e., in excess of 1,000,000 tons TNT equivalent), as well as of low-yield, small, easily carried devices useful for limited war or at least for almost conventional types of troop engagements.

The emphasis on the specialization toward pure retaliatory weapons is a direct consequence of the growing inefficiency of the defense. *The weaker the direct, passive defenses get, the stronger is the need for retaliatory power.*

That retaliation, with its different target system, needs no great accuracy—certainly far less than the attack on strictly military targets—accounts for the arrival of the ICBM's and related systems. It is obviously more difficult from a distant country to destroy, say, an aircraft carrier at sea, than to aim a ballistic missile with an error of $\pm$ 5 miles at New York City.

The burden placed on the defense is now greater than ever: instead of merely having to ward off an attack on one's strictly military targets *one also has to defend one's own retaliatory power.* This is where the principal difficulties of military planning lie at the present time. It is here where new devices and new strategic concepts have to be developed.

The destruction of the enemy's retaliatory power becomes the overshadowing aim of military operations. If this can be accomplished or if the enemy can be convinced that he should under no circumstances ever use his retaliatory power, war can proceed along conventional lines *even though nuclear weapons may be used.* It is a frequent misconception that the use of nuclear weapons is identical with retaliatory mass destruction. We have unfortunately contributed greatly to the fact that the world falsely associates the use of nuclear weapons with mass destruction only.

Defense of the Retaliatory Force

Even though defense becomes in general more and more difficult, the problem of defending the retaliatory force has to be faced squarely. There are several ways to accomplish this.

The condition of the retaliatory force can run the entire scale from *vulnerable* to *invulnerable.* These two states are relative to each other: nothing is by itself totally vulnerable or totally invulnerable. Clearly the answer depends on the strength of the opponent, on the kind and quantity of weapons at his command. Merely to possess weapons but not to be able to *deliver* them does not give strength to the enemy nor does it make us vulnerable (except in a purely hypothetical sense). Thus even if we had no weapons of defense at all, but if the enemy could not get at us, we would be safe. This extreme condition does not exist any longer. The enemy in some form or other can over time always reach us with *some* weapons but not necessarily with those he would like to employ, nor with decisive quantities.

In order to estimate the enemy strength we must rely on intelligence and make assumptions where we have no firm information. That means essentially the latter, especially considering the poor record of some of our intelligence work. The principal assumption is to attribute to the enemy at least our own strength (in regard to retaliatory power) and at least our own knowledge about nuclear weapons. With this in mind we can assert the following:

(1) *Absolute vulnerability* of the retaliatory force and an absolutely untrustworthy and powerful enemy are an extremely unstable combination. Growth of one's own retaliatory force cannot easily compensate for vulnerability, although it will do this to some extent, since a greater force by necessity occupies more space and therefore gives somewhat better security due to the associated dispersal.

The essential point is that in case of a hostile act by the enemy, or if rightly or wrongly some phenomenon is taken for a hostile act, *the vulnerable retaliatory force has to attack its specific targets immediately and in full strength.* This is the application of the principle of involuntary reaction and of the principle of the need for the complete kill (cf. p. 22 and p. 33). Should the attack wait, the force, being extremely exposed, is likely to be destroyed and the chance of bringing the enemy to terms, or at least punishing him, is lost. Note that the enemy's *first* act is a purely military one: the attempt to destroy—if possible by surprise—our retaliatory force, i.e., the installations, planes, missile bases, etc. But *our* reply is necessarily (apart from the direct defense mounted and whatever counterattack is possible or still meaningful against the bases from which he draws the strength for his attack) the immoral terror of retaliatory devastation.

Our own vulnerability forces upon us the complete unleashing in the most ruthless manner of whatever power is at our command. We have no choice. We cannot graduate our action. We cannot wait. We cannot deliberate; we have to react by reflex.

Our decision to do so is to a large extent dependent on our susceptibility to *surprise.* There is a premium on surprise. If our retaliatory force is highly vulnerable, then it is so particularly to surprise attack. This is why one must pay great attention to different known forms and possible new techniques of surprise. In that respect a great deal of imagination is needed.

(It is my impression that we are as much lacking in cunning and ideas in anticipating surprise in this area as we are in the general politico-diplomatic one.)

Absolute vulnerability of the prime power with which we hope to hold an enemy at a distance and to deter him from attack introduces a strong element of suspicion in our relations with him. We will be inclined to interpret his every act, every shift of policy as of extreme danger for us. Again, there is hardly an alternative. But it also shows that an untrustworthy enemy under such circumstances has greatest difficulties in mending his ways, in adopting a different attitude and in coming to a stable, peaceful settlement with us. As long as we are highly vulnerable, we will find it almost impossible to come to an understanding with an enemy: his every conciliatory move will have to be studied to determine whether it is a ruse to allow him to attack us more effectively later on.

So far we have considered only one side as having an absolutely vulnerable force. It is easy to project the argument to the situation where both parties are in this position. This is the present condition of the world. The instability of the situation is increased; it is extreme.

But first let us consider case (2).

(2) *Absolute invulnerability* of the retaliatory force and an absolutely untrustworthy enemy. Assume that our retaliatory force fulfills the minimum requirements, i.e., that the part which can get through to the enemy country can inflict such devastation that even if he destroys us first, he will be destroyed too. If the enemy knows that our retaliatory power is absolutely invulnerable in this sense, and if he cannot raise significantly the effectiveness of his defense, then there is a situation of our successfully deterring him. Surprise attack on our force is virtually excluded—unless there be a tremendous technological development, which we shall neglect in this hypothetical case. Though we must be wary of every move the enemy makes, politically or militarily, there will prevail a feeling of safety; there will be absent the fear that an instantaneous

reaction may be required from us at any moment but not come off successfully. If under such conditions the enemy should propose a settlement, it will be possible to examine it at leisure, in an atmosphere of growing trust.

Mixed Systems

As a rule the retaliatory force is made up of several component systems. This is so because there are several ways of delivering a retaliatory blow and each one has to be explored. As never before in history, swift technological changes make the transition from one system to another possible or even imperative. While a new system is being introduced, the older one is still available and will become superseded and be replaced only gradually. We still have planes though IRBM's (Intermediate Range Ballistic Missiles) and ICBM's have been developed. A further part of our force is represented by aircraft carriers. Each component part has specific characteristics which determine its own vulnerability to attack, to surprise attack, to blast, to radiation, etc. This essay would turn highly technical and become voluminous were we to enter into all aspects of this situation. But we need not be exhaustive. In the following discussion we shall not lose anything essential.

In the preceding discussion we saw that susceptibility to surprise is one of the chief characteristics distinguishing a vulnerable from an invulnerable force.

It is common knowledge, indeed notorious, that the Strategic Air Force is exceedingly vulnerable. This is why we sometimes keep as large a part of it as we think we can afford financially and operationally always in the air.

Aircraft carriers are also highly vulnerable. They can be followed by submarines even in peacetime and can be sunk without warning. This danger is great, especially in view of Russia's rising submarine capability and the increasing power of each submarine's capability of firing missiles instead of its having to come within torpedo range. That is why carriers usually have

to be surrounded by large screening forces. These would, however, be far from effective against a surprise operation carried
out in deep peace.

Today's ICBM's stand exposed above ground and have to
go through complicated count downs lasting many hours before
they can be fired. During this time they are obviously highly
susceptible to blast even from misses rather far away. That is
why one now would like to simplify the missiles in order to
shorten the exposure time or even better to put them underground. Another method of protection is to build many bases
in order to get high dispersion.

At the present we have only the strategic bombers and the
aircraft carriers, but we are moving toward the missiles, of
which the shorter-range intermediate missiles, placed overseas, will be the first to become operational. These two or, if
we anticipate by quite some time, three systems have each
their own individual properties as far as vulnerability is concerned. Possession of more than one system is definitely advantageous. The advantage increases the greater their operational differences are. Although SAC, as well as the carriers,
uses airplanes, they are placed far apart, the carriers move
about in different areas and the planes themselves have different performance characteristics and therefore different missions. The crucial point is this:

*Any one weapons system, if its properties become known,
generates over time methods to overcome and defeat it.*

This is, of course, a simple statement but its application is
not always easy. In particular, it may take a great deal of time
to develop a countermeasure. This time lapse is the reason for
the seesaw between the alternating predominance of offensive
and defensive power. We are now in the phase of the ascendancy of the offensive. But airplanes, whose properties are well
understood by both sides and whose strategic and tactical uses
are bounded by their performance characteristics, are beginning to find their match. So it is now becoming clear that the

manned fighter plane as an answer to the fast, high-flying bomber is on the way out; the ground-to-air missile will take over.

We have encountered this phenomenon before, when it was shown that adoption of a system in strength forces the opponent to adopt a countersystem whether he desires to do so or not.

The point now is that if a country is economically strong enough to employ simultaneously several widely different systems for the same purpose, i.e., establishes a *mixed system,* it complicates the problems of the opponent enormously.

The greater the difference among the weapons systems, the better. There is some difference between land-based bombers, with their fixed bases, and carriers, but the difference between both on the one hand and ballistic missiles on the other is still greater.

It is seldom, if ever, the case that one system is clearly better than, or "superior," to another in every respect. But a mixture of several such systems will, as a rule, be superior to any single system alone. Since, furthermore, each system allows for a variety of uses (naturally within bounds) it is easily seen that a mixed system, or rather a mixture of systems, enlarges the scope of operations enormously. If such mixtures are adopted, there is great freedom to choose the exact composition, i.e., to determine whether it should be, say, 50:30:20, or 30:40:30, etc. The determination of the best combination is a scientific task of great complexity, and even if it is determined, it may be difficult to obtain it within strictly given economic bounds. There exist exact mathematical methods which allow the determination of the optimum mixture or combination. They should be used. The fact is, however, that decisions of this kind are made in an entirely haphazard manner; often they are the consequence only of the political effectiveness of different pressure groups.

When the opponent is confronted with a mixed system, in particular when the exact proportions of the component systems are not well known to him, he is faced with grave problems. He must decide on the hardware best suited technologically to take care of each one and the systems may differ widely. He must decide, in particular, how much of the appropriate kinds of hardware he should produce, and he must allow for the possibility that his opponent will switch his proportions frequently. If at all possible, this will be good policy for the opponent.

One easily concludes from the above that the retaliatory force ought to be varied, frequently variable in strength, and that the exact allocations among the different component parts be kept as much under cover as possible. A mixed system is *per se* not invulnerable, certainly not if made up of vulnerable subsystems, but the manner of composition can greatly reduce the vulnerability. A mixed system is also superior to the mere enlargement of a single system, which is also a method, but not a very effective one, of reducing vulnerability. The present American retaliatory force fulfills none of the demands for an invulnerable force in an acceptable manner.

If the mixed system contains at least one invulnerable component, then it is definitely superior. Can the whole system be made completely invulnerable?

If there is more than one invulnerable system—which we would expect by necessity to be a mixed system—the task is to find among the different systems the one that is:

(a) technologically the most advanced (and thereby minimizes the speed of technical obsolescence)

(b) cheapest (either regarding acquisition or upkeep, or both)

(c) politically acceptable, given political constraints arising from the nature of alliances, geography, etc.

The solution to this formidable problem is demanded of the Joint Chiefs of Staff, the Department of Defense and the State Department. What we have now is their "solution." It was good enough for the past, when we nearly had a monopoly of nuclear power, and even later, when we had an overwhelmingly larger stockpile though were no longer in exclusive possession of atomic weapons. But the tendencies it embodies in regard to the current technological changes are definitely unsatisfactory.

Methods for Decreasing the Vulnerability of the Retaliatory Force

The present system of our retaliatory capability is highly vulnerable. We shall therefore ask ourselves what changes and developments are possible to make it less vulnerable. This is best done by setting up a table of alternatives:

Retaliatory Force with:

A. *Fixed bases*   (a)   domestic
                  (a′)   in foreign countries

B. *Variable bases* (b)   domestic
                   (b′)   in foreign countries
                   (b″)   oceanic   (1) on the water or
                                          water-based air
                                     (2) underwater

All arrangements except b″(2) can involve, with more or less difficulty, both planes and missiles; b″(2) can only be missile launching.

"Space" is neglected for two reasons: *first,* because the technology is still in such an early stage that many years will go by before a clear conception can be had of what objects are feasible; *second,* because it stands to reason that a missile fired from land or sea poses far fewer problems regarding accuracy, cost, etc., than one launched from several hundreds or thousands of miles above the earth, not to mention the moon. A retaliatory force of any size and power floating in space is only a distant possibility. We have to solve a minor problem for this interval: how to survive! The decisions we are concerned with deal with the next ten to fifteen years.

If for each year that passes we can keep such a time span ahead of us safe for survival, as we have done in the past, we accomplish more than we have any right to expect.

We must now *order* the different types of retaliatory forces according to their desirability. The less vulnerable system is preferable to the vulnerable. This leads to the following ordering (> sign means "preferable to"):

In general: B > A; a movable base is preferable to a fixed base; variable bases are more easily protected than fixed bases. Or put differently: The movability of a base is itself already the desired protection. It is possible to make up for the inferiority of a fixed system by special efforts and devices. The chief one is now called "hardening": i.e., any base can be made harder to penetrate, for example, by special defenses, by placing equipment underground (fuel, planes, missiles, etc.). Under certain conditions and at proper costs a fixed base may be hardened so much that it will be less vulnerable than a nonprotected variable, or movable, base. But the latter too can be hardened.

Specifically: b″ > b′ or b; a movable base on the oceans is preferable to bases moving about on land either abroad or at home. Oceanic bases are distinguished according to their being on or below water. The latter are clearly more difficult to find and therefore securer than surface ships such as aircraft carriers. But it is necessary also to consider seaplanes which, if they will work, could be superior to the carriers because of their greater dispersion and vastly greater mobility.

Just as fixed bases—which are by necessity land bases—can be hardened, the vulnerability, if any, of variable bases can be reduced by increasing their *mobility*. In addition they can become invisible by operating below the surface of the ocean, which is a form of hardening.

There are, therefore, for each of the two basic systems possibilities of combining properties. Should SAC keep a substantial number of planes constantly in the air, it would acquire the advantages of mobility. But it is gravely limited in that effort by the high fuel consumption, the expense of refueling in the air and the respective time coefficients which show this to be a rather ineffective makeshift compared with a truly mobile dispersion. Mobile aircraft carriers are "hardened" by the already mentioned screens, but effectively only against weapons of the recent past, not against those already in development.

The mobile oceanic systems also need bases from which to operate. But the staying power of the individual units is vastly greater than that of the land-based airplanes. This was true even before nuclear propulsion, but with its introduction a discrete jump forward has been made. There simply is no comparison between the endurance in battle readiness of a nuclear submarine and a conventional jet plane, however well and often the latter may be refueled. It remains fixed-base dependent after a short number of hours. The submarine can remain submerged for weeks on end. Plane and submarine can acquire the same strategic target; therefore, they can be substituted for each other as far as that target is concerned.

These hybrid characteristics must not be considered as equivalent to the mixed systems that were discussed above. A mixed system need not have hybrid components in order to be properly mixed.

Hardening Draws Fire

Our Strategic Air Command is at present the mainstay of our retaliatory power. It is exceedingly vulnerable to all principal types of attack. So it is only natural to protect it as best we can in different ways:

(1) It should be ready for almost instantaneous action. This expresses the previously mentioned fact that a vulnerable retaliatory force has to go into operation at full strength the moment an attack is launched against the country. Consequently the extensive readiness preparations, the alert systems, the planes constantly in the air and supplied with nuclear weapons, the Distant Early Warning line (DEW line), etc.

(2) It must be protected against sabotage. Thus extensive precautions are being taken against saboteurs' entering and harming the bases. One hopes that the most dangerous forms of sabotage or clandestine attack are completely nullified. (This is exceedingly doubtful.)

(3) The bases must be hardened, to different degrees. This should serve to beat back an attack on the bases themselves, an attack on runways, depots, planes, fuel dumps, personnel. To harden means to acquire ground-to-air defenses, air-to-air defenses, to place as much of the equipment as possible underground, to make bombproof shelters, etc.

We shall deal with (1) farther below, say nothing about (2), leaving this to the imagination of the reader, and here discuss (3).

Hardening may indeed accomplish a great deal: Fuel and nuclear weapons may be safely stored deep underground. Runways can be made thicker to withstand greater blast (but which planes can take off on deeply pockmarked runways?). People can be put into shelters. The planes themselves can be dug in, although they are very delicate and easily subject to damage. Active defense can be concentrated there: fighter planes with air-to-air missiles equipped with nuclear warheads, ground-to-air missiles equally equipped against planes and—if we are thinking of ICBM bases—anti-ICBM's (though the latter are, various official announcements notwithstanding, only something for a distant future—if they can ever be made at all).

Some of this hardening conflicts with the state of extreme flight readiness in which the force should be held. There will be no time to refuel, to rearm, to fly many missions. The planes that take off may even be shot down by their own defenses—especially those of nearby cities, if they are defended.

The following fundamental principle ought to be self-evident: *The harder the bases, the heavier will be the attack.*

It is immaterial whether the enemy attacks with planes or missiles or both. Only a nuclear attack with all its side effects, in particular widespread fall-out, need be considered.

The increase in the weight of the attack is a direct consequence of the hardening. The weight will increase more than proportionally, because the defense, active and passive, makes aiming more difficult: thick shelters require greater bombs, poorer anticipated aiming will be compensated by bigger bombs (all in the multi-megaton range, of course), shelters call for ground bursts with correspondingly vastly increased fall-out compared with that for high-altitude bursts, etc. The enemy may even want to produce fall-out deliberately. This he can easily do.

Let us leave aside for a moment the question whether we have got most of SAC safely into the air before or during such a period. Instead consider the general situation around the SAC bases: These are, in the United States and in many allied countries, located near large cities, which are *soft* targets (i.e., not especially defended, certainly much less defended than hardened SAC bases). Given almost any bombing pattern to be used in such raids, the population centers are exposed to blast and fire and in particular to radiation.

Hard SAC and missile bases are legitimate military targets. But they cannot be attacked effectively without important soft targets also coming under the influences of the attack.

The enemy, being the aggressor, has no reason to attack our soft targets, the big cities, first. His primary aim must be our retaliatory force. Only after he has destroyed it will he consider going on to annihilate the rest. But why should he, if he can get the cities intact, with all the industrial power they represent, which he may want to use for his own purpose? He will attack them if he wishes just to kill, or if he has failed to reach our retaliatory force. The frequently drawn picture of an initial, all-out attack on our cities as the primary event of a war is fundamentally faulty. But that does not make the cities safe.

Our choice of SAC and missile bases condemns the nearby soft targets. An enemy attack will not be stopped by the fact that SAC is partly in the air or that some missile salvos have been fired. The enemy will attack the bases in full strength in any case for several reasons: *first,* his attack instruments, i.e., the bombers and ballistic missiles, are not suited for his active defense against our counterblow; hence, he will use them at any rate; *second,* our power may not be great enough (in his estimation of our capabilities at least, which alone matters), so that our planes will have to return to their bases for repeat missions, or he may think our missile-firing rate to be low enough so that his attack would interfere with it successfully.

The distribution of SAC bases in the homeland and, to a lesser degree, that of future missile bases, being what it is, guarantees tremendous casualty rates for nearby soft targets. "Nearby" must be interpreted with great latitude considering speed of operations, megaton yields of weapons, aiming errors, and confusion of combat. We must add also that the enemy will surely see to it that not a single bomb he ever succeeds in getting over this country will go to waste. Unless the *warhead* is destroyed each will go off, even if the carrier should be destroyed far from the target. It is technically easy to make such arrangements. Thus "success" of defense, once the plane or missile is over the United States, simply means the substitution of another place for devastation than the (possibly military!) one the enemy had chosen. This is a peculiar dilemma for the defense of the homeland.

What was said about bases in the United States applies even more forcefully to bases in allied countries. There the population density is much greater than here (England!). The more American, British or other bases in those countries are hardened, the greater the possibility of side-devastation. This goes for the Intermediate Ballistic Missiles there too.

Yet, how can we avoid hardening? Of course we are not pleading for a vulnerable retaliatory force in order to give some indirect and tenuous protection to our cities.

Hardening is also very expensive. Again an alternative has to be considered: instead of spending effort and material on hardening—which does not *increase* our striking power; at best it *preserves* it!—we may choose a different system. The weakest way out is to build the system, though in itself vulnerable, to such strength that, with what would be left of SAC and ICBM's on fixed land bases, we would be assured of a modicum of strength. This is what we are doing now and what we are counting on.

Hardening of bases means a smaller system in more concentrated form, it being impossible with present equipment to harden a great number of units (needed length of runways, communications, servicing, etc.). Now concentration instead of dispersal is precisely what is wrong when considering exposure to nuclear attack: the concentrated units make the best targets and the large-yield bombs are best suited for them.

There is a race between more hardening and heavier attack. The basic fact is that there is no other limit to the megatons that can be placed in bombs except their weights. But weights have constantly gone down per megaton and will do so further while the lifting capability of planes and missiles increases. For each new degree of hardening of any type of base, and in particular missile bases, a heavier attack can be made. Computations quickly show that it is easier and cheaper for the enemy to build and launch an additional missile than for us to increase hardening to an extent that would nullify the use of that additional weapon.

Hardening imposes a greater burden on a country than the burden the opponent has to assume in order to raise his striking power with which to offset the effects of hardening.

To restate: Cities are vulnerable even if our retaliatory force is invulnerable. But part of their vulnerability is, at present, a direct consequence of being near SAC bases and that degree of vulnerability becomes larger if the bases are hardened to a high degree. But *not every* form of an invulnerable retaliatory force increases the danger to the cities: if the retaliatory force is nowhere near the cities then they are at least that much safer.

If the enemy wishes to destroy a city, it makes no difference whether our retaliatory force is vulnerable or not. He can do it.

There is still the following observation to be made: The danger to the soft targets is naturally reduced by the deterrent which the forces on the hard bases represent. In other words, if SAC power is such that, no matter what the enemy does, he is "destroyed" to a degree which is entirely inacceptable to him, then in spite of being near a hard target of prime importance, the soft target is protected for the simple reason that no attack will take place. This could be achieved also by SAC's being softer, provided there were no surprise; but this assumption would be of ever-decreasing validity for the future. Of course, it is impossible to give SAC this degree of power and provide this assurance. Ideally there could be one single impenetrable point from which, at a moment's notice, any enemy could be totally destroyed at will. Such a force would then have the effect of a complete deterrence; even more, it could subjugate any other power. Nothing of this kind exists anywhere in the world, nor has it ever existed. It is doubtful that one should strive to develop in that direction, but we cannot foresee where technology will take us.

How pathetic it is to consider that the more "effective" we make our present ineffective retaliatory system, the more we are endangering our people: precisely what we most want to protect. The rigidity with which we adhere to a technologically antiquated strategic concept endangers the entire country.

But observe that the situation is more favorable to Russia. Their more thinly populated country with large waste areas more easily allows embedding and hardening of all kinds. The bases of her retaliatory force are mostly far removed from important centers of population (of which there are few anyway) and they do not generate, as in this country, great satellite settlements after having been started in comparatively remote areas. Russia can disperse more and do it more safely. Russia can give dispersal rather than hardening a greater role; Russia can change the complement on each base more freely (and in great secrecy) and thus achieve some advantages of a mobile system even though it is landlocked.

If, instead of moving the base, one can move the weapon freely and continuously, one has a superior system.

Early Warning

The higher the vulnerability of defensive installations and the greater the vulnerability of the retaliatory force, the greater is the pay-off for surprise. This is an inescapable relationship. The attacker will do everything possible to achieve the utmost in surprise. Consequently one will be willing to pay a great price for early warning. It must come early enough so that the active defense can do something about the announced attack: counterattack, "man the bastions," get guns ready, get planes into the air, fire the missiles, get steam up in warships —whatever the technology may demand. Otherwise, there is no "hardening" at all. Or, SAC must immediately get into the air, which is not possible while a great, nearby battle is fought between the active defense and the oncoming aggressor. The shortage of time available between early warning and the actual attack forces us to make greater and greater efforts to push the early-warning installations as far north and as far toward the sea as possible. (This, of course, puts a high premium on enemy attacks via the Caribbean, the southwestern shore of the United States, and Mexico, attacks of which the Russians are capable if we attribute to them, as we must, our own ability to refuel bombers in the air.) At any rate early detection becomes increasingly more difficult because of the increased speed of incoming planes and missiles, their different altitudes, their smallness, the possibility and effectiveness of decoys, etc.

Early warning makes sense only if the one who receives the warning can actually do something about the announced peril.

This obvious requirement is by no means properly built into our present defense system.[1] It is certainly not fulfilled for civil

---

[1] Early warning for the NATO forces until quite recently was functioning only 5 days a week from 8 A.M. to 5 P.M. (It has now been placed on a 24-hour basis.) What greater absurdity can there be? This was sanctioned by the military leaders of many countries. One wonders what other absurdities exist at present here or in the NATO world! We may assume

defense. SAC can get part of itself into the air, although this becomes increasingly more difficult in spite of great efforts made to obtain almost instantaneous take-off. Furthermore, the scientific and technological difficulties of obtaining early warning (with proper identification) mount steadily and approach an impasse, if it has not already been reached. Now we even desire early warning against ballistic missiles—almost hopeless. Yet we are making increasing efforts in that direction instead of concentrating in another direction altogether: to make our retaliatory forces *in*vulnerable, i.e., to produce a condition where early warning is by virtue of the situation much less important and certainly not as vital as in the present situation.

So we see that a basically faulty strategic concept generates the need for special devices, equipment and services for which great effort must be made. If, instead, a different system were chosen, a reassessment of effort would be indicated, leading to an overall improvement in our capabilities.

This is not to be construed as stating that warning, or early warning, is not desirable. We did discuss the role of intelligence above. It is one of the prime aims of military operations. But it is one thing to *improve* operations by intelligence and another to make them wholly *dependent* on special information. Systems of the latter sort cannot survive.

I shall digress for a moment with a remark on civil defense: What good does early warning or any warning do in our case of multi-megaton attacks? Especially for the large cities? Do we just wish to sink to our knees for prayer while awaiting the death blow? Or do we want to send a last curse to the government, or to the Civil Defense Administration in particular, for having let us down? Do we suffer more or fewer agonies knowing that we cannot do one single thing to stop the attack, to

---

that similar mistakes are made in Russia somewhere in her military establishment, but the point is that we cannot bank on them.

join our loved ones to die with them, to seek nonexisting shelters capable of rendering protection against blast or at least against radiation? Would one not rather prefer to die without being "warned," without having the impotency of our defense system driven home in the last moment of life?

Civil defense warning without even remotely effective civil defense, as at present, is nothing but a preposterous, blasphemous farce. It is an insult to the intelligence of the whole people.

Superiority of Offensive Power Versus "Invulnerable" Forces

It may seem impossible to talk of an "invulnerable" force in view of the present ascendancy of offensive power.

First of all, "invulnerability" is a relative notion. Nothing is completely, absolutely and forever invulnerable if a determined, powerful enemy, shunning no effort and expense, is bent on destruction; but for some military forces this cost is much higher than for others. For some it is forbiddingly so; for some, finally, new scientific discoveries have to be made which, while it is not unreasonable to expect them, have not yet happened and are nowhere in sight.

An attack on a military force is successful only when the part of it that remains is no longer a power. This means that SAC, for example, can suffer the destruction of some bases; or perhaps that a single base can survive, after a fashion, if part of it is gone. SAC may still be a power, it may still survive. But no city can. A megaton weapon hitting part of an SAC base will do great damage, but some believe that the situation may not be absolutely hopeless. Therefore it makes a lot of sense to defend SAC bases, to ward off the attacker by heavy fire from interceptors or from defensive ground-to-air missiles. If only a part of the attacker's force is destroyed, much is accomplished, or, to put it the other way around, if only some of the enemy's bombs get through there is a slight chance that the attacked part of SAC can still function. How large that part is depends on the degree of hardening: how many planes have been put in shelters, how many extra runways are usable, and how many defensive missile batteries still exist. But there are quite different, vastly superior, forms of invulnerability, as we shall see in the next chapter.

As far as cities are concerned, the situation is quite different: *The defense of a city must be perfect or it is no defense at all. Even if only one single megaton weapon gets through to New York or Washington or Chicago or whatever city you may wish to name, that city is gone completely.*

There must be no illusion about it: A 90% successful defense of a city is no defense and who can even dream of 90%. In ancient times (World War II) a 90% effective defense meant that the remaining 10% of the attacking planes could do perhaps 10% damage, if that much. Now one single bomb that gets through does *all* the damage. A successfully defended city means large numbers of people surviving under conditions that allow them to go on living, perhaps to rebuild, or at least to remain at a level at which a reduced but continuing existence is their reasonable prospect. Anyone who has even a cursory knowledge (gained, for example, from the publicly available book, *The Effects of Atomic Weapons,* issued by the Atomic Energy Commission, and many other such releases of more recent date) of the probable effects of a 10- to 25-megaton explosion over a large city will agree that it is not an idea of perfection which causes us to state once more: *City defense against such weapons must be 100% perfect or it is no defense at all.*

The burden of proof that any city, let alone the thirty or fifty most populous cities in the United States or Russia, could be defended, or indeed *is* now actually defended, to 100% against bombers, or against missiles fired from bombers, or against ballistic missiles, or against clandestine operations is of course on those who make this assertion. How statements to that effect can be made seriously by responsible persons or agencies is beyond the understanding of the present writer. Since they cannot possibly fool themselves they must be trying to fool others.

Alarms, Errors and Attacks

So far we have discussed the condition of a single force. Now we must aim at understanding the interplay between the forces of the opponents. There it will happen that both will have retaliatory forces, either each one vulnerable to the other's attack force, or one may have an invulnerable force while the other has not. Finally, both may have invulnerable retaliatory systems. This is a case of particular interest. At the present time we either have the first case or are going over into the second one, with Russia undoubtedly having a less vulnerable force than the United States.

The correct evaluation of our strategic situation is possible only if the interaction of these different types of forces is well understood.

Leaving aside for a moment the case of the absolutely perfect surprise attack for which there is not the slightest warning, we have the following typical time sequence:

$$\text{Signal} \longrightarrow \text{Identification} \longrightarrow \text{Alarm} \longrightarrow \text{Attack}$$

If signal and attack coincide, i.e., if the attack is the only signal, then we have perfect surprise. This happened when, during World War II, German V_2 missiles fell on London; their explosion was the only signal received. This may obviously happen with the new Intermediate or Intercontinental Ballistic Missiles; nevertheless, they might be detected in flight provided some stringent requirements are met.

At each point in the above sequence, up to the attack, there is the possibility of a failure:

The *signal* (which is also a warning) may not occur when it should, or there may be a signal without a cause.

The *identification* of the object, of the attacker and of the severity of the attack may be wrong: i.e., planes can be mistaken for geese or vice versa; planes, though hostile, can be identified as one's own or vice versa; the numbers involved may be over- or understated. The attacker will make every effort to produce malfunctioning, for example, by decoys, by electronic countermeasures (disturbance of radar, etc.) and by the use of deceitful tactics.

The *alarm* may not go off at all or go off for no cause.

After the attack begins, further errors and mistakes are possible.

Each of these defects has a certain probability which one wishes to reduce as much as possible. Of course one would like a system with complete certainty.

Absolute reliability has not been attained by the human race in any of its undertakings. Nor has it been necessary, even in weapons systems. But now it is required in some cases, for example, in the defense of large cities as was shown above. Yet in this case it is impossible to attain reliability.

Perhaps the highest degree of reliability for complex systems is reached in high-speed electronic calculators. But these are logically designed constructs and, apart from the uncertainties of a nonmalevolent nature, there are no deliberate countermoves being made against their functioning. Yet even there things go wrong, despite the fact that computers exist by now in large numbers and are in continuous use—and have provided valuable experience on the basis of which to improve the operation of existing devices and the design of new devices.

But no combat has actually taken place which would have tested even a small fraction of the design of the world's retaliatory forces. Exercises, though indispensable, are only a pale image of the real thing. *So there is no immediate guidance from experience. There is only hypothetical construction.* The new systems are so different from those used in World War II that the experience from there hardly carries over to the present. This is to a large measure true for the carriers of weapons, especially for the ballistic missiles. It is unrestrictedly true for the nuclear weapons, especially for the multi-megaton hydrogen bombs.

In previous times, when a war was followed by technological developments, these were never of the magnitude we witness now: it was easy to extrapolate from past experience. The difference between a crossbow and bows and arrows was important; the transition from crossbows to gunpowder was a very big step; but nothing was remotely as large as that between conventional explosives and the hydrogen bomb of several megatons. For the latter case we cannot simply project past experience—something different *in kind* has happened. This does not make us completely helpless but the danger of erroneous reasoning is vastly greater than ever before. Military writing is full of valid illustrations showing the disasters that were caused by "preparing for the last war." Yet the transition in technology was never nearly as abrupt as it is now almost every five years compared with the preceding five years.

We consider now the following principal cases of hostilities:

A. *The "ultra-attack":* The enemy achieves total surprise, i.e., there is no warning, no identification, no alarm. The power of the attack is *critical*, i.e., obliterating. Our own force is completely vulnerable and hence destroyed. This is the complete end; we cannot even damage the enemy. His only losses are those suffered by whatever sporadic local defense we can muster.

No major power is now in either position vis-à-vis another major power. However, a large power could deal in this way with almost any small country and destroy its military installations completely—provided the attacker is not put under pressure from other powers. It could, obviously, also destroy the rest of the country.

This case is possible, but its occurrence is improbable. The small countries are indirectly protected by the interests of other large powers. It will be different if in a few years more countries acquire large-scale nuclear capabilities. Small countries will then not be safe from other small countries.

B. *The identified and sub-critical attack,* hence spread out over time: In this case there is the possibility of alarm and the preceding events of signaling and identification with the chance of errors. Neglecting those sub-cases, we find that, if our own retaliatory force is vulnerable, we have to strike back fully with everything that is left over after the first phases of the enemy's attack. The enemy will concentrate his attack on the sources of our retaliatory power: the bases, airfields, weapons depots, personnel. Such an attack will cripple our vulnerable force, but some part of it will be able to rise. Whatever that part may be, this is what has to be used. Nothing will be held back. There is no point in keeping reserves. However, this should *not* be interpreted as being necessarily identical with a short war!

Our force will strike at the bases of the enemy's force if it is vulnerable, provided the enemy has some force left in a form that can still be attacked. If on the other hand the entire enemy force (assuming planes only) is in the air, and if the part that gets through our active defenses in several phases is already powerful enough to obliterate the bases of our own striking strength, and if we are aware of this, then our attack of his bases is pointless and wasteful. Instead, our remaining force will be used for retaliation and therefore we will attack his cities. It will be swift revenge and punishment. It will have only moral and political significance. It can have no military significance any more.

It is possible to envisage the following case: The attacker's approach is properly observed and identified. Our defenses can get into action, having been duly alarmed, and our vulnerable retaliatory force can be got under way before the enemy can destroy significant parts of it, let alone destroy it completely. Thus we have at least a significant part of our force heading for the enemy country. In that case his force and ours might pass each other in the air, his force naturally nearer our frontiers than ours to his since he had the initiative. Each side then delivers what blow it was prepared to deal to the other, diminished only by whatever toll the respective defensive forces can take of the aggressor and the retaliator.

In this situation the further events depend on the following: *Has each side mounted the maximum power of which it is capable? This will certainly be true for the attacked.* He will now have to decide whether the attacker has done the same:

(a) If the conclusion of the attacked is *positive,* this means that he believes that the attacker cannot increase his present attack by repeat strikes. Consequently, the retaliatory force will make for the enemy's cities and try to inflict the largest possible population damage. The attacker will easily conclude that this is the aim of the retaliatory force. If the attacker received early intelligence of the successful departure of the retaliatory force he will, instead of heading for the bases of the retaliatory forces also aim for the cities of the country he attacks. Originally, he may have had a purely military strike in mind, but the successful evasion of the attacked country's vulnerable retaliatory force has made an attack on those bases meaningless. It is ironic: *The attacked country, under these circumstances, has by virtue of its own successful operation brought devastation upon the nonmilitary, civilian targets it offers.*

(b) If the conclusion of the attacked is *negative,* this means that he believes that the attacker can mount repeat strikes. Therefore, whatever great damage the attacker will inflict, it will be less than what he can do by coming back. Consequently the retaliatory force will try to destroy the attacker's bases to prevent repetitions of the attack. The destruction of cities will be incidental but welcome as punishment and deterrent for the attacker. It will not be attempted unless the primary aim, the elimination of further striking power, is accomplished.

It is clearly difficult for either side to have adequate information. Each will certainly try to prevent the other from getting it. So each has to go by assumptions and try to outguess the other. The parallelism of these efforts with what goes on in games such as poker is apparent. One should therefore expect that an understanding of these games would be helpful. This is the domain of the mathematical theory of games of strategy. It has, indeed, produced rules of behavior which are directly applicable to military problems of the kind outlined here. We shall have opportunity to draw at least one fundamental lesson later (cf. p. 76). The important point to make at this juncture is that each side will have to choose that strategy which is optimal for him in the sense that it is his best action no matter what the other side can do to hurt him.

Observe that the above examples refer to a *vulnerable retaliatory force*. This imposes a sharp limitation for the actions of the country that is attacked. We have stressed it before but it needs to be restated: The retaliation has to be immediate and to employ the full power available. In the preceding discussion there was only an appearance of invulnerability—the force was assumed to be in the air or able to rise before and during the attack. But it has no staying power. It has to return to bases which in the meantime were exposed to the enemy attack and probably destroyed. It cannot be spaced out over time. The situation is different with an invulnerable force.

In addition we have made very optimistic assumptions, in particular that there are no mistakes and that the time interval between the first signal and the actual *in-flight state* of all planes suffices. That interval is now rapidly tending toward zero. This applies in particular to the case where one side has planes (SAC) and the other already possesses missiles with a warning time of less than five minutes after they have been spotted by radar—if they are spotted at all! These and other asymmetries in the relation between two opponents will for a long time to come be of great importance. They cannot be neglected in studying the nuclear parity conditions.

Assume now that we have an *invulnerable retaliatory force* and that the enemy attacks us, for whatever reasons. Clearly the deterrent which we would like to see our force exercise did not work, perhaps because it is too weak or the enemy believes it to be too weak. Be that as it may; what are our courses of action? "Invulnerable" is only a relative term, meaning mostly that surprise is virtually impossible and that our counteraction is assured. The enemy will want to minimize the effects of the latter. He will therefore concentrate his efforts on neutralizing our retaliatory force after having penetrated our perimeter defenses. If "invulnerability" has been achieved by hardening, the hardened bases will come under heavy attack. It will make some difference whether we have planes or missiles on the bases. The former should rise eventually, but the more effectively the bases have been made invulnerable the less urgent is the need for instantaneous reaction.

If the enemy is unable to destroy our bases in one mission our force will be used to attack his bases to make a repetition of his first strike impossible or less effective. The time we have available for this action is shorter than the time he needs to mount his next strike—whatever the concrete time intervals may be. They differ for planes and missiles.

If the enemy is unable to destroy our retaliatory force—for example, because it is hardened beyond his expectations or so far dispersed that he cannot reach it—our counteraction need not be imminent. Indeed, if it is not, his country has the threat of vengeance and punishment hanging over it. This may be meted out piecemeal or in concentrated fashion. City after city can be taken under fire, one at a time if we so choose, especially from our mobile missile bases. Threat can be followed by threat, thereby possibly weakening the people's will to resist and employing the rising forces in the enemy country against its government. But let us hold these considerations in abeyance for later (cf. p. 139). Now we have not asked about the rationale of each party's actions; rather we are discussing technical possibilities and strategies, not trying to find the optimal strategy for either side. There are obviously many alternatives corresponding to the technological possibilities and the different ways in which each can be exploited. This gives many courses of action; we may call each of them a "strategy."

There remains the possibility that the enemy may strike from invulnerable bases. This has a bearing upon our response: we will not waste effort in trying to find and destroy his bases even if he should have to engage in repeat strikes. We would do this only if we were *very* much stronger than he —but we have assumed nuclear parity throughout! We will, instead, try to deter him by concentrating on his population, though possibly spacing the retaliatory action over time, as described above.

Thus we have another paradoxical result: An invulnerable retaliatory force, if strong enough, is a powerful deterrent, but if a country possessing such a power *becomes an aggressor* it exposes its soft population targets to the primary response of the attacked country.

Or stated differently: Under conditions of nuclear parity a country having unprotected open cities and possessing itself an invulnerable retaliatory force cannot become an aggressor without inviting disaster on its population unless—contrary to the assumption—it can overwhelm the opponent's retaliatory force in such short order that it is destroyed.

If we make this symmetrical for both sides we are led to the determination of the optimal strategies for both sides. This is done further below. But first another point of prime importance.

Geese and Meteors

It is definitely unpleasant to have a *vulnerable* retaliatory force. SAC therefore makes many efforts to become less vulnerable. The principal device would be, as already mentioned, to keep a substantial number of planes constantly in the air, to disperse planes on the ground as widely as possible, even by using civilian airports, to move them about frequently, to protect itself against the obvious kinds of sabotage and by other means to make the enemy's unobserved penetration difficult. Future ICBM bases will be kept in a high state of readiness, but that state will be a far cry from the push-button readiness of future solid fuel missiles.

This is not a handbook on military operations (in which case it would have to be many thousands of pages long). There one should find details about reduction of vulnerability. Unfortunately I cannot tell the reader to go and look it up, for the simple reason that it does not exist—at least not for the public —in spite of the creation of so many large military research organizations. Perhaps there should be none in the public domain. But we can briefly deal with one point that should be covered in that mythical book in greatest detail and with utmost care: The problem of *identification* and its relation to vulnerability of the retaliatory force.

We recall the sequence on page 56 from the signal to the enemy attack. The time between the two is the *warning time*. The longer it is, the better the chances to activate the defenses, to get SAC into the air, to prepare and fire the ground-to-air missiles. It has already been stated that this interval inexorably goes toward zero.

This extreme shortness of time makes the disposition of every minute that elapses between identification and attack tremendously important. Identification and *alarm* can be made almost identical given modern electronic equipment. But between the first signal and identification some time will be lost. It must be minimized. Hence there will be a tendency to give alarm unnecessarily rather than take frightful chances of missing the true approach of the enemy by even only a minute. Yet are there systems which can stand a false alarm? And how often?

Here is the crucial point that distinguishes SAC from a missile force—though both are vulnerable.

We shall find another dilemma: the more technological progress drives us toward higher speed of planes or missiles, the less stable will our system be in respect to mistakes and errors. These are bound to occur. Yet we cannot stop being driven in the direction of speed. Ultimately only the design of different *systems* which are not upset by these technological tendencies will lead us away from the troubles in which we have become so deeply enmeshed. Such a system is the "Oceanic System" (cf. page 80 ff.).

Distance also plays a role, as is obvious: The difference between fast-flying planes and missiles is practically nil if a Russian attack on Western Europe is considered; it still matters somewhat for the United States. This means, of course, that the NATO countries cannot afford *not* to understand *instantly* that they are being attacked, if such an event should occur. As we shall see presently, neither must they ever falsely imagine being attacked.

Recently a flock of geese was spotted on a radar constantly and dutifully poised to discover a possible Russian fleet of bombers heading for the United States heartland. They were believed to be bombers, an alarm was promptly sounded, and a sequence of operations set into motion which would have led to an attack on Russia had not, as was to be expected, the true identity of the radar signal been discovered in time. This is the type of error which is still compatible with the operation of SAC forces. Should airplane speed be doubled—which is not impossible if we think of such advanced designs as the supersonic B-58, the B-70 and superfuels—we may exceed the limits within which such errors can be tolerated without a catastrophe. This works both ways: If Russia has this higher capability the time is so shortened that our inclination to mistake geese for bombers will be increased. The result will be a severe disturbance of the system, which will produce a tendency to decrease its efficiency in a dangerous manner. Repetition of errors will be discouraged though there can be no lessening of the tendency to commit them.

If we send up our bombers needlessly under present conditions, we will soon discover that geese were geese. *There is time for recall.* There is an upper bound within which the complete identification has to be made: our planes must never get into the Russian Early Warning System. They will not be geese in the Russian radar! They will be the real thing, though they will be there by mistake. The faster our bombers become, the shorter the time for recall. Naturally we are driven to make them faster. The advantages of the increase in speed can, of course, offset the disadvantage of shortening this time interval for recall.

Should our force mistakenly get into the Russian Early Warning System, the consequence is clear: If the Russians have a vulnerable retaliatory force composed of planes, then these will rise immediately and start for the United States. This is one of the cases discussed above. They would hit the United States probably after we have either proceeded with our attack or have frantically and perhaps vainly tried to convince the Russians that we didn't mean it and that all was a ghastly mistake. Everything might still be called off by both sides. But if the Russians have vulnerable ICBM's, they would have to fire them instantly and with their vastly greater speed than that of our planes, the missiles would hit the United States before any explaining could be done, or even before our planes could go through with their flight!

Our forces, of course, have to obey orders. None would be allowed wantonly to attack anyone, merely because some geese have been sighted. The existing system of controls is as tight as one can make it and the danger is therefore none too great. But in every system there is always a danger of malfunctioning.

The case of SAC, as briefly outlined, changes fundamentally if our principal retaliatory strength, or a substantial part of it is in the form of *ballistic missiles* fired from vulnerable domestic or allied bases. We do not yet have these missiles in operation, but when they are in position they will unquestionably be in highly vulnerable installations—at least as much as present SAC bases. There is no easy, obvious way of provisionally protecting the missiles. SAC planes can be kept continually in the air (i.e., a part of the force, and at very great expense) but not ballistic missiles. A very serious drawback! Missile bases can, however, be hardened, mostly by underground installation. The pressure to do this will undoubtedly become very great since it is doubtful that the advantages of mere speed of the missiles over great distances completely outweighs the safety that SAC planes in the air provide.

Assume now that we expect a Russian attack on the United States will be by means of ICBM's, possibly followed by planes. Whatever type of retaliatory force we have, provided it is vulnerable, can produce this type of possible error: we spot in our radar screens *showers of meteors,* satellite debris and electrical phenomena and mistake them for Russian ICBM's or at least we are exceedingly suspicious that they might be such.

This is the situation of the flock of geese all over again with a cardinal difference. Time for verification has shrunk to only fractions of minutes, to almost zero. But the real difference is this: If we decide to respond in this short time interval we have no choice but to fire our (presumably ready) ballistic missiles. If we do not fire them and the radar signal is indeed of Russian ICBM's, then our retaliatory force is crippled or completely gone and we have lost. If we do fire them and the signals were those of meteors (or similar astronomical or terrestrial phenomena) the missiles are on their way. *They cannot be recalled.* We have attacked Russia without wanting to do so. We have fallen prey to technical tricks.

What targets would these missiles aim at? If we think that the meteors or rather the alleged missiles are meant for our missile bases and would be powerful enough to destroy them in a short series of salvos we would aim in retaliation for the Russian cities. There would be no reason to destroy empty bases. If we think the enemy "missiles" are aimed in force at our cities, then we would know that the greatest damage is about to be done to our population and we would retaliate against their cities. The reader will observe the parallelism with the above case of the bombers we failed to recall. Naturally, if we attack Russian cities by mistake, we are done for, since even during the attack the enemy would retaliate by destroying our cities.

Consider again the meteor case. There are such showers and some occur at regular times of the year. If Russia wanted to attack us, would not those periods be most suitable? Certainly then the distinction between missiles and meteors is greatly complicated. However, meteors have distinct magnetic echo wakes, well known to radio astronomers. If ballistic missiles do not have them, would it not be wise for the Russians or for us to build them so that they produce this phenomenon too? Assuming it could be done, is this to our advantage, if the Russians should know about this? Perhaps it would then not be, because this might make them inclined *not* to bypass present meteor signals as quickly as they may be doing. They do have a fairly vulnerable retaliatory force and would therefore have to fire right away.

Yet concealment of the true nature of a weapon has always been a standard military procedure, believed to be of great value. Should we, therefore, once we have ICBM's, perhaps on the contrary be anxious to convince Russia that our missiles make unmistakably individual tracks, have a clear signature on their radars, so that no other accidentally occurring phenomenon of nature could ever possibly be mixed up with one of our missiles? But how are we going to convince the Russians that we can do this, and that, if we can, we will stick to this idea? Why should we not stick to it, since we do not want to attack surreptitiously? Or are we bluffing? Should we have an international inspection system? Are not the Russian interests in that respect parallel to ours, though otherwise the two powers are poised in a deadly manner against each other?

These are just some of the questions which arise. There seems to be no end of them and of the complications they produce. But how far do these matters penetrate into the government? While they are perhaps discussed among some scientists and officers, they are never considered in that detail—vital though it is—by the highest functionaries of government. For them there are so many similar problems elsewhere—and there is simply not enough time to go into everything as deeply as could and should be done. This is precisely the moment when these people, not knowing what to do and not able to estimate the consequences of their decisions, begin to talk about having to take a "calculated risk." The use of this or a similar empty phraseology cannot cover up for the lack of knowledge. So all over the world we constantly go on building systems of devastating physical power without a proper understanding of their inner nature and the high degree of instability they possess.

All that was said in respect to the United States could be restated, allowing for a few appropriate modifications, as far as the Russian side is concerned. Of course, most of our analysis will look very different once we drop the restriction to vulnerable retaliatory forces and can, instead, assume "invulnerability." Although we know that the difference is one of degree only, even a few degrees bring about a big change. And the fact is that the two types of forces are really very far apart from each other.

To sum up: *Accidental, large-scale war is a distinct possibility when one side has a highly vulnerable retaliatory force. The situation is correspondingly worse when both are so equipped. The dangers are particularly great when vulnerably placed missiles are used.*

Fortunately the missile age is not yet with us; but we are moving into it with increasing speed. We shall then look back —if we ever make it—upon the comfortable, comparatively unproblematical age of the jet bomber with the usual nostalgia we have for the "good old times." Such is the fate the human race has brought upon itself.

The Mythical Major

It is sometimes asserted that a new world war could be started by an inadvertent or a deliberate action of a single officer, not even one placed highly in the military hierarchy.

There is no doubt that under present conditions a world-wide war could be started, on each side, by very small numbers of people, *"legally"* or *not*. In the United States war has to be declared by Congress, but few people can have the illusion that hostilities could not be started directly, long before Congress has any chance of action. The use of nuclear weapons is —theoretically—predicated upon the word of the President of the United States, and there are many situations possible where he may have to act before he can get a declaration of war. There are even situations where the commander of SAC may have to give the order to proceed to attack, for example when we are attacked and the President has been killed or is incapacitated. The action would be legal, provided we are attacked. But what if it is based on error and there is no time to ascertain whether it was an error, or to recall the missiles, which can never be done? Be that as it may, the technical conditions of automatic, reflex response are as we have described them.

In Russia it is even simpler for a small number of men to set the war machine in operation. This applies to the offensive, the willful attack. Just as the machine gun has made national dictatorships easier to establish and maintain, nuclear weapons with their coming missile-delivery capability make it possible for small groups of men to terrorize other nations.

Since there is no doubt possible about the abilities of governments to plunge the world into war, the really interesting question is whether that can be done lower down the line, either willfully or by accident.

A distinction has to be made: A government, whether that of a dictator or one temporarily empowered, wishing to start a war would do so only by unleashing full power against the enemy. Anything else would be foolish. An underling, however, cannot set the whole war machine into operation, *except by an individual hostile act of a type which inevitably commits his own and the other side to an extension of hostilities*. The commitment is mechanical and automatic, rather than one based on honor, pride, national feeling, etc. The latter type of commitment belongs to past ages. The present is too full of mortal danger to allow nations to indulge in such luxuries—no matter what high-sounding, hollow words may be used for a disclaimer.

Previously no junior officer was in peacetime ever poised so that he could have technically produced a catastrophe in a foreign country such that the latter would have interpreted it as a major hostile military act. Today many are placed in this position and in future there will be many more.

This does not state anything about the probability of occurrence; it merely describes a technical possibility. Therefore safeguards have to be devised to give the occurrence a probability approaching zero. Now we are no longer concerned with the type of error previously discussed, which, if committed, would set one's whole war machinery into motion.

SAC has created a complicated system supposed to be capable of safeguarding against the kind of accidental action under consideration here. It is called "Fail-Safe" and governs the behavior of its fully (nuclear) armed force that is actually in the air, or is being put into the air, following an alarm and may be approaching Russia. When a plane reaches a distant critical point, the commander either has to receive specially protected signals ordering him to proceed, or he has to return.

Assuming that no error is possible in coding, transmission, checking, etc., there can still be malfunctioning: The (mythical!) major in command of the plane may disregard orders, proceed and drop a 5-, 10- or more megaton weapon in enemy country, not necessarily on target, since he may never reach it. This will set off retaliation. It is doubtful that we have machinery which would serve in time to explain away the nature of the incident and to offer amends. It is even doubtful that such machinery can be set up in advance. But the problem would bear thinking about.

Will our mythical major ever act this way? Will his crew go along with him? It is not likely, at least not as long as the alarm was based on possibly false radar signals (of which fact he would get confirmation). But suppose the international situation is very bad and the United States has accepted, for the sake of peace, humiliating setbacks. Perhaps planes have been shot down and ships have been sunk, and still we have done no more than to issue protests. Even graver incidents can have happened. The country may feel utterly frustrated, many sections of the population may clamor for revenge and stern action. The point is that formerly nobody in the major's position could have done anything decisive; now he can. This introduces a new element of uncertainty which must not be lost sight of.

If we have missiles, the situation is peculiarly different. With the present type of liquid-fueled missiles, which need many men and a long count-down time before they are ready to be fired, there is less danger of the above type of malfunctioning. The military fabric of the country would have to disintegrate substantially before anything could happen there. But when more advanced solid-fuel missiles of true push-button readiness become available, as they will be sooner or later, the danger increases. Again missile bases will remain sufficiently complicated so that it is unlikely but not impossible that a single individual officer or a very small group of officers could set off a catastrophe. This possibility makes for exciting reading of a fictional character but we may feel fairly safe in this respect. Nevertheless it is clear that small, highly efficient installations in which the greatest imaginable power is concentrated require a singularly stable political setup. If revolutions or civil wars occur, the dangers involving such countries, their neighbors and, indeed, the rest of the world, rise immeasurably.

The point is that the danger is greater as fewer people are involved (as in the plane with a crew of three). It diminishes if the individual can function only within a large and complicated machinery. But the danger rises again for the entire unit as such (missile base, missile-firing submarine, etc.).

All this is independent of whether the retaliatory force is vulnerable or not.

We dismiss the matter with an uncomfortable feeling: On the one hand we have confidence in the stability of those officers and men who are directly involved in situations where the above-mentioned deviations could technically occur. Our major remains mythical. On the other hand, exceptional political and psychological circumstances can arise which might trigger a behavior of individuals or nations that is outside any easily foreseen pattern. The poor showing of some American soldiers who fell captive to the Chinese in Korea is an illustration from another, though still military, area.

The situation is further complicated by the fact that what was said for one side applies obviously also to the other. Our understanding of Russian mentality, discipline and sensitivity in regard to national pride is not particularly firm. Although in such circumstances it is proper to make those assumptions which are least favorable to us, it is difficult to go beyond expressing uneasiness in regard to the stability of the Russians and stating the hope that these trigger conditions will never arise for the two chief antagonists.

All of this appears in a much more ominous light if large nuclear weapons, together with a delivery capability, should ever be given to some smaller nations, prone to revolutions, possessed by nationalistic aspirations and of correspondingly excitable temperament. It is not unreasonable to contemplate that such nations may believe it to be to their advantage to involve the large powers in war with each other. This they could do by clandestine operations, causing nuclear explosions, not attributable to any particular country, but producing tensions, countermoves, war.

When this time comes the big powers may discover that their conflicts, grave as they are, do cover up some elemental common interests. It is the duty of statesmen to discover what is common and what could form the basis of agreements. It is the duty of the military to prepare for the case when all other efforts fail.

There can be no complete enumeration of all possible accidents that might start a large war, given the new weapons capabilities. Even if we were able to make a complete list, what could be done about each individual item? Clearly probabilities would have to be assigned to each possible event and accordingly joint controls would have to be invented to deal at least with those receiving the highest probabilities. This requires a degree of coöperation for which the opposing powers are not prepared at this time. But even the highly improbable happens sometimes: In 1908 a very large meteor hit Siberia, devastating hundreds of square miles by fire; in 1947 another one almost destroyed Vladivostok. Neither in 1908 nor in 1947 did anyone think that this was a missile with a nuclear warhead. What if the third meteor falls on Stalingrad or Minneapolis? How will the countries with vulnerable retaliatory missile forces react? How much time will they feel they have available to make sure that this was a meteor and not the first missile from the other side?

Invulnerable Retaliatory Forces on Both Sides

The effects of possessing an invulnerable retaliatory force have been described in preceding sections. There can be no doubt whatsoever that, so long as we have to be armed and be prepared for retaliatory action in order to have an effective deterrence, an invulnerable force is vastly to be preferred to the present, vulnerable one. Now the question arises of how the United States is affected if the enemy too has an invulnerable force.

We are now ready to state the followng *first principle:*

In order to preserve a nuclear stalemate under conditions of nuclear plenty it is necessary for both sides to possess invulnerable retaliatory forces.

It was shown previously that the optimal strategy for the United States is to put its retaliatory force into a position of invulnerability. What the above statement means, essentially, is that this is also the best strategy the opponent can adopt and that if both use their optimal strategies, then the stalemate is more likely to be preserved than not.

It sounds odd that it should be to our advantage to have our (potential) enemy have an invulnerable retaliatory force. But in view of the preceding analysis, this is not difficult to understand: our primary interest is to protect ourselves. This we expect to do by deterring the enemy from attacking us. Clearly the deterrence is the greater the less vulnerable our retaliatory capability is.

Since we do not plan to attack the enemy it is at first blush indifferent to us whether his retaliatory force is vulnerable or not. Of all countries in the world, only we could now be attackers of Russia. None of the European powers could do this singly or in any European combination whatsoever and still hope to survive. China is still in too early a state of its industrial development to count as a possible independent antagonist of Russia with aggressive intentions (but times will change!). In spite of all this, Russia cannot afford to be without effective deterrent. Even if she were to believe our nonaggressive intentions, if she were without that power, it might set forces into motion, not now visible, endangering her very existence. But she does not believe us in the first place.

Russia's position is therefore in no way different from ours; she needs a deterrent force and she needs it in as invulnerable a form as possible. This is how she will build her force. She will use those forms of invulnerability best suited to her geography, her economic capabilities and the weapons systems she has chosen. It is immaterial at the moment what this choice actually is.

An invulnerable deterrent force on each side makes any attack by either one less likely since the ordinary means of surprise fail. Surprise is, as we saw, the greatest inducement and temptation to stage an attack—when all other conditions are favorable—provided the attacked country has a vulnerable retaliatory force.

There is a *second principle:*
In view of modern technology of speedy weapons delivery

from any point on earth to any other, it is in the interest of the United States for Russia to have an invulnerable retaliatory force and vice versa.

The first principle is not hard to grasp; the second one, which is merely a restatement of the first in a somewhat different form, sounds paradoxical. It is, however, possible to give a rigorous proof. The argumentation is complicated and difficult; it makes use of notions of the mathematical theory of games of strategy. However, we have already stated the crucial result: each party must stick to its optimal strategy or be sure to lose. Also, it is advantageous to each that the other adopt his own optimal strategy, which is that plan of action which secures for himself the best possible outcome no matter what the opponent does.

Leaving these statements aside, we can argue on an intuitive basis, as in preceding sections. We recall the extraordinary and steadily increasing danger of misinterpreting natural phenomena of the most varied kind as signs of an attack. Again, if the enemy with a vulnerable force does conclude falsely, even if only once, that he is being attacked and if we are in the ballistic missile age of nonrecallable action, a world catastrophe cannot be avoided.

We do not want to live under conditions so precarious. We want to protect ourselves against accidents and errors where these have consequences of the magnitude of an all-out thermonuclear war.

The invulnerability of the force removes the need, as will be recalled, to launch a "counter"-attack when no attack is being delivered in the first place. This would be the inevitable response of an alert country with a vulnerable force. To avoid this is where one of our chief interests lies.

Conferences on how to avoid surprise attack will never resolve the present deadly dilemma. But the fact that they have been arranged at all shows a beginning awareness of the magnitude and imminence of the danger. There is here a germ of recognition of common interest among the hostile camps. But the time is short to let it develop.

Our other aim is to be as well protected against willful attack by effective deterrence as technically possible. Our invulnerable force protects the enemy (and indirectly us) from the accidental catastrophe and it protects us from the enemy should he try to act deliberately.

There should be no misunderstanding of what it would mean for Russia to have an invulnerable retaliatory force. *We would lose nothing* thereby—absolutely nothing except the ability to stage a successful surprise attack against the enemy. This we do not plan to do in the first place, the time for such action having vanished at any rate. We have never planned a surprise attack; therefore, this inability to carry it out deprives us of nothing. Neither do we expose our cities and our population to any greater danger than the one they are facing at this moment. On the contrary, it is reduced *first* by the invulnerability of our own retaliatory force and the greatly increased effectiveness of the deterrent, and *second* by the virtual removal of the possibility of accidental war being started by either side.

So the task is to find suitable methods for building invulnerable forces.

A Stopgap Device

Before we examine better systems a word about SAC operations: The 15-minute, certainly the 5-minute, alert being insufficient, we can nevertheless immediately protect SAC by keeping a substantial part of that force constantly in the air. By "substantial" I mean something like 50% of the force in being. This is expensive. It will cost per year anywhere between 1 to 3 billion dollars to do so. But this is a small price to pay compared with the results achieved. This country will spend in 1959 alone approximately 2.5 billion dollars on pleasure boating, to give some idea of the relative magnitudes involved. The measure would also decrease somewhat the importance of early warning, one of the most expensive and least reliable measures, thus making possible a balancing of costs, though there can be no doubt that we can absorb this additional amount without any great trouble.

A vulnerable SAC is practically worthless, offering no protection to the country. SAC properly invulnerable is a totally different instrument of defense. The fact that as soon as a critical international situation arises SAC takes to the air in order to be safe is a clear indication of the value of the operation.

But a good surprise attack would not take place in the midst of a critical situation. On the contrary, there would first be created a harmonious, peaceful atmosphere with plenty of high-level negotiations going on, if Russia really wanted to strike at us.

No amount of speeding up the time it takes to get into the air—and much effort has been made in that direction—can ever match the advantage of actually having the planes in the air.

Clearly, if our planes are kept in the air, they have to be refueled; the tanker planes themselves which would normally accompany the bombers for refueling have their operational ranges also reduced by being in the air, etc. (We assume, of course, that the bombers would always be fully armed with nuclear weapons with the warheads in place—otherwise the whole procedure would be meaningless.) All this complicates matters, but not hopelessly. However, we are ill-equipped with tankers. There has been no foresight to order them in proper numbers. Yet there is no deep problem here. At most it is a financial question of minor importance. (But this aspect probably appeared to be "crucial" to the first Secretary of Defense of the Eisenhower Administration—if he ever came to grips with the problem. Today too many think the budget to be more important than our life and the nation's future.)

There is, however, a profound difference between SAC in the air and a truly invulnerable retaliatory force. It is nothing but a stopgap measure. *This "invulnerable" force has no stay-*

ing power. It still has to be used *entirely* and *immediately;* it cannot spread out its operations. It cannot choose its own timing. This is a grave limitation. The effectiveness of the force as a deterrent is limited and it is much less valuable as an instrument of politics than would be the case with a truly invulnerable force. For these inherently stable forces we must search and these we must introduce with all conceivable speed.

In the meantime, we must hope that the order will be given immediately to put at least half of our Strategic Air Command into the air no matter what the cost and trouble. However, we can be sure that this measure will not be carried out: the worship of the sacred cow, the budget, will prevent it.

What a world we live in, that we need hundreds of fully armed bombers constantly over our heads so that we—and the world—may feel "safe."

4 The Oceanic System: The Invulnerable Force

In this chapter we shall search for the best form of invulnerability under the constraints of present technology.[1] "Present" must be interpreted somewhat broadly, i. e., to allow for technical devices which are at least on the drawing boards, though possibly not yet in production. The devices must not be so remote in time that nothing can be planned for them on a production basis. In that sense solid-fuel firing rockets are admis-

[1] We shall not discuss various other types of invulnerable retaliatory forces such as bacteriological warfare. Such devices seem to be little considered, just as gas was during the last war. One must suspect that this restraint is primarily due to the imperfection of the methods, the great possibility of "backfire" to one's own country, rather than to ethical-moral reasons. The latter, however, are the ones which are given. This is how the world is made: it is acceptable to transform humans into gas, burn them, destroy them by blast, by bullets, maim them, but it is not acceptable to let them die by means of microörganisms. It is difficult to fathom the reasons for such behavior.

sible, although they still have many difficulties to overcome, but platforms in outer space do not enter the picture. We neglect constraints of monetary costs for two reasons: first, they are not known and not knowable before concrete ideas about the magnitudes of programs have been formed if these involve new devices; second, the estimation of monetary costs is too narrow at any rate, since it leaves out of account the military worth of alternative defensive schemes. This is a complicated and very important topic, much neglected in the study of defense problems. (Costs and production are considered on p. 187.)

Whatever the costs might be, the first and overriding aim is to build a strategic force which takes us out of our present dilemma, gives our country a superior deterrent to aggressors and thereby makes the strongest possible contribution to world peace. Let the moneymisers explain afterward why some dollars saved are more important than the fulfillment of these goals. But we shall see that an acceptable system is economically within easy reach of this country.

Hardening the Zone of Interior

It was shown how hardening of SAC and missile bases draws fire and how the better the hardening the more the fire increases. Heavier and heavier bombs with yields in the high-megaton range have to be used. The better our anti-air or anti-missile defense becomes, the more bombs will be used in any onslaught. This goes for fixed installations. Air bases will always be fixed, and if the placement of planes is to be made mobile they have to travel from one base to the other, requiring many bases. Or they have to be kept in the air. At any rate, they retain their dependency on fixed bases which they must use at intervals of a few hours.

Missiles could conceivably be moved around within the country. This would be a formidable operation and is out of the question at present, since the missiles require large towers, complicated electronic gear and long count-down periods before being ready for firing. Neither can they remain long in a ready position. This may change somewhat when solid-fuel missiles are further developed, but their movability on land is of doubtful value. Such clumsy and conspicuous operations invite sabotage, which is anyway reaching into a new and as yet little appreciated dimension because nuclear weapons have become so small.

The attacker's fire is drawn to the Zone of Interior[2] if we hold our main force there and harden it. This is the tendency now developing. We also hold some of our retaliatory forces in allied countries. Their consent is only grudgingly given for the same plausible reason: The presence of our force there draws the attack to their countries. This is no pleasure to contemplate, especially as it could happen that the United States might become involved in a great conflict seemingly extraneous to the immediate interests and policies of these allied countries. Yet they would inevitably come under attack; they cannot disengage themselves. They are wary of indefinite commitments and as a consequence our relations with them are difficult and tenuous.

Where shall our retaliatory force then be held? The answer is simple. It must be placed on the oceans of the world, in the oceans and in the air above them. I shall call this the *Oceanic System*.

This will be a system that either alone, or more likely in conjunction with forces held in the United States, should constitute our main deterrent to Russian attack. Instead of hardening bases in the continental United States we should make extensive use of the vast opportunities offered by the free oceans of the world. Their waters cover more than three quarters of the earth's surface. This is one of those basic, elemental facts, glaringly evident, but unrecognized as such.

When we try to combine these facts—extension and free-

---

[2] In current military parlance the "Zone of Interior" or "ZI" describes the interior of the continental United States, or more generally the interior of any country, if the reference is to another nation. We shall use it only as referring to the continental United States.

dom of the waters—with the latest technological advances and
the tremendous changes in the weapons field, we are naturally,
but forcefully, led to the construction of systems that would
give us an invulnerable retaliatory force without drawing
dreadful devastation on our homeland should the enemy ever
want to destroy our retaliatory power.

The United States occupies the better part of a continent but
is on two sides bordered by great oceans while the land mass to
the north is in the hands of a friendly power whose fate is inex-
tricably linked to ours. Still farther north only ice masses bring
a link to Russia. This constellation of size and separation allows an integration of sea and land power that no other nation
can match for a long time to come. It is unique. In Latin America there is not one big country touching both oceans and none
is powerful. The same is true of Africa, which is only beginning
in its development. China is restricted to a fringe of the Pacific.
Russia is practically landlocked; if she wants to do what we
can do easily, she will have to make vastly greater efforts than
are required of us. As we know, it is good strategy to choose a
system that the enemy cannot easily duplicate and that forces
him to involuntary efforts.

So instead of hardening and confining our main retaliatory
power within the Zone of Interior we shall obtain this capability by dispersing it all over the world, by hiding it in the depths
of the oceans and, if need be, by striking from mobile bases
whose locations are constantly changing and can never be subject to mass surprise attacks by the enemy.

The New Extent of Sea Power

I shall not even attempt to summarize the historical role of sea
power. So much has been written about it, and so clear are the
lessons of history, that the military strategists in this country
are quite aware of the traditional functions of a powerful
navy. Yet there have been first subtle, then drastic, changes, all
due to the changes in technology. The progress from sail to
steam to Diesel only enhanced a navy's capabilities, but the ad-

vent of the airplane began to threaten it, until the United States Navy developed the aircraft carrier. It brought it to perfection in the war against Japan. But then the power of the land-based plane increased, its range vastly improved, especially due to refueling techniques; and in lifting capability it outstrips anything that can be flown from a carrier.

This was of tremendous importance until quite recently because atomic weapons were so large and heavy that they could not be lifted easily by carrier planes. It is common knowledge that the weapons are becoming smaller and smaller without losing any of their power—on the contrary. This seems to bring the carrier back again, even to the extent that nuclear propulsion might be used. But the ups and downs are not yet over. The large carrier is in fact doomed in the long run, while small carriers may have a limited future.

The end of the large aircraft carrier is determined by a variety of factors: It represents probably the largest concentration of nuclear weapons in any one accessible spot that can come under fire. The carrier is therefore a most valuable target, inviting and justifying the greatest efforts by the enemy to destroy it. So it has to be protected by large forces made up of destroyers, missile ships, submarine hunters, submarines, etc. In other words, a carrier is by necessity a whole fleet, operating together as a unit. The carriers can be detected and identified. In particular they are exceedingly vulnerable to sneak attack at the outbreak of hostilities. Even far misses by megaton bombs dropped into the sea are deadly. Their mobility is virtually zero compared with the speed of the planes that will be looking for them. They violate the basic protective principle imposed by nuclear weapons: dispersion. The concentration of power they represent is an outgrowth of the conditions imposed by conventional weapons, by ordinary, nonatomic explosives.

The large aircraft carrier is a representative of a vulnerable retaliatory force. Should the signal of war be given, the carriers —much less their accompanying ships—are among the prime targets of the aggressor. Therefore the same applies to them that applies to SAC: All carrier-based planes have to take to the air immediately and must proceed to their targets. This is a no-choice situation. When they return, they most likely will no longer find their carriers afloat, just as the SAC planes will find their bases destroyed. The entire force is spent. There is only one strike; it is a very costly one.

Neither can carrier planes be used for the stopgap system of keeping a significant part constantly in the air. Logistic considerations forbid this: there is no way of solving the problem of the great fuel consumption. This fuel could never be supplied from tanker ships, and if it has to be done by air then the whole effort might just as well be concentrated in the SAC operations.

Those who have grown up with a particular kind of sea power find it hard to imagine that it will be superseded by other forms. The battleship died in World War II and there is no chance that it will be revived. The large carrier is dying before our very eyes. To anyone who has ever seen the wondrous, magnificent spectacle of day and night carrier operations—perhaps the most perfect interplay of men and machines ever designed and executed anywhere—this is indeed saddening. But it would be fatal not to read the signs of technological development. These point to small units, to submarines and to seaplanes based directly on the water.

One of the standard formulations of the mission of a navy is to "control the sea lanes," i.e., to secure the flow of men and goods across the oceans. This assigns the navy a protective duty for something else, namely, the transport function as such. The navy therefore has to clear the seas of enemy forces, to convoy if necessary. It also has to contribute force in landing operations, and the classical bombardment from ships has, for ages past, been a formidable threat. Naval power therefore has been interdiction of enemy fleet movements and supplies, accomplished by sinking or fending off the enemy fighting strength on the waters. The naval supply services are something else, vital of course, but not part of the strictly fighting navy.

Without navies it would not have been possible for some powers to occupy other countries, to survive in war and to prevent wars. The navies until recently, however, have not reached directly deep into the country of the opponent. They have had to stay on the fringe.

Fleets were designed with this limitation in mind; in fact, there was hardly any alternative. Until the airplane arrived. If planes, first lacking in range, could be brought near enemy fleets or countries and flown from there, not only could the fleets be neutralized more easily but deep penetration of the enemy's homeland could be accomplished. Now the fleet could reach the hinterland and destroy sources of power. If the enemy country were islands, as Japan, the whole country could —theoretically—be held down. But the carriers were not numerous and powerful enough to do so; land-based planes had to be combined with theirs. Nevertheless a new dimension of sea power opened up. Navies could do what had never before been assigned to them.

This tendency can be strengthened even though the form in which this expresses itself changes: it will not be expressed in the carrier, which had the dominant role in the last war. This role will be assumed by the submarine and the seaplane. Both will take their strength from nuclear propulsion and, of course, nuclear weapons.

The problem is to find forms, technically feasible and within temporal and economic reach, that embody the essential features of the new naval concept of extended power.

Basically this amounts to moving our main strategic, retaliatory force out of the United States, out of the Zone of Interior, but not into the lands of our allies. This is the alternative to hardening the Zone of Interior.

If this is technically possible—and it is—a side effect of greatest importance is achieved. We saw earlier that existing SAC bases and many ICBM launching sites under construction are uncomfortably close to large concentrations of population. If they are not, they inevitably produce considerable satellite settlements. Even with fairly accurate delivery by the enemy of large megaton weapons, these centers are doomed. Scattered forces at sea exist in isolation; they continuously move about and they endanger no civilian population. No one has solved the problem of protection of the cities, the exaggerated, even fantastic, claims, especially of the Army, notwithstanding. Here, however, is a chance to redress completely the worst aspect of the situation: the civilian population can be protected effectively from the side effects of an attack on our main retaliatory strength. And this can be accomplished *without new specific installation,* without new cost attributable to the expenditures on civil defense.

Holding our main retaliatory force at sea makes the greatest immediate contribution to the defense of the country: it protects the force proper and it frees the country thereby from direct and indirect effects of a possible attack on this force itself.

The Early End of Known Fixed Bases

There is no getting away from it: the technological development of the last few years and the perfections in weapons delivery, by missiles fired either from the ground or from the air make all fixed military installations of any size anywhere in the world obsolete. Such is particularly the case for the heavy, strategic force of retaliatory power, the form of military organization we are primarily concerned with at this point. This is also true of our conspicuous and well-advertised missile bases here and abroad. This will apply furthermore to the planned future hardened bases, even to the still distant Minute Man installations.

This is unpleasant to contemplate. We possess many fixed bases and now would not be able to dispense with them. Indeed, we build more here and abroad and the building expenses have been nothing short of fabulous. Yet the tendency away from fixed bases will prove to be inexorable. We have ac-

cepted mobility as one of the main features of modern life. Increases in speed of transportation and communication, made
possible by new sources of power, have changed the face of the
earth. They will also mold weapons systems accordingly.

Nuclear energy has had its impact on weapons; but it has
not made itself felt nearly as much on the availability of energy
in small quantities wherever needed. The Atomic Energy Commission has unfortunately paid only negligible attention to the
fact that small reactors can be made and should therefore be
developed. These would allow the same kind of miniaturization of individual power sources as that of nuclear weapons. It
is now comparatively easy to build huge, stationary power
plants; it is difficult to make small, mobile units. But all these
things are interdependent and their influences will reinforce
each other in the same direction: mobility at speeds greater
than ever, virtually unlimited range, independence from fixed
bases, smallness of individual units, but each exceedingly
powerful because of the spectacular reduction in weight and
size of atomic weapons. Instead of concentration of power we
can have dispersal of the small individual units with the ability
to direct them wherever they are needed and to pull them together swiftly wherever wanted. The dispersion is their greatest
protection, together with the fact that dispersion is not to stationary, fixed bases.

*The individual units can be moved around at will, in fact
randomly.*

Randomization of movement, of deployment of strength,
and use of such randomized forces are the most formidable
ways of exploiting one's opportunities. This lesson, sometimes
learned from experience, but capable of rigorous proof, must
be applied to our own principal strategic concern: to find the
proper form of retaliatory power.

The statement that fixed bases are doomed in the long run
must be properly interpreted: somewhere, naturally, there have
to be fixed installations—the factories where weapons, ships,
planes are manufactured, the depots where spare parts are

held ready, houses where personnel live, etc. This, however, is something different from, say, the nature of a nuclear-propelled ship, which has an unlimited radius of operations, restricted only by the endurance of its crew, but packing a force hundreds of times in excess of that which a ship could deliver previously even when *returning frequently to a fixed point.* Even ships had stripped off much of that dependence by being supplied at sea, a service that the United States Navy has developed in an admirable manner.

Dependence on fixed bases is necessary when the survival ability and the power of the weapon carrier are weak relative to the tasks to be performed. This is therefore the case when a long and continuous pipe line has to be maintained in order to keep it going and when overhaul in large installations is necessary. Planes have been in this position; nevertheless, the movable aircraft carrier could give some types of planes accommodation where they otherwise would have been helpless. The seaplane has a greater independence, needing no landing fields, runways, etc. It can be serviced and repaired at places far from its area of operations. But neither has its development been pushed very hard by the Navy, nor does it at present represent a distinctive step forward. This will be very different when nuclear propulsion for aircraft has been developed. (Our program for this is one of the weakest, most grossly mismanaged of all our military development work. And this is saying something!)

In stating that *fixed* bases are constantly losing in significance, we do not mean that *no* bases are necessary. The point is to make them *movable* with high speed. The fast seaplane gives an excellent example: by using water, it dispenses with the most expensive and vulnerable part of land-based planes— the runways. It still has to be supplied frequently with fuel (if it is not nuclear), with food, fresh crews, and with weapons, if they have been spent. But, a moving base can take care of many of its operational needs. The flexibility of the system increases. This is one of the surest ways to reduce its vulnerability.

Provided there is any technological feasibility at all, a choice has to be made between large, fixed installations with their well-known, impressive capabilities and their great drawbacks of being easy targets, on the one hand, and on the other hand, many small units, widely dispersed, susceptible of frequent, erratic, speedy movement, most difficult to catch. They are more difficult to organize than the fixed bases; for example, because of a great problem of communications.

From the point of view of strategic principles, there is no doubt that the latter system is vastly superior. In its new technological appearance it is novel, less tested than the system of fixed bases. But this constitutes a challenge to our ingenuity. There is absolutely no justification that we should stick to, and even further petrify, our present system when we do have the possibility of putting into reality a superior strategic principle on whose adoption our very survival may depend.

The principal aim of shifting the weapons carrier, of putting it one moment here, the other there, below the water and in the air, is of course to hide it. As already mentioned this is achieved by combining the properties of speed and depth of water with erratic movements, with randomization. Instead of deploying forces to carefully selected places, of giving their placement a pattern and formation such as fleets had to adopt by necessity even in the last war, probability alone should determine the geographical spot where the weapon carrier (submarine, floating missile base, seaplane) is next to appear. This is what the combination of nuclear propulsion of ships and seaplanes with nuclear weapons and solid-fuel propulsion for missiles is making possible. Never before in warfare could a system be envisaged where mobile dispersal is combined with great power in each unit, the ability for all to act together from their dispersed points according to some previous plan, and be directed from a central point of command. It is the task of the military to set up systems incorporating all these elements.

Hiding of this type brings the most drastic form of reducing the vulnerability of the retaliatory force. Missiles can also be hidden on permanent installations provided these are kept secret. Russia may be able to do this, in view of the vastness of the country and the strictness with which Russia controls all information. Secret fixed bases still have a chance of survival until high-resolution inspection of the earth's surface from satellites has been accomplished. No base in the United States would remain secret. We can keep no secrets; certainly none of this kind. The Russians will quickly discover them, and their missiles, placed on bases unknown to us, will be "zeroed-in" (i.e., precisely aimed at those points). This is an asymmetry which need not be tolerated, especially when the solution to it is so glaringly apparent.

Mobile Dispersion of the Strategic Force

Having established the need for a mobile dispersed retaliatory force, it remains to be seen how feasible the scheme is. Fortunately the affirmative answer is already in part provided, but there is a grave question whether the effort we are making to put the system into being is commensurate with the benefits it provides.

There are now *two forms* in which we can express the principle: *first,* the *fleet ballistic missile* fired from submerged submarines now over distances of up to 1500 miles; *second,* the *nuclear-propelled seaplane,* supported on the oceans from submarines acting as tenders (or from surface tenders, at great distances from Russian and satellite coasts). The first system is known as the *Polaris* project and is in a modest state of development. It has received high priority within the Navy, but the Navy efforts and the support given it in the Department of Defense are entirely inadequate. The fundamental significance of the system has apparently not yet been recognized by the Administration. Exceptions are a few influential members of Congress, notably Senator Henry M. Jackson who, in several important speeches, has clearly outlined some of the contributions Polaris can make to our national defense.[3]

These are the characteristics of Polaris: It consists of a nuclear-powered submarine force which is able to deliver ballistic missiles with hydrogen warheads of great power (presumably in the megaton range) over distances at least equal to those of the Intermediate Ballistic Missile for which bases are now either under construction or discussion in various European NATO countries. The missiles are fired while the submarine is submerged and, according to published accounts, as many as sixteen missiles can be delivered from one single submarine. There exist, as yet, no operational units fitted with missiles, but progress could be swift and assured. This would not have been possible without the development of solid fuels since liquid fuels not only require a vastly more complicated missile, but are much more dangerous to handle. Liquid fuels could not be handled on board a submerged ship.

In order to be accurate the submarine has to know its position precisely. The navigational difficulties are therefore considerable. But, though it can move at great speeds, the submarine need only fire from a predetermined position in which it can lie in wait before its retaliatory attack. This has also the advantage of reducing the chances of its discovery, because the sound it generates is reduced to a minimum. Nuclear submarines have been operating continuously submerged for over sixty days. This, coupled with the large battery of missiles they command, gives an idea of the endurance power of this weapon.

Here is an illustration of the increasing independence from fixed bases that was discussed above. The submarine is itself a movable base, vastly superior to an IRBM base located in the heart of, say, densely populated industrial England, drawing fire upon itself and its surroundings the moment a war should

---

[3] A clear statement of the strategic concept is found in the *Report of the Underseas Warfare Advisory Panel* to the Subcommittee on Military Applications of the Joint Committee on Atomic Energy, 85th Congress, 2nd Session, August, 1958.

start. Naturally, the submarine sometimes has to go back home from its cruise or location in order to exchange crews and be serviced. Much of this can be accomplished by servicing the submarine at sea from equally mobile surface ships and sending them to well-protected, isolated pens carved out on rocky shores only for major overhauls. Such flexibility, in several stages, is possible only because of nuclear propulsion. It would be hopeless to try to achieve this with conventionally powered ships.

Nuclear propulsion is not just a better way of propelling submarines. A *discrete,* discontinuous, step forward has been taken in technology. Whenever such occasions occur the accompanying functions also undergo discrete and not simply minor changes. It is for the military planners to understand them. Certainly some advocates of the Polaris system are aware of this, but few of them appear to see the wider implications for the country as a whole. If the system were better understood the Navy and the country would press harder for it. And we seem to be a long way from the point where the other services, the Department of Defense and the National Security Council, realize how profoundly our entire strategic situation can be improved. To them Polaris is apparently only another weapon system.

It is only gradually becoming apparent how difficult it is to find, identify and destroy hostile submarines. The last war has given some idea of these difficulties, but then the individual submarine did not pack very much power, had to surface frequently and to return often to bases in order to fulfill its mission. The nuclear submarine is speedy and can stay under water for very long periods. Both factors militate against its discovery. Its speed and the depth to which it can safely go will both increase, compounding the difficulties of discovery. Even when found, the submarine has to be identified as hostile, and when the identification is assured it still has to be destroyed, which is not an automatic consequence of the identification. Few who are not intimately acquainted with anti-submarine warfare can form a proper idea of the immense problems involved, which are much greater than those arising in combat against airplanes.

The mobility and dispersal of the units at sea have another consequence. If the enemy wishes to attack the system he has to go after small, individual moving units. There are no conspicuous airfields covering many square miles, no large, conspicuous missile sites. There is just the water, with an unknown number of submarines in unknown locations deep in the sea changing their positions at random. Fixed bases can be attacked by ballistic missiles containing megaton warheads, or from planes. But ICBM's are completely useless against submarines; they are also far too expensive to dispatch in great numbers against such small and elusive targets. The enemy would therefore have to develop totally different lines for attack. He would have to find and destroy our submarines one by one. This is an exceedingly difficult task and not easier for Russia than for us.

The reader should note that the enemy's missiles can be applied alternatively against our cities *and* against SAC bases, be they hardened or soft. So long as we hold on to fixed, large land installations, wherever they be, the enemy has a dual-purpose weapon in his hands.

If we switch a large part of our retaliatory force to Polaris and related systems, we deprive him of an enormous advantage which he now enjoys. Instead, we force him to use his resources in a different, unwanted way. We force him to split his strength, with the consequence that he is weaker in each. Or he has to burden his people more, at a time when they seem strongly to demand more consumers' goods. Perhaps, even, he might give up his aggressive tendencies to everyone's benefit. Not that this is likely to happen.

Since this is not a treatise on weapons systems and technology we can forgo a more detailed description of the Polaris system. Suffice it to say that the technical problems it offers are considerable, but far from insurmountable. The two chief obstacles are our inadequate knowledge of the ocean floor and the difficulties of communicating with submerged submarines. The first can be overcome easily, if only we will equip enough oceanographic survey ships, sufficient at least to match the current Russian effort, which exceeds ours enormously. This knowledge is necessary in order to navigate properly under water and to wage undersea warfare. The communication problem is difficult. But even now it is partly solved (some would too optimistically say: solved) and its complete solution may not require a scientific breakthrough of absolutely first order.

The Polaris system is strictly a matter of effort and determination.

First we must build in large numbers the types of submarines already foreseen. Then the missiles must be developed and produced. But most important for the long run is to accommodate the system to missiles which have the full range, so that the Polaris force can be deployed anywhere, in any ocean. Then the weapon is no longer dependent on deployment along geographical limits dictated by the present insufficient missile range. When this point has been reached the hour of perfection has come to the Polaris concept. There are hardly any other tasks in the field of weapons systems deserving a greater effort of our scientists and engineers.

Now consider briefly the *second* possibility: This is a system of *nuclear-powered seaplanes supported by ships or submarines*. These planes have the following capabilities: practically unlimited endurance, ability to fly very low without wasting fuel (as jet planes do at low altitudes), ability to land on water and always to find quiet water without running out of fuel. They would be very large planes of great lifting power. They would be, if not carriers of bombs, carriers of air-to-ground missiles, and could even be used as carriers for ballistic missiles.

This system has still greater flexibility than the present Polaris with its limited range, since a possible retaliation against Russia could use more routes and avenues than Polaris has, as long as the latter is restricted to about a 1500-mile range (although this would bring all of the important centers of Russia under fire). Therefore the Polaris force has to be deployed in some vicinity of European or Asiatic shores. Even though nuclear submarines will eventually be the fastest ships in and on the water, they are slow compared with planes. And their ballistic missiles are less easily handled than the variety of bombs or long-range missiles the planes can carry and dispatch.

The nuclear plane may choose routes of penetration where Russia at present feels completely safe, e.g., over the Himalayas, or via China. So far Russia has not needed to make preparations of defense in those regions, has needed no radar and no early warning systems there. Much less does she have to place defensive forces in those regions to cope with this kind of threat. It is obvious that she could not protect herself everywhere equally along her immense frontiers. She therefore has to make difficult decisions as to which parts of the country to protect. In short, a great and new burden would be placed upon her, distracting from whatever aggressive efforts she may be making now in other directions. We have here a beautiful illustration for the "principle of the imposed, involuntary reaction" of which we make so little use. Clearly all that was said above about the uselessness of Russian ICBM's against this type of force applies again.

We have no nuclear-powered plane at present. It is reported that Russia will produce one shortly. They may have one in the air by the time these words appear in print. As mentioned earlier, our program for nuclear propulsion of airplanes has a very bad, confused record, beset by difficulties of "on again, off again," approximately seven hundred million dollars wasted, absurd conflicts between the Air Force and Navy and the total inability of former Secretary of Defense, Charles E. Wilson, to make satisfactory decisions and make them stick. It is, however, not too late to obtain results. Unfortunately even the post-Sputnik reorganization of the program has not led to any decisive progress. At any rate there is no doubt that a plane, in particular a safe seaplane, can be developed.

The possibility that such a plane can be adapted to the above-mentioned strategic purpose would appear to be self-evident. Since the benefits for the country would be large and since the weapons system incorporates correct strategic principles our efforts in this direction should be increased, after a thorough review and overhaul of the project. And in addition there are other uses of nuclear-powered seaplanes, especially for cargo purposes. Such planes would give us a great capability in limited war situations, again making us independent of scarce airports, since there is water practically everywhere.

Suppose we had both systems, Polaris and the seaplane. Suppose further we could for once stop advertising how much we have of each, what our future detailed plans and production schedules are, and what share of our retaliatory force we propose to keep in this form rather than in SAC and ICBM's. In short, suppose that we really behaved intelligently: then we would have added phenomenally to the strength of the country. And we would have done this without further exposing the civilian population.

There is a high probability, based on certain indications, that Russia is developing both systems. Since we are, or shortly will be, at any rate exposed to their power of attack with only negligible active protection, there is no other task for us of even remotely similar importance than to make our retaliatory force as invulnerable as possible by adopting what I have called the *Oceanic System*.

Should both sides develop an Oceanic System there is this to say: Each side gains an effective deterrent. Our side gains in attacking power, but Russia might gain more, mainly because of our geography and the closeness of so many of our cities to the sea. This is dangerous for us, but there is nothing we can do peacefully to prevent Russia from getting this capability (which is not much different at any rate from her ability to reach any point in the United States by ballistic missiles from Russian soil). Our proper "reaction" to the still hypothetical Russian move is a voluntary one: we anticipate the possibility and do this effectively by constructing precisely the type of invulnerable retaliatory force which is strategically optimal irrespective of the opponent's moves and embodies the most advanced combination of technological components.

It would take scientific discoveries of great magnitude to make this scheme obsolete. Years will go by before space exploration may lead to something new, and should this happen and be militarily valuable, more years will be needed to manufacture and position whatever the new something might be.

If both sides adopt the Oceanic System the most curious consequence is that *both parties gain together:* in making their deterrence effective they protect themselves against accidental war by enabling the opponent to verify signals of attack and to filter out the false ones. Clearly, as the reader will recall, an invulnerable force does not have to rise immediately when a signal of attack, which may be only a false alarm, is accepted as real. Even if the signal is true, the retaliation can be spaced out over time, giving all the favorable possibilities mentioned earlier.

Political Consequences of the Oceanic System

The Oceanic System has political implications of a magnitude that forces us to consider it in a broader framework than a strictly military one. The consequences are beneficial for the whole world, since they would help reduce those unnecessary tensions which arise from adhering to faulty strategic concepts.

The present system, with fixed land bases in the United States and abroad, is by necessity also politically rigid. We still need the overseas SAC bases and we are even building IRBM bases in Europe, since the ICBM is not yet operational. It is well known what political difficulties, delicate alliances and great monetary expenses were and are associated with building and holding these bases. When they are located in countries

like Saudi Arabia or Spain we have to give at least indirect
support to political regimes which are not necessarily to our
liking. This support spoils our style when we talk about "freedom" and "democracy" as the ideals we live by and fight for.
In Morocco we get into such problems as the country's desire
for independence from another of our allies, France. In this
case we lost the bases after having invested in them several
hundreds of millions of dollars. England does not like to see
our nuclear weapons stored there; Denmark is wary of an
IRBM launching site, etc. Russia feels that every new SAC
overseas airport or launching site is another link in the chain of
bases around her. This intensifies her intransigence in dealing
with us. We, on the other hand, find it impossible even to consider giving up one single overseas base lest we weaken our
position materially, which would possibly cost us allies on
whose willingness much of our strength depends. Although our
strength supports our allies, our bases also put us in their
hands.

The Oceanic System can change this situation profoundly.
There is less need, or ultimately even no need, for American
fixed bases in European and African countries, though they
should not be given up now, of course, and never without due
compensation from Russia. The Polaris force is out of sight,
even more than the Sixth Fleet, and the Polaris deployment is
unknown to the Russians. Without loss of face the Russian
government can easily play down to its own people the strength
and the positioning of the United States force, and the
United States government can do the same. The Russian government can never play down to its people, even if it wanted
to, the threat presented by a ring of SAC and IRBM bases.
But it is easy for both parties to come nearer to fruitful negotiations when a United States Polaris-type force is in existence—
even though it is militarily more effective because of its invisi-
bility. Thus a new door is opened in the political arena. The
Oceanic Force is flexible and becomes a suitable tool for political
pressure and negotiation.

Should both countries or groups of countries have a large Polaris force, new political complications arise which are difficult to describe at present. Their signs are already faintly discernible. The transfer of even a few conventional, non-nuclear submarines to Syria and Egypt has changed the situation in the Mediterranean in a subtle manner. The appearance of Russian submarines 50 miles from the Eastern Seaboard of the United States poses a new political problem. There is nothing illegal about this deployment, but the threat is there. Soon they may stay 500 and even 1000 miles away and yet have longer-ranged missiles poised at our eastern and inland cities or, better still, zeroed-in at our fixed SAC and missile bases. But these submarines cannot at the same time threaten our own Polaris force which may be cruising, in part at least, in the same waters, presenting the same problem for Russia.

It would be tempting to go deeper into these matters but space forbids this at present. The evolution of new weapons systems necessarily produces new political problems. One of the poor features of United States policy has been that the political implications were not seen early enough, mostly because the activities of the Departments of Defense and State proceed in almost watertight compartments (in spite of the existence of coördinating committees), the State Department in particular making only faint attempts to learn the fundamentals of military capabilities, weapons technology and future developments, perhaps subconsciously fearful of the problems they pose to the conventional, outdated modes of thinking in the politico-diplomatic field.

Other Systems of Mobile Dispersal: Space

The two forms of Oceanic Systems described so far, the ballistic-missile-firing nuclear submarine and the bombing and missile-firing nuclear seaplane, are not the only ones to incorporate the basic principle of mobile dispersal away from the Zone of Interior. They are, however, the most tangible at present. It is up to our military planners to add to them superior forms. It is a safe guess that they will not be superseded soon, as long as we must contemplate warfare using essentially blast, fire and possibly willful radiation (incidental radiation being inseparable from most types of nuclear blasts), and as long as we restrict ourselves to the conventional forms of delivery of energy through the air by bombs or missiles.

There remains *space*. But space is not only far away in geometric terms, it is also distant in time as far as quantitatively significant military uses other than reconnaissance are concerned. Leaving this aspect aside, it is possible to dream of satellites equipped with nuclear weapons, manned or unmanned, circling the earth, a last-resort weapon to be called upon when the infinitely simpler earth-based missiles have been spent, or methods for their detection and destruction before they ever get off their base or hit a target have been discovered—thereby rendering them useless. All this is in a rather distant future, distant not for a prototype perhaps, for an occasional shot at or around the moon, but for the construction of weapons systems in quantities that have any meaning at all. Before satellites by the hundreds and thousands are floating around the earth, equipped with large nuclear weapons and capable of reëntering the atmosphere and being directed to their targets without fail and interference, a great deal of time —perhaps as much as two decades—will pass during which we will have to solve the problem of survival on the present basis.

Space research goes on under mutual pressure—nothing in sight will stop it; but it will offer no solution to our more immediate problems. Indeed it may well distract from our needs. Let us leave this alone, for the time being. Let us just state that the principle of mobile dispersal with the utmost amount of hiding is certainly preserved in these space efforts. There may, however, be other systems between these schemes and those discussed above—the latter we do not yet have in sufficient quantities although there is no other difficulty connected with them than the lack of determination by the government to get them. By far and away the greatest vehicle of war deterrence we have now is the missile-launching submarine. Its capabilities are only gradually becoming clear; it represents a technology in ascendancy already getting under firm control.

We note, finally, that either side can put nuclear weapons into space and that eventually both may have them up there at the same time. Should a war occur then and should they represent the main threat, then each side would be bound first of all to try to locate and then destroy the other's space capability. If we are lucky, that war would then be mercifully fought away from the earth, and whoever loses would have to surrender an intact country.

Perhaps the human race will have enough time to contemplate the meaning of all this. The futility of future large-scale wars begins to be written in such large, clear signs that even governments, the alleged leaders of men, should be able to read them. But in order to appreciate these signs and to devise methods to prevent war, they will have to take time out from conferences, briefings, meetings, hearings and cocktail parties in order to sit down and think. And think hard and long.

A Second Stopgap Device

Although we must strive for a mobile, dispersed force away from the Zone of Interior, we will not get it quickly in satisfactory strength. Even if great efforts are made to build a sufficient number of Polaris submarines, precious time is consumed. So the question arises whether, similar to the transitory measure of keeping a large part of SAC in the air, another stopgap device is possible.

The principal feature of the Oceanic System is that dispersal is combined with mobility at sea. Of these two components the former is more easily obtained. Therefore our missile placements, so long as they have to be stationary, should be as widely spread as possible and outside, or at least on the fringes, of the continental United States. ICBM's can be put in the Aleutian Islands, on islands in the Pacific which are firmly in our hands, in remote parts of Alaska, etc. Missiles should also be put temporarily on ships or platforms distributed over the oceans until the properly designed submarines become available. This would be far more important than to keep hundreds of ships in moth balls, sitting idly on the water, vainly waiting for a type of naval action that will never come again.

The statement, made elsewhere, that known fixed bases are doomed in the long run still applies. The same is true of the fact that it will always be easier to make more powerful missiles, directed against bases, than to harden the missile bases. But this stopgap device recommends itself nevertheless, especially if such a program were carried out swiftly and secretly. I doubt, however, that this will be done, and if it is, the Russians will probably be presented with all details of the operations in newspapers and commercial magazines, through the publication of articles based on the stream of unnecessary and foolish news releases constantly emanating from the Pentagon.

5 Attrition, Shelters and Recovery

Long War or Short War?

Should a major war occur, will it be long or short? Will it last a few hours, a few days, or will it again stretch over years? These are important and delicate questions. How we answer them now determines the use of our existing power and the planning for future weapons systems, which in turn influence our strategy in the future should no war have broken out up to the time when they become available.

Estimates made before both world wars were mostly on the short side. It was argued that modern weapons were so powerful and plentiful that countries could not stand a protracted conflict. The burden on the economy was believed to be so great that if for no other reason hostilities would come to an early end because of economic factors. This leaves completely out of account the many people—eminent men of their times among them—who thought that there simply would be no more war because of the dreadful power of machine guns,

battleships, etc. It is tempting to argue the same way now.
There would seem to be much more justification. Having been
wrong twice, people might be inclined for that reason now to
argue the other way. But looking at currently available statements one finds that a total war is believed likely to last at
most a few days. The big "thermonuclear exchange" is to be
done with quickly. Much of our previous analysis would support this view. But we have seen that the question of duration
is primarily dependent upon the existence of vulnerable retaliatory forces. The moment this condition changes the whole
picture is transformed: then there is no absolute need to throw
all you have at your enemy immediately.

A short, violent thermonuclear exchange is clearly not to be
preferred over a longer-lasting war if only for one reason:
during those violent days and hours all other contact is lost between the fighting powers. This means that the battle cannot
be stopped before it is spent. One side may want to give in to
the other but cannot communicate during the holocaust—the
fight is governed by the automatic responses built into each
side's war machine.

Therefore it only appears to be a paradox that a short war
should be more disadvantageous than a long war. For during
a long war we could gather strength and mobilize. The result
is only a consequence of the relative power of the weapons
themselves and of the power a single massive strike can deliver. If nations should succeed only in avoiding conditions in
which they have no choice but immediately to throw everything at each other, they would have succeeded in very much.
Their mutual chances of survival would greatly increase while
otherwise the doom of the largest part of their people is virtually assured.

I know as little as any other man whether the next war will
really "be over" in a few days, as so many believe. My belief is
that, with vulnerable forces on both sides, there would be a
fearful, sharp battle in which each side would be left gravely
wounded, but that the war as such would not be ended thereby.

Rather each side would make a supreme effort to show that it could salvage so much from the ruins that it could after all impress its will upon the opponent if only by its ability to survive. This might go on for years, if not decades. How do we stand in this respect?

We are not prepared. We have nothing to protect us, the people, the economy. We have not even thought about the problem much. Indeed, it is most unkind to raise the issue. It is in bad taste to do so. The idea even has a pinkish tinge. The fact that the Russians too are not far advanced along these lines is no excuse. But as far as one knows, they are ahead of us in this respect also, though the level they have reached with their civil defense preparations is totally inadequate in view of the devastation we could bring upon them. But do we have to wait for the Russians to show us the way? To what depth has this country fallen if we cannot any longer make decisions freely, but make them only after having been forced to take steps by virtue of the superior action of an implacable enemy?

So the problem poses itself whether a country can and should take measures for passive defense, by building shelters, by storage of food, medicines and equipment. It may be that there is no point to this—that the only salvation lies in the avoidance of war since, should it occur, it would be of such violence that no amount of passive protection would be effective. Efforts made in this direction would therefore be merely wasteful. The question so far is one of feasibility. The other questions have to do with the costs—should protection be possible—the timeliness, i.e., how long it would take to secure protection in view of the imminence and type of the danger, and finally with the strategic implications of acquiring this protection. I shall discuss all of these, but first we turn to the problem of *attrition*.

Attrition Strategy

It is customary to distinguish between a strategy of *annihilation* and of *attrition* (*Ermattungsstrategie*). This is not a very sharp distinction. Military writers, no matter how famous, are often imprecise in their terms and are usually better in describing past battles than in formulation of "theory." In fact the theory of military strategy as developed by the military themselves is conspicuous mostly by its absence. Therefore it is not surprising that frequently used terms such as those above are ambiguous and do not readily fit the needs of precise thinking.

Annihilation is the aim—speaking of our times—when the whole of the retaliatory force is thrown against the enemy. There are no holds barred. With modern weapons the issue will be decided in the short thermonuclear exchange as far as military power can decide it (i. e., leaving out of account a possible recuperation over the years). Modern weapons can produce annihilation in a very short interval of time. In earlier wars an enemy could also be annihilated, but it would frequently take long periods, repeated blows at his forces in being, at the forces being assembled, and at the sources of his power which perhaps were remote from the battle. Annihilation in the modern sense means utter destruction of a whole country, with tens of millions of people killed within a few days. Annihilation in a previous era meant the destruction of a country's military power in the form of the armies in the field and the fleets at sea. In World War II this was widened to the *gradual* destruction of war industries from which combat losses could be repaired and new strength be added. Great losses among the civilian population also occurred, notably in Russia. When gradual weakening of the enemy's power is intended we have attrition strategy at work. It can be applied against a country as a whole or against specific forces, weapons and industries.

Consider conventional anti-submarine warfare: only about one third of all submarines are actually at sea. The rest are coming from and returning to base and under repair there. Thus the actual combat strength is much smaller than the available total might suggest. What is the proper manner to deal with these submarines? Those at sea should be destroyed as well as their bases. But if the latter are gone, all are helpless. This was the classical procedure adopted in World War II (only the bases proved very hard to destroy).

If we now introduce modern missile weapons into the picture (not even necessarily nuclear submarines!), there is a profound change: an initial deployment of the force can launch weapons even in excess of the requirements of all conceivable strategic targets ever to be assigned to the entire submarine force.

Let us discuss this somewhat hypothetically: A Polaris submarine is designed to fire 16 missiles; let us assume that each carries a megaton warhead. This is equivalent to one city per missile. Assume that only 10 missiles reach their targets, and let there be only 10 submarines at station. This finishes more cities than there are worth-while as targets in the United States. (Naturally, there are other targets besides.) A total of 10 submarines at station is a negligible force. Russia now has about 500; let only 1/5 of these in the future be of the Polaris type. They need not even be nuclear-powered submarines. All that matters is that they are fitted for ballistic missiles. This would provide 1600 missiles; assume 1000 hits with 1 megaton each. How many American cities would be left?

Nuclear submarines, of course, add immensely to the possibilities of the situation because of their great endurance. This gives an idea of the magnitudes involved, even if the missiles should be capable of only, say, 100 kiloton, 1/10 of a megaton (Hiroshima was destroyed by at most 20 kilotons!).

Now it is clear that in this case "attrition" means nothing. No attack on our part on Russian submarine pens and bases would have the slightest bearing on the situation. Only destruction of the deployed submarines themselves *before the firing* is of value, and only destruction of the missile, or even the warhead itself, matters *after the firing*.

It is a disturbing experience still to encounter among many high-placed officers the idea that in case of all-out war we have to attack the "bases," those "sources of power" of the enemy. This thought is completely out of line with the facts of the present time.

We can put the matter concisely:

If the weapons carrier, e. g., the plane or submarine, has to return to base in order to accomplish its mission of target destruction (i. e., if it can accomplish it only in repeated strikes that are not self-contained in their own capabilities), then and only then is an attack on its base strategically meaningful.

In modern large-scale war the "force in being" is large enough to accomplish the assigned mission. And the "force in being" may even be the warhead itself. This is what has to be destroyed—the bullet has to be caught in flight and be destroyed before it explodes since wherever that might happen over the home country it will do profound damage. The concept of attrition, on the other hand, grows from the belief that an operation along a long chain:

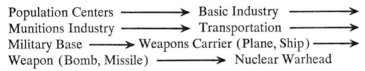

Population Centers ⟶ Basic Industry ⟶
Munitions Industry ⟶ Transportation ⟶
Military Base ⟶ Weapons Carrier (Plane, Ship) ⟶
Weapon (Bomb, Missile) ⟶ Nuclear Warhead

is possible and will become effective, because the power at the end of the chain (weapons carrier to warhead) is less (e. g., in number or yield) than what is needed by the enemy in order to bring us down in a shorter time than the one needed for the attrition measures (the partial breaking of the above chain) to become effective.

The reader will judge for himself what value there is in destroying the enemy's munitions industry when his bomber and missile force, ready for launching, can already destroy the essential parts of our country many times over.

Attrition in Limited War

Limited war will be discussed in the next chapter. But even without having clear concepts on hand at this moment, the following remark can be made: A limited war does not aim at the total destruction of the opponent. It has more restricted political objectives, and there is, most likely, a great selectivity of targets as distinguished from the holocaust unleashed by the actions of retaliatory forces in a thermonuclear exchange. It does not matter whether conventional weapons are used or small, so-called low-yield, tactical nuclear weapons—here the planes have many sorties to fly, the troops have to be supplied with food and ammunition over long periods of time, and this material may have to be hauled for great distances. In short here we have situations which more nearly correspond to experiences of the past. Therefore attrition is one of the possible forms to weaken the enemy; he must never be allowed to organize.

As soon as a war stabilizes, because there is a discrepancy between the power of the individual weapons used and the hardness or diffusion of the targets, there is a rationale for the destruction of parts of the whole chain on which the continuation of the operations depends.

Thus we see that there is no unique answer as to what strategy is appropriate. It is certainly misleading to apply the same thinking that proved valid in the last war to the widely different conditions of a large thermonuclear exchange. This would be truly subject to the familiar criticism that a current war is often fought with the principles of the last.

It has never before happened that the warhead of a missile has had to be destroyed and not only the missile itself!

Shelters

Even in a short war, i.e., one mainly consisting of a single, fierce battle of a few days' duration, shelters for the population may be of tremendous significance. In a long war, with intermittent action, they are even more important, partly because the life of the population can perhaps be adjusted to devastation, as people gradually become accustomed to a form of existence which otherwise would be hard to bear. The problem of shelters is so immense and so little understood and appreciated that not more than some rather summary remarks can be made in the compass of the space available.

There are *two types of shelters:* against *blast* and against *radiation*. They require different construction and have different functions. It is, of course, possible to combine both types into one, but it is better to discuss them separately.

Protection against *blast* from large nuclear weapons is very hard to secure. It requires very deep and strong shelters. Even then it is doubtful that much is gained because of the fearful heat, the post-explosion rubble and the intense radiation near the center of the explosion. There may be blast without much radiation but the chances are small, except when "clean" bombs, i.e., those with a minimum of fission products, are developed and used cleanly (the latter does not necessarily follow from the former!). We may neglect this point entirely since there is no evidence that Russia is interested in developing clean weapons.

The construction of blast-proof shelters for a large city like New York, Chicago or Philadelphia would be an undertaking of phenomenal difficulty, not to mention expense. One would obviously have to go very deep into the rock, excavate great caverns, provide good ventilation, fall-out filters, food, sanitary facilities, light, power, medical supplies, and all this for millions of people. It is possible that people might have to stay in such shelters for weeks on end. On emerging they would find a completely shattered world as far as their eyes could see, with no other transportation than their own feet, and a distant countryside where help might either be unavailable or not be tendered because of the breakdown of the social structure that must be expected in such tremendous catastrophes.

It is one of the peculiarities of our time that there exist hardly any qualitative descriptions of these conditions even though such descriptions could easily be based on the precise, quantitative data which are available, such as for bomb blasts, for bombs of different sizes, for fall-out effects and the types of radiation sickness and deaths, etc. And yet the destruction of Hiroshima and Nagasaki—nothing, absolutely nothing, compared to what is now possible—has left deep scars on the Japanese population and in an abstract sense has shocked large parts of the whole world. If such popular descriptions were available and if the national leaders were really aware of the nature of the possible and not improbable disaster, the public mood might change from the present indifference to the demand for action and protection no matter what the cost.

Shelters against blast for isolated communities, individual farms, even small cities are probably a lesser need than for the large cities, where they are so difficult and time-consuming to construct. These small places are not worth-while targets for blast. They will be reached only incidentally if they are near SAC and future missile bases, and because of the entirely unpredictable misses of bombs or missiles against primary targets.

It is quite different with *shelters against fall-out*. These are useful even if the population is not directly exposed to blast, and a very large percentage will not be. But these people will succumb to fall-out unless protected. Now fall-out shelters are comparatively easy to make. Fundamentally a few feet of dirt is all that is required, but without organization and information, sanitary measures, air filters, food and water storage, etc., nothing of value can be accomplished. Without this organization and information, the few feet of dirt will only become the cover of a grave. With moderate support from the government most people living in individual houses could provide an adequate fall-out shelter for themselves. The financial burden would not be excessive and it could be eased by loans, tax write-offs and so forth. Naturally people would have to forgo other expenditures and why should they not? The sacrifices would reach even farther: so much cement would be needed all over the nation that our highway program could not be carried out as planned. But why should it be carried out? Why is it not more important to protect large parts of the population rather than to have them careen around more swiftly in gaudy motorcars before their premature death by radiation?

This choice will have to be made consciously. The present government has not faced up to the facts of the situation. Neither has Congress, usually so far ahead of the Administration, seen fit to take action. Perhaps this is due to the sad circumstance that our civil defense organization is a shambles. Having had a bad start in the hands of a political administrator, Val Peterson, at the beginning and for so long, it cannot be put in order without a completely fresh start and without the most energetic backing from the President. This is not forthcoming. In the meantime the few good people in the organization suffer from the burden of their task and the lack of support.

So we are restricted to the absurd, ludicrous civil defense "exercises," to the sad spectacle of small children sitting for ten minutes in school corridors stupidly designated as "shelters," mayors of big cities, wearing steel helmets, proudly strutting through empty streets and feeling important, sirens that no one hears or knows how to interpret, if he does hear. What do the sirens tell the people (would they ever sound in time)? Where are they to go? How long should they stay? What are they to eat? Who will tell them when the fall-out danger is over? And so one could go on asking questions, all of which could be answered sensibly if only the government were to do its most primitive duty.

Yet when these exercises are over the Civil Defense Administration triumphantly and unfailingly announces a great success and congratulates itself and the misguided, well-meaning and ill-informed volunteers. And it announces in the same breath some hypothetical casualties running into the tens of millions. *Difficile satiram non scribere.*

The people themselves are totally lacking sensible instructions as to what to do, how to discern fall-out, how to get rid of it (if they can), what preparations to make and how to start life again should they have survived. Neither do they themselves ask for any help now. They do not urge Congress to come up with legislation, to press upon the executive. Like children whistling in the dark, they keep their eyes glued to the soporific banalities of the television screen or their ears tuned to music by Muzak.

Suppose this very minute, while you are reading these lines, wherever you are, the sirens sound and a real attack is under way. It is no test. It is the real thing. It would come out of the blue. Do you even hear the sirens? Do you wonder whether it is a fire, or an exercise you know nothing about? Perhaps you turn the radio on, if you are already suspicious. You learn that an attack is coming. What do you do? You have no instructions, no place to go, you have made no preparations. You can merely stop and wait. Only if you are lucky enough to be on board a warship, at an exposed military post, or in an unusually important government building (not the Pentagon!) having a deep shelter, only then do you know what to do, and a few of the things you are expected to do actually may make some sense.

Not even the paper plans for civil defense are worth anything. More funds would not help. They would merely mean that inadequate, unrealistic ideas would be put into practice. The situation is not comparable to that of, say, the Polaris project: There an excellent concept exists but the effort behind it is inadequate for want of its proper appreciation by the Administration and, consequently, for want of sufficient financial support.

Once more we have to note that Russia is farther along the road to preparation: Millions of people have received stern training in civil defense, are instructed in first aid and have at least a rudimentary acquaintance with tasks that have to be performed after attack. We do not even teach our children in high schools how to give hypodermics, how to care for wounded. (But we do have courses for them in dancing, driving, table setting, etc.). The Russians, living a much more Spartan life than we do, would find the new hardships nearer their present existence and have shown in the last war how well they are able to cope with the grim life of wartime destruction. In the United States no family has experience of this kind; each would have to learn, starting from scratch. Even neutrals, such as Sweden, are far ahead of us. That country has devoted much energy and large means to carving huge shelters out of rock, placing whole factories as well as arms in ready state into the caves. But we, who are in far greater danger, have done nothing.

Shelter Time

I have stated before that warning without shelters is meaningless, but will warning *with* shelters have any significance? If the warning time is in the order of hours, there is a chance that many will reach them before the attack starts. Not all will be able to go to join their families in shelters, or otherwise exercise a choice—however, they could not in the last war either. But they may reach some shelter. If the warning time is in minutes only, as it will be at best, almost no one will reach the few shelters in the large cities if these come under attack. But not all cities will be attacked at the same instant; therefore, some people will be saved. Fall-out shelters in suburbs, in the country, in small communities can be more safely reached if only because it takes the fall-out some time (in the order of hours, under favorable circumstances) to arrive. Again, many people will be lost, but many will be saved who would have no chance to survive without fall-out shelters. That difference in the United States may very well be of the order of fifty million people or even more.

While we can show that shelters are no guarantee against loss of life, they do offer a great deal and are—apart from avoiding attack altogether—the only chance of saving people by the tens of millions. It is paradoxical: on the one hand we know that tens of millions will certainly be lost, no matter what we do; but on the other hand tens of millions who would surely also perish can be saved. Are the latter worth a great effort? Or is the disaster of the loss of the others so great and unthinkable that it is not possible to conceive of an effort to preserve the life of some? The dilemma is real. But I fail to see how one could argue that nothing should be done. Perhaps one should resign oneself to the possibility that this fate will overtake us, but the mind resents this attitude.

No one alive has any experience with these matters. No one speaks with authority. But we may venture the guess that posterity will condemn us for not having tried the utmost to preserve the continuing life of the nation.

Therefore we shall once more take a "realistic" look and see what the difficulties and possibilities are for carrying out a very substantial shelter program.

There are two principal time factors involved in judging the effectiveness of shelters and planning for them. The *first* was already briefly discussed: Is it possible for people *to reach the shelters?* Here the answer is that this will be possible only for some. The more shelters exist, the more people will reach them; but even so, shelters cannot be everywhere, and many will be caught away from them and die. This is a statistical matter of the distribution of the population at the moment of attack, which depends on the time of the year, the hour of the day, on previous alarm, and on the degree of surprise.

The *second* is the capacity of people *to stay in shelters for the period of danger.* This time the situation is quite different from that of the last war. Then, after a night of attack, people could emerge from their hide-outs, go to work and work hard, perhaps go back to the shelters the next night, and so on. In a few extreme cases successive day and night attacks occurred, adding gravely to the difficulties of the people. Sometimes shelters were altogether neglected by the people because of a growing indifference to danger, or the realization that bombs fell in patterns, isolated from each other. They could be indifferent or defiant because the individual bomb was only a 'blockbuster' (while now it would be a 'metropolisbuster'). The point is that no uninterrupted, continuous occupancy of shelters, for weeks on end, was ever necessary for the civilian population. For atomic attacks, with heavy fall-out, the situation would be quite different. Now it would be necessary to stay put in shelters until radiation has dropped to "safe" levels. No one in the millions of individual shelters can determine for himself when the safe level has been reached. A good organization is necessary, requiring a foolproof communications system that will reach all with information of radiation changes.

Fall-out even from only a single large bomb can spread, as is well known, over thousands upon thousands of square miles. It is dependent on the speed of wind, moisture, nature of the soil at the place of the explosion, height of burst, and other circumstances. Fall-out may last a few hours, a few days or many weeks or months, the latter in particular if the enemy deliberately so chooses. Duration of the fall-out determines the length of time it is necessary to remain in shelters. These are small and cramped; people will develop claustrophobia, run out of food and water or fall ill. In short, the point may be reached where in despair they prefer to venture outside, only to succumb to radiation sickness, probably to die. One can barely imagine the psychological situations that would arise and the problems the occupants of shelters would have to solve for themselves. In the minds of the persons in the shelters would be the shattering knowledge of being involved in the greatest disaster the human race has ever seen.

This would indeed be so: The black death, the massacres by the Mongol hordes, or any other large misfortunes either have been spread out over many years, or have involved isolated, widely separated cities, small by modern standards. Here disaster would cover great areas, be *concentrated* in time and still *last* indefinitely, if the enemy so chose.

In current discussions of fall-out we find statements such as those made over television by Dr. Libby of the Atomic Energy Commission: "If a bomb destroyed Philadelphia, people in Washington could come out of their shelters 48 hours later possibly." True, perhaps, but so limited in concept! Would not

Washington too be bombed, and Baltimore, Pittsburgh . . . ? In what intervals would these bombs fall, how would their radiations mingle, what would be the weather trends in these different parts of the country? Mostly, however, would not the enemy *space his attack in time* so that when the radiation effects of one bomb would die down another one would start spilling radiation? It is clear that, given certain conditions, he could do this easily. He could deliberately produce long-lasting radiation even with single strikes. Possibly this would become his strategy in order *to nullify the existence of fall-out shelters.* Assuming that, his aim would be to destroy as many people as possible as a consequence of his aggressive or retaliatory action.

Indeed shelters are not a perfect answer, but they are better than no shelters. The *chances* of survival increase for tens of millions of people who otherwise are *certainly* doomed in the case of even one single large-scale thermonuclear attack. This should be reason enough to construct shelters.

If we decide to restrict ourselves to fall-out shelters, which can clearly not be built for large cities (without also being blast shelters), a new and grave social problem arises. It may produce serious troubles: People living in the large cities will know that they are to be sacrificed in case of large-scale war, while those living in the country, on farms, in small communities will have a better chance of survival. This chance would not be due to a limitation of the enemy's weapons and capabilities. It would be due to our own protective measures, which could be applied only to a part of the population. This would cause social stratification, privileges and advantages, which cut across all existing ones. Something more vital would be touched than the possession of more or less money, the color of the skin or the religious creed. It might well be that unforseeable trouble would arise when the government started protecting the lives of only some of the people and by necessity gave up those of the others.

But there are still other problems: (1) Can we "afford" shelters? (2) What are the strategic implications? Are they all favorable to us?

Shelter Cost

To the first question there is but one answer: Of course the United States can afford shelters. This goes for both types and *a fortiori* is positively answered for the simple and more immediately available and useful fall-out shelters.

Perhaps a simple shelter program would cost thirty to fifty billion dollars, spread over some years, about 10% of one single year's Gross National Product. But the shelters could not be built within one year anyway. Perhaps the absolute cost would be much higher. What does this matter when the alternative is to lose some *additional* fifty million people or even more? If the capital outlay for shelters reduces the likelihood of war, this will always be a cheap insurance against war costs. In our time we are not even able any longer to talk of "costs of a war" in any sensible manner, since the expected destruction would go beyond all bounds where the term and concept of "costs" has any meaning. Therefore we must do what is required of us and not try to think in inapplicable economic terms.

This is not an economic problem at all. It is a problem of the estimation of the danger we are in. That is all. If it is judged low, then we need no shelters. If we think that we are in mortal danger, as the government tells us from time to time, then there is no problem of feasibility. But to assert that we are in danger, yet to do nothing about it, to think only of the sacred budget, shows a unique incongruity of behavior.

No one can doubt that the American economy can produce enough cement, steam shovels, bulldozers, employ sufficiently large labor forces, and make the necessary organizational effort to procure at least fall-out shelters in a really short time. There are neither technological nor economic problems. There is only the question of whether the government, once having decided to go ahead with this business, can persuade the people to accept the burden and the temporary disturbance of their pursuit of happiness (and profits).

There is one aspect to costs of shelters which bears repeating. If we need shelters at all, it is because we deem our deterrent power too weak. As stated before, if the deterrent were perfect, nothing more would be required. No deterrent can of course be perfect; but it can be much better than what we have now. The principal weakness is not that our retaliatory force is not strong enough—we are told that we could destroy any conceivable opponent if our force is intact—but that the force is vulnerable. In other words, this strength is in grave doubt after all. Hence, we come back to our point that the force must be made as invulnerable as possible *without endangering our civil population,* i. e., by other means than through hardening of the Zone of Interior. We know that this can be achieved by means of adding a large Oceanic System of defense. We also know that this will be costly. But if its adoption increases the deterrent power of the United States, then it correspondingly decreases the need for shelters and the cost they represent for the country. Shelter cost has therefore to be weighted against the cost of making our deterrent more effective.

Both programs have a common element: if no war occurs, our effort appears to have been wasted, but so is the premium on every accident insurance wasted if the expected accident does not happen. The deterrent force *prevents* the accident, the shelters *protect* us from it. We are conditioned to accept the "waste" of military preparations as long as that means the maintenance of large armies and navies. But we would look with different eyes upon countless holes in the ground and consider them a singularly undesirable way of spending the national treasure. So all we need is a different attitude: fall-out shelters are part of the deterrent force and have an almost imperceptible rate of obsolescence compared with that of the other weapons. Besides, when will be the day when we can say with assurance that shelters are no longer necessary, that the danger has passed?

Evacuation

Quite apart from the pitiful signs "Shelter" and "Shelter Area," which one finds in so many official buildings (including the Pentagon and the Executive Office of the President), signs signifying nothing but the total lack of an understanding of events in case of nuclear attack, one finds further posters. These are on many highways leading out of our large cities, designating the roads as having been set aside for civil defense in case of enemy attack. Precisely who would use them or for what purpose is obscure, except that they figure in another scheme, namely, evacuation. It is not easy to find out how seriously evacuation is being taken at present. The views about its desirability are certainly divided. Thick books and manuals exist; these are about all. But there can be only one conclusion: Evacuation is useless, even where possible, and for the most part it is quite unthinkable. It is nonsense.

We have discussed the ever-shrinking warning times, especially for the coming missile age. These few minutes hardly would make it possible to take an elevator to a deep shelter after the alarm sounds, let alone to get outside a large city in a rush of panic-stricken people. To evacuate the Los Angeles area from the sea on across the Sierra would surely take many hours at best, but the warning time for a missile fired from under water, say 100 miles distant, is zero. But suppose there were time. Where would the millions from New York, Chicago, Los Angeles go? How would they survive? How would they be sheltered (perhaps in the desert around Los Angeles or in zero weather near Minneapolis and Chicago), fed, organized? How long would they stay? How are they protected against fall-out? Have fall-out shelters for the millions been built around cities in the presumptive evacuation areas? Would they return if the attack did not materialize or were beaten back? And a few hours or days later the whole exodus would perhaps be repeated if the enemy persisted in his attacks?

One can hardly imagine a more pathetic scheme for trying to save people in the case of unrestricted war. Even in the Second World War evacuation was limited to children and some sick people, and where it was tried the total number was negligible compared to the whole city population. Besides, people would evacuate only *after* the first attacks were made. But this time there is only *one* attack.

In the present fall-out world of high-speed planes and missiles, a successful and meaningful evacuation of large cities is entirely out of the question.

In the early days of the atomic bombs it was said that the best protection against a bomb was not to be where it exploded. Alas, these good old times are long since gone: that was ten years ago. Now one is caught by fall-out even hundreds of miles away from the explosion, even when "evacuated."

Together with the absurd and ludicrous "Shelter" signs the evacuation announcements about highway use should also be removed. Let us put up signs that have real meaning or no signs at all. Let us confess that there simply does not exist any civil defense whatever. There exists only a microscopic item bearing that designation in the Federal Budget.

Looking at everything together, it is clear that a reasonably significant result can be obtained from a great effort toward civilian defense. No individual can be sure of protection, even many of those in shelters would perish; but in the aggregate tens of millions would be saved who are certainly doomed if a large attack should occur at this moment when we have no protection.

It is a most complex scientific problem to evaluate probabilities of single events which have never happened before, but I think it is safe to state the following: The probability that this country will suffer an attack by 500 to 1000 ten-megaton weapons is *greater* than the probability that the country will rouse itself to get whatever little civilian protection is still possible against precisely this catastrophe.

Recovery after Attack

Life resumes after the attack in whatever fashion it can. If we have made provisions, recovery can be swift. Everyone was impressed by the astounding resilience of modern industrial societies to get on their feet again after World War II. No two countries have made greater strides forward than Germany and Russia. The former relied on a system of free, private initiative but produced only civilian goods; the latter relied upon central direction of the economy and was engaged in heavy arms production. Each system has worked because the essential feature of its development was that the investment level was kept as high as possible, or, to put it differently, consumption was first held down, savings were forced, in order to strengthen the capital basis of the economy. When that had become larger, the goods began to pour out.

Depending on the degree of destruction and the skills and determination of the survivors, the question is largely what stocks of commodities, especially food, will be on hand so that the new economic basis can be found. After the last war Germany was helped greatly by enormous infusions of food and material from the U.S., while similar help offered to Russia under the Marshall Plan was refused. So it is clear that stockpiling during times of peace may materially help in securing a faster recovery after a disaster than if no such action is taken. This is, of course, still another and rather formidable expense. It seems as if there were no end to what should be imposed on the ordinary citizen-taxpayer and as if the economy should not be able to support such further measures. Whatever his complaints may be, they would be bigger still should a communistic regime take over instead. The well-to-do and the rich who look with horror at still higher taxes should meditate for at least five minutes, and they will come to the conclusion that higher taxes are after all preferable to extermination.

It is possible, however, to design a stockpiling system that minimizes costs—and furthermore it must be pointed out that we already have carried enormous stocks at great expense for many years: our agricultural surplus. Since food would be among the most important components of a well-designed stockpile, the primary task, as far as food is concerned, is to protect the food stock against blast, fire and radiation, rather than to accumulate it from scratch. This can be done without too much difficulty. A great deal of food can be stored underground quickly with only little additional cost. Even stored above ground, it can be made reasonably secure against radiation spoilage. Another important form of food storage is processing so that the physical volume of the stock is greatly reduced (by dehydration, for example), which in turn would reduce the underground storage needs and lighten the difficulties of transportation to stricken areas. Progress has been made in food processing, but not nearly as much effort is put into the problems as their importance warrants. Since this is not primarily a business interest in our "normal" times (i. e., before the attack) the government must support this research area vigorously.

It is obvious what else should be stored in strategically selected places, i. e., outside the large cities, but within their reach: medicines, medical and surgical equipment, clothing, tools, etc. Such lists, of course, have been worked out. But this is about all. How could the negligible resources of the Civil Defense Administration even begin to cover the needs? The Administration is incapable of impressing Congress sufficiently to appropriate even research money; so how could they be doing a job that could by any stretch of the imagination be called adequate? The situation here is as bad as for the shelters.

It would make little sense to stockpile, unless the population were expected to survive. It makes just as little sense to secure survival from the attack but not to provide for the resumption of life afterward. The sheltered population must be provided with more than the shelters, which they, for a large part, can provide for themselves. But nobody can on his own secure so much storage of so many different things as he will need in order to rebuild his life together with those of other survivors after the battles are fought.

If there ever was a time for coöperation, it is now.

Active Storage: The Sub-Economy

So far I have discussed only *dead storage*. Important items are simply put away to be used when the time comes, always in the hope that that time may never come. This aspect of the uselessness of the storage during peacetime combined with the fear of disaster makes the whole idea of storage distasteful to many people and prevents action.

But it is possible to think of other forms.

It will be recalled that in the first flush after the initial atomic explosions many writers suggested that our whole country be rebuilt, for example, in the form of linear strip cities, in order to get away from the heavy concentration of our present global cities which offer such easy targets. Others even suggested rebuilding our industries underground, or at least putting each new factory away from existing concentrations, preferably underground.

As was to be expected, nothing was done. The factories that moved into the country did so for entirely different reasons. President Truman discouraged the feeble attempts made by some of his aides to promote dispersal, and the present Administration says and does nothing about dispersal. The rebuilding of cities spurred by nothing more profound than road-building, motorcars and the desire for the good life, resulted in Suburbia. The old 20-kiloton atomic bomb has been forgotten, and the new multi-megaton hydrogen bomb has not yet made its appearance in the consciousness of those who decide these things.

Now it is a drastic suggestion, to rebuild the whole country, and it is not surprising that no one can give the orders to do so. This idea goes too far and therefore spoils the good features it has. I shall therefore modify the idea and instead make the following proposal:

Some part of our economy ought to be put underground. This is the alternative to dead storage—though some supplies will have to be held in this form anyway.

The questions are which part of the economy should go underground, and whether it is possible to determine that part in a scientific manner.

What can be envisaged is the following: It is possible to determine within our present economy a sub-economy which provides at least a certain number of interdependent essential activities, free from all luxuries, all frills. It will secure the very barest *but continuing* existence of a part of the population—that part which may be assumed as saved by shelters or by-passed in a large-scale attack. Economic science can make a vital contribution in determining the exact nature of this sub-economy, this "nucleus" or "kernel" of our present economic system. Methods for identifying such "kernels" exist and can be further developed. It is this sub-economy which should be put underground, properly dispersed in its parts. And this should be done immediately, preferably together with the construction of fall-out shelters.

The sub-economy must be a surplus-producing economy; hence, it must at first have ample stocks from which to expand when called upon to do so. This means that, together with the particular factories to be put underground, stocks of the raw materials and intermediary products they use must be stored at or near their sites. This would give a good plan for the selection of what to store, which otherwise is very difficult to determine. At present in the case of conventional factories this is done on a somewhat haphazard, mostly intuitive basis, totally inadequate for securing a continuing functioning of the post-attack economy.

The sub-economy, on the other hand, must form an integrated system which can live by itself and which, if properly put underground, is virtually bombproof. No part of it need be important enough for the enemy to find it a desirable target. Its underground location would make it hard, i. e., expensive, to destroy.

The proper design of the sub-economy should not only accomplish the construction of an economy which can work by itself when the surface economy is knocked out or gravely wounded. It should be able to rebuild the country gradually from the remnants left over. Therefore it must have the power to expand greatly, for which purpose the already mentioned stocks of different materials are to be kept in readiness. The intention would never be merely to have an economy underground which would work by itself, for itself. It would be a servant of the much larger economy above ground, or rather of what would be left of it.

I have said that this is "active storage." It is so in the good sense that what is put underground is a living thing. Now it is easy to extend this concept to peacetime. Instead of being viewed as something separate from the entire ordinary economy, the underground sub-economy can be integrated with it. This will have many advantages, some of which will be briefly mentioned.

First of all there is a reduction in costs. Instead of being an expensive stand-by set of idle factories and other installations, it will be a working part of the present economy, producing, selling, undergoing technological development whenever it occurs. Only it will happen to be located underground and be compensated by the government for some higher costs arising therefrom. It will be restricted to the making of certain simple but fundamental products. It will have to keep inventories both of its raw materials and its own products in excess of what other installations would normally keep. It will have to stay in close touch with the other components of the sub-economy and coördinate its growth with them. But for the rest it would be a normally functioning component of the economy as a whole.

The sub-economy would probably contain machine-tool factories, nuclear power plants and installations capable of producing atomic power plants, pharmaceutical plants, hospitals, refineries, etc. These factories should be able to maintain themselves in functioning condition even if the economy above ground is essentially destroyed. In that case they would first of all take care of the people working and living underground, then supply the survivors of the attack with necessities, with organization, and information. They would then set out to piece together what could be salvaged above ground and provide power for expansion so that the whole economy could once more in some fashion arise from the shambles. The astounding capacity of modern industrial societies to revive after seemingly irreparable damage would be put to its most formidable test.

The cost of the sub-economy would be great—but only the initial investment. There are many ways in which costs could be met, not all of them wholly dependent on government subsidies. On the contrary, even with small tax advantages, private investors might very well eye with favor the opportunity to insure themselves against losses from war damage in a manner no insurance company now can possibly offer.

On the ability of the country to reconstruct itself after a large thermonuclear battle the survival of the nation will undoubtedly depend. If both antagonists are grievously wounded, the one that can rebuild will be the true survivor: I avoid the word "victor" which in the face of catastrophes of these dimensions has lost all meaning.

Recovery

With stocks alone we will not recover. With an active sub-economy it is possible.

Recovery is imperative because otherwise the survivors will slowly perish, even if they have fortunately escaped the bombing and fall-out by means of shelters. It will be imperative to organize them out of the confusion after the strike. No one may assume that "private initiative" will suffice, that a few tricks with "stable money" and the like will do. Those will be needed but they will be too little. Where they worked after World War II, it was only because there was a government, there was American help, there was a world with which to resume contact. Nothing of this kind is assured now.

Recovery for the purpose of resuming military operations can hardly be considered. It is not likely that a country after a big thermonuclear exchange will be able to mount any new military power at all. What matters is the force in being when the war starts—this we have seen. A modern force is so highly technical and requires such specialized personnel that the chances of filling lost positions is practically nil. You may give a rifle to an adolescent boy in the hope that he can step in where a soldier fell; but you cannot turn a ballistic missile or a jet plane over to him! Even those who produce modern weapons are completely separated from the users. This is true for both camps: What we have not got in the way of specialized personnel at the beginning of a war we will never get, except of course in the case of limited wars.

Recovery is therefore something much more elemental. It aims at continuation of life, on a simple and primitive basis. From mere survival, in view of perhaps a hundred million people killed within a few days, to the construction of a society which adheres to the lofty ideals we cherish today is a long way. And the survivors may develop ideals so different from ours that we may not recognize the country—should we live to make the comparison, or, living, should we care to make it even if we could.

Still, we now believe that some values of our civilization should be preserved. Therefore we must make this possible. At present we do only a partial job poorly.

Shelter Construction as a Provocation

The building of shelters for the civilian population has important strategic consequences: soft targets are hardened. This is entirely apart from the moral question of whether it is legitimate to attack the civilian population. The stark fact is that with shelters in existence it is harder to destroy population. Retaliation is more difficult to accomplish. True, cities can be turned into rubble as before, and if only fall-out shelters exist, the city population will also be lost. But tens of millions away from cities who would necessarily perish in the side effects may now be saved. This reduces the effectiveness of the retaliatory threat. If in one country 50,000,000 people survive and in another none survive, the first is the victor, though amidst terrible ruins.

Of course, if even a very much *smaller* threat, say the destruction of New York City alone, used against us, is fully effective, then nothing more needs to be said. It is very doubtful, however, that this threat would be effective, no matter how horrible the decision would be to sacrifice New York. We would not surrender then, just as we would not surrender if only some American Embassy were held as pawn, or a ship were sunk. This was discussed above, p. 17, and it was pointed out that the evaluation of the survival of one's own nationals will be estimated differently in different countries at different times.

Since we are always being told about the high respect for human life which we are supposed to have, our own motivation for building shelters ought to be much stronger than that of the Russians or Chinese. Whatever the true circumstances, the basic fact remains that shelters make it harder to kill people and that this has an effect on the strategy each country would employ either as an aggressor or defender.

We can now state the following:

A speedy and large-scale shelter construction upsets the strategic balance existing at the time of the initiation of the program in favor of the shelter-building country. Its effects are the same as those of any other weapons crash program.

After the construction period has passed, the country is definitely better off. Now each nation wishes its strategic position to be superior to that of its opponent—a goal that clearly cannot be achieved by all at once. This is why new weapons are introduced and new defensive devices are designed continuously. Shelters have to be viewed on par with weapons systems. Though called "civilian" defense, they are part and parcel of the picture of the whole strength of a country.

We started in Chapter II from the premise that there exists, at the present, approximate parity at the highest level in the nuclear striking power of Russia and the United States. We also saw that any *discrete,* discontinuous, change by either country is exceedingly dangerous since it invites preventive action by one party (which is going to be left relatively weaker) *before* the strength of the other increases materially.

To make this quite clear: if we introduce a superior missile, Russia is thereby forced to do the same in approximately the same time period or to find a superior defense against this missile, thus re-establishing parity or stalemate. If it is not feasible for her to do either, then the possibility of a preventive attack on us while we are working on the new missile will be weighed in spite of the enormous risk involved. This is where speed enters again:

The time interval needed for the introduction of a really important new weapons or defense system is critical. The longer it is, the more dangerous is the period.

Applying this principle to the shelter program, it is easy to see that it would take very long to build shelters against blast, not so very long to get fall-out shelters. A country engaging in a large shelter program is literally "digging in" and may well give the impression that it is getting ready to attack. This interpretation will be unavoidable, no matter what peaceful intentions are officially declared at that time. A shelter program is a *major* change in the balance between the two countries and therefore can not be viewed with equanimity by the enemy.

It suffices to ask what our own reaction would be if we learned that Russia had decided to go all out regarding shelter construction. Would we not very quickly decide that we have to do the same? Would we not want to be ready with ours at least not later than they? Would we not desire immediately to improve the power of the bombs and missiles we might use in a retaliatory attack? Would we not feel only then that the present, precarious balance had been restored? I exclude the possibility that we might attack before the Russians had finished their new enterprise. There are, however, historical illustrations for precisely such situations where this consequence was drawn. There are also instances where this consequence was *not* drawn: For example, when Hitler armed Germany, the balance with the West was upset. During his long period of preparation there was ample opportunity for a showdown or for a preventive war.

To sum up: Any substantial improvement or deterioration of the position of either side is dangerous for the preservation of peace. On the one hand the weaker side is tempted to stage a preventive operation if it cannot hope to nullify the advantage the adversary is gaining and do this as rapidly as the former. On the other hand the stronger side is tempted, if it reaches the position of greater strength, to use it in order to capitalize from what may be only temporary advantage.

There is nothing stabilizing in the situation. Needed is an invulnerable retaliatory force strong enough to destroy as large a part of the enemy's population as would certainly be an unacceptable price for him to pay for any big adventure he might contemplate. This holds unequivocally for both sides.

Whether we build shelters or not is therefore overshadowed by the need for the invulnerable force. But the risks involved in our present state are such that we hardly have any choice. In spite of the risks involved, we should build fall-out shelters immediately, backed by the proper organization. I do not believe that deep shelters will be built for our large cities—not because of the expense of several hundred billions of dollars, or the time it would take, but because of the emotional conditions involved. We may dig small shelters in our back yards individually, but whole cities will not go underground. Their life depends precariously on the effectiveness of the deterrent. In the meantime, the stopgap solution of keeping large parts of SAC continuously in the air would, at any rate, be the first, though halting, step toward a truly dispersed, mobile retaliatory deterrent force flung over the wide oceans of the earth.

However, such is our schizophrenic behavior that though we are in various degrees aware of the tremendous danger to the country, one can safely predict that nothing decisive will be done. There will be much comforting talk from high places and the usual little stabs in this and that direction: a negligible Polaris force, a few more SAC planes in the air, a little more noise about "Civil Defense" and some hardened missile bases. Far from being a truly mixed force in the sense of our previous analysis, this hodge-podge will add up to nothing more than a standing invitation to an implacable, risk-taking enemy some day to try it after all.

6   Limitation of War

Is the Question Absurd?

War is violence. How can violence be limited? Strange and absurd as the question may sound there are limitations. In boxing, fencing and any other sport involving a fundamentally hostile attitude of the contenders certain rules are observed and they are enforced by the umpire. But in war there is no umpire. "World conscience," the "moral law," and whatever other pious names there may be, belong to the verbiage surrounding war but have little operative significance. What meaning they did have, the increased brutalization of war over the last hundred years has practically eliminated. Gallantry, chivalry and even heroism all sound hollow and false in connection with thermonuclear weapons that can in the near future be directed by push button from thousands of miles away against the civilian population anywhere.

Yet even under such conditions wars need not necessarily get completely out of hand. There is after all the fundamental self-interest of the contestants, which sometimes may dictate to them a behavior somewhat different from use of the full potentialities of their weapons. The failure to use gas in the last war is possibly a case in point; why it was not used in the Korean war is perhaps more obscure. The situations where both contenders may lose significantly—which occupied us in the preceding pages—are becoming more numerous, more easily discernible and may eventually be recognized even by the statesmen in power. But it is a long way from a general awareness that both may lose to relating this fact correctly to the employment of special types of weapons and to the choice of particular targets. Given the multitude of weapons systems and the manifold ways in which they can be combined and interchanged, this is not a simple matter.

The real trouble is, of course, that the recognition of the fact that *both may lose all* must spread to both sides and be equally convincing for each party. This then will impose the self-restraint one is looking for, which cannot be secured by appeal to moral and ethical values and the constraints these theoretically might lead to. Even when wars were fought within the same world of values, say among the Christians, they were often particularly bitter and ruthless. The religious wars offer ample illustrations. Then the differences were often very sharply defined, but minute, theological issues. Present conflicts tend to involve the Western world and Communism, between whom cleavage of values is much broader. In this there is some hope, insofar as one may discover that one has fewer specific principles that come into direct conflict at any given moment.

That both sides lose everything is not a normal outcome of conflicts that have led to war. One hears frequently that "wars don't settle anything," which is a way to express the belief that all wars have been in vain. This is simply not true. There were many wars in which there was a clear victor and in which the issue over which the war was fought was definitely settled. The Third Punic War was one of these; the battle of Tours secured

Europe from the Moors; that of Salamis saved Greek civilization and removed the threat of the Persians; the War of Independence established this country—to name only a few at random.

The most effective way of limiting war is to prevent it from occurring in spite of conflicts and antagonism. In this case either one country imposes its will upon another without resort to arms, or two countries abstain from war because of its futility under the given circumstances. The submission of Austria and Czechoslovakia to Hitler are illustrations of the former; in fact, the Western European powers also submitted on these occasions. The present "peace" is an illustration of the latter; it is born out of the nuclear stalemate which the powers believe to exist at this moment.

Sometimes operations are carried out which are hostile in intent but do not involve shooting and shedding of blood. The blockade of Berlin by Russia in 1948-1949 is an example: a primitive semi-military unfriendly act was intended to produce the submission of Berlin. The Western powers answered by the air lift, which was also semi-military in nature, and aimed to nullify the Russian action. The "weapons" used in these operations were partly the display of military power, partly economic pressure, partly an organizational device— the costly but completely effective air lift. It is questionable that our reaction was a sound one precisely because of its great cost and complication. With the aid of a simple roadblock the Russians succeeded in imposing upon us an effort totally out of proportion to their investment. It would, of course, have been easy to meet their challenge in kind.

Over the centuries such instances can be found, yet it is doubtful that there is a tendency to be seen in them. But at any rate the possibility of recurrence of one or the other type of limited war cannot be excluded.

Limitation of war by prevention of hostilities is perfectly feasible and has happened many times. The problem is, therefore, whether some new elements have been introduced into the present scene which make such limitations more difficult or even impossible. The reasons would have to be found in a stiffening of the attitudes of the antagonists, that is, *in a sharper definition of their ideological differences,* or in technological changes, notably of course those resulting in the new nuclear weapons—or both.

The ideological antagonism between the West and the Communistic powers is strong, but one may question whether it exceeds or even approaches the enmity between Protestants and Catholics in times of the religious wars, or that between Mohammedans and Christians a few centuries ago. There are no objective ways to measure the intensity of those conflicts and to compare them with those of the present. The desire for world domination evidenced by the Communists is also easily matched by the craving for world rule and subjugation of all peoples by the Mongols, the Romans and others.

Since not even the Russians can seriously believe that the soft-living United States is set to conquer the whole world—or indeed any part of it—the only present force tending toward world domination by hook or by crook is Communism. Though this forces us and others to our defensive steps, it does not introduce an element into the situation which would clearly make it so different from any previous experience that the thought of limitation of war in our time would have to be shrugged off *a limine.*

Not a Precise Notion

We have a general idea of when a war is "limited" and when it is not. But we cannot state precisely the point in the whole gamut of different forms of violence where a war stops being limited and begins to be unrestricted. Mathematical rigor in these areas is not to be expected. Perhaps it can be rightly argued that the violation of an entire country by a mighty neighbor without firing a shot, as in the case of Czechoslovakia, is worse than a fight costing many lives but leading to some sort of independent existence afterward, as in the case of Finland.

This is a matter of opinion about which one may talk endlessly without settling any issue. But people feel what the above opinion expresses. Indeed, few will agree that the freedom and independence of their own country should be sacrificed merely because great pressure is exercised. They would rather give battle, hoping for some decent settlement on the assumption that the cost to the opponent would not be worth the objective he would gain. Yet when this battle means virtually the instant loss of 50, 75, or 90% of one's own people, the doughty sentiment may well become softened.

No matter from what point the problem of the meaning of "balance" in the time of nuclear plenty is approached, one is led directly to the central theme of retaliation and deterrent discussed in the earlier chapters.

Even though the notion of limitation lacks in precision no one will fail to see a significant difference between a complete thermonuclear exchange between two countries or groups of countries and an action like that in Korea, or Indochina—or the difference between the last world war and the war in Korea.

Limitation of Aims

We saw above that there are two conditions when—given fundamental hostility—no shooting war will occur: (1) when a country surrenders without fight to another, and (2) when the enemies are so matched that neither can move.

The *first case* is not a true "limitation" since it describes the involuntary end of a nation as an independent entity, as happened to Czechoslovakia in 1939. However it is limitation in the sense that it is a different end from that which a country may suffer when its own people are killed and its towns destroyed.

The *second case* describes essentially a technical situation. Presumably one country may want to destroy, subjugate or push back the other. This desire may be mutual or one country may be purely on the defensive. Whatever the intentions on either side, their power is so distributed between them that a hostile action by either one of them is futile. Thus there is a mutual limitation of the freedom of action. The advantage that can accrue from action is negated by the dangers that accompany such action.

This kind of limitation can, of course, be vital but it is not the one associated with "limited war."

Limited war requires a limitation of the aims pursued by the opponents. The limitation of war aims must be declared immediately.

This is the crucial condition. Hostilities and bloodshed occur but the fighting goes less far than technically possible.

The most exacting war aim a nation can have is to demand the *unconditional surrender* of the enemy. If this is being fought for, and if the opposing forces are very nearly matched, the war will be violent and tend to transcend all bounds regarding types of weapons used, target selection (e.g., open cities), fighting past the point of reasonable resistance of the loser. The demand for unconditional surrender will bring forth, in the enemy country, forces in support of that government which otherwise might be used politically or militarily to the advantage of the government demanding surrender, helping to shorten the war. Thus the demand that Germany surrender unconditionally made it difficult, if not impossible, for a powerful resistance against Hitler to develop, leading to his removal and to the conclusion of an earlier peace on terms less unfavorable to that country. This would, incidentally, have been a victory less costly in blood and materiel to the Allies than the one that was actually achieved. The limitation of war aims, therefore, also may work to the favor of the winner who restrains himself. It is questionable whether there can be many situations where the total destruction of the enemy is vital to the interests of the other party. Total destruction is not desirable when it is clear that—barring the complete extinction of life in the other country—one will have to live with the opponent after the war. Sometimes he is even shortly thereafter needed as an ally in newly developing situations. There are ample illustrations of this occurrence from history: Germany and Japan are the most recent.

The war aims are always political. Once formulated, they have to be translated into military terms—such as exclusion of attack on open cities, respect for political or other boundaries where their violation might otherwise be convenient, adherence to international agreements even of a nonmilitary nature, etc. Military actions are thus contained within these politically set bounds, and thus are hampered. But the political leadership gains advantages: it can negotiate more easily, with a view to further restricting military operations, or, on the other hand, it can threaten that it is willing to expand the war—whatever might further the attainment of the war aims and thereby bring the war to an end.

The limited objectives must be made known, if possible even before the start of hostilities, and they must be reiterated often during the fighting. This procedure is necessary in order to impress upon the enemy the possibility of settlement substantially short of conditions threatening his survival and his honor (if this matters to him) and to give him the opportunity of adjustment. The idea is not a new one; it was stated clearly and forcefully thousands of years ago by Chinese writers on military affairs.

The limited objectives must be substantially *smaller* than the demand for unconditional surrender. But they must be *greater* than the conditions the opponent strives for, i.e., the ones for which he would settle (without hostilities) at the outbreak of hostilities.

The limited objectives must be adhered to by the winning party. In other words, if the fortunes of war go to one side they must be exploited in a limited sense only. The winner must not allow himself to be carried away by success, raising the demands he has made initially regarding the conditions for which he would settle. The loser must admit defeat and not go on fighting beyond the point at which he would initially have conceded loss. In other words, *the limited response to a limited challenge* must never be lost sight of. Even the preservation of the *status quo ante* must be considered as a solution.

The question of limitations raises problems of strategy, tactics, political adjustment, of admissibility and inadmissibility of particular weapons. The latter are at present, of course, the nuclear devices.

Historical Experiences

Limited wars have been fought frequently. One might learn a great deal from their course but unfortunately little work has been done in this area. If the State Department were as far-sighted as the Navy is in promoting basic research with its Office of Naval Research, we might be in possession of careful exhaustive investigations of the precise circumstances in which certain wars were limited and remained so, and of why the conventions or military forces which kept other limited wars in bounds narrower than those the weapons and forces would have permitted broke down from time to time.

At times there existed standards of behavior accepted by both sides which regulated the extent of hostilities. Occasionally there were strong economic reasons why battles were not fought as violently as they could have been. For example, expensive mercenaries were frequently used on both sides. Being mercenaries, they were little involved in the ideological or dynastic conflicts that led to hostilities. They had no intention of dying gloriously, for another country, for another king. When such forces faced each other and one side was clearly stronger than the other it became profitable for the weaker force to cede some territorial or other advantage rather than risk the very existence of a valuable, specialized force which could play a significant role in some other engagement where the situation might be reversed. When people's armies became available, as in the French Revolution, idealism rose, and as a consequence the price of human life immediately fell. Large casualties became acceptable because the combination of patriotism with conscription allowed more soldiers to be raised cheaply. A cheapening of weapons and the ready availability of men tend to enlarge conflicts and to make them more bloody. We live in a time when this is true as never before. Hence, the difficulties of containing conflicts are great.

Thermonuclear Stalemate and Limited War

When two opponents match each other in their thermonuclear capabilities in the sense of the preceding discussion, but their antagonism continues, conflict tends to shift to other areas. It is natural for the more aggressive of the antagonists then to seek those areas where he is by nature better endowed, and where active conflict imposes a greater strain on the other. This is the situation which produces the types of limited war which have happened over the last few years.

Russia and the United States are matched regarding bombers, and if we are lucky, may be so in a few years regarding missiles (in the dangerous in-between time, we are fearfully lagging in missiles). But we are not matched in respect to land armies, tanks, navies, etc. If there has to be fighting, Russia would naturally try to use that form which makes the most of her advantage in regard to, say, land armies using conventional weapons. Better still, she would prefer to equip allies and satellites with such weapons, saving her own men. This policy would be combined with an intensive campaign against the use of nuclear weapons, especially small-yield weapons, which would be the technically proper reply to massively concentrated troops and tanks. There would be pressure against weapons tests, since the small, clean weapons are precisely those which the United States would need and which require an active test program. It would be natural, in particular for a United States force, to choose this type of nuclear counteraction when it has to fight at a great distance from home and therefore is primarily beset with enormous difficulties of transportation and supply.

This tendency to transfer the conflict from the stalemate

area to others is perfectly natural. It also happens, of course, if one party has a clear-cut advantage over the other in a particular geographical area, or in a weapon. In the latter case this specific weapon will be denounced by the other as immoral, inhuman, etc., in order that another weapon in which the enemy has the edge can come to the fore. The strength one party may have may also be circumvented or annulled by unconventional means, tactics and operations such as infiltration and subversion.

All this is also observed in civilian life in any country: if the police are strong enough to prevent open robberies, the criminals will steal, for which operation the police may not be well prepared or cannot use the arms and equipment which make robberies unprofitable. Or the criminals will go over to forgery, etc., which requires again a different police technique and so on. The conflict between the police and the criminal world persists, but the area where it emerges shifts, depending on the distribution of relative strengths.

The lesson to be drawn is that, given the thermonuclear stalemate, the United States must expect that limited wars are more likely to happen and that consequently we have to prepare for the specific conditions under which they are to be fought. There is now a great deal of discussion of limited war. But the fundamental fact that such conflicts are more likely to happen in the future than they have in the recent past and certainly more likely than a big thermonuclear exchange is still not recognized in leading government circles. It is even expressly denied. So it is no wonder that our preparations for these types of actions are woefully inadequate and that very little has been done to develop new systems for limited-war situations imaginatively.

Given the relationship between the stalemated capabilities of the antagonists and the subsequent transfer of the conflict to areas where they are not likely to be matched, we obtain an important result:

The matching of technical capabilities must be preserved

from strategic bombers and missiles on downward to the specific limited-war capabilities in order to shift the area and domain of conflict primarily to the political, diplomatic, economic and ideological sphere.

Wherever we succeed at least in matching and stalemating the other side, we have, with a high degree of probability, removed that particular area from becoming active. It is clearly to our interest and that of the world to have the unavoidable conflict areas restricted to the nonviolent politico-economic type of warfare.

It follows equally that if we should have the upper hand in one of those areas we are well-advised to use that advantage. For example, we could even now exercise so much economic pressure, which Russia could not hope to match, that we would relieve her pressure upon us in other fields where we feel it more strongly.

Since at present we are ill-prepared for limited wars—official statements to the contrary notwithstanding—a great effort must be made as fast as possible to close the existing gap. This requires reorganization and even the construction of novel equipment.

The lack of a limited-war capability that matches that of the opponent increases the danger of all-out war. The side having no such capability is then always confronted with the only alternative: either to give in to a comparatively small challenge or to go to all-out war in order to stop the demands of the limited aggression. Local provocation can then be met only by all-out action. This situation encourages more and more "little" demands, none of which, taken by itself, is "worth" a total war. Repeated defeats of this kind encourage the aggressor to step up his demands. In the end the peaceful party will see that the sum of all losses is greater than what he would have accepted had they come in one package. The next demand may then bring the big war. The series of events leading from the Saar, to Austria, to Czechoslovakia ended in Danzig and in the Second World War. Only if the challenge can be and is being met in kind will this road to total war not be traveled the entire way.

Wherever a stalemate exists along the entire scale of types of conflict and weapons, it must never be allowed to slip away from us. This is the principal guarantee we have against an expansion of a strictly limited war, and it is a most troublesome and difficult problem. Clearly the principal stalemate must be with the completely devastating thermonuclear exchange.

It stands to reason that if the United States and Russia are mutually protected against the outbreak of all-out war by virtue of their mutual ability to annihilate each other at short notice, they are also protected even if they are engaged directly or indirectly in a limited conflict fought somewhere in the world not involving the territory of the main antagonists. Mutual destruction, however, is mutual destruction even if it should spring from a limited situation that might develop involving anyone else. The deterioration of a limited situation may produce some expansion of the conflict—especially if the more favorably placed party behaves foolishly, i. e., presses its advantage too hard—but the motivation which prevented a wholesale exchange in the first place still exists.

If the deterrent works, it must work also against the expansion of limited conflicts.

It is just as unpleasant to be annihilated with something first having gone wrong in, say, Indonesia, as when nothing at all is happening there!

Weapons Systems for Limited War

The great diversification of modern weapons and especially their great differences in power raise the questions whether some of them are particularly suited for the type of limited operations associated with borderline wars and whether some are not only not suited but definitely taboo. This latter possibility raises a very difficult problem which has not yet been solved. Furthermore, the issue is being deliberately beclouded by intensive propaganda against the use of all nuclear weapons. Many well-meaning but naïve groups have quite clearly fallen prey to a clever and subtle Communist effort to make it impossible for us to use nuclear weapons in limited wars. But let us look at weapons without any thought of restrictions and bear in mind the enormous advantage in manpower that the Communist countries have over us.

Although the population of the Western world, or even of the NATO countries alone, is impressive it is smaller than what the populous East can muster. This includes Russia, although limited wars directly adjacent to the Russian border are less likely than in other areas. Furthermore, all probable areas of conflict are at great distances from the United States. One conflict may arise in the Middle East, the other by design soon thereafter far away from there. Keeping us hopping around from one place to another is, of course, sound strategy for Russia to use. It is easy to foresee that strategy, and it is also not too difficult to counter it in a defensive (but positive) way.

Russia was able to force us in the Korean war to violate a classical principle of warfare, which is: *Never fight an inferior army on its own terms.* This refers to weapons as well as to the type of fighting and the battleground. We did not fight the American Indians with their own bows and arrows, but used the most advanced weapons of that time.

It is imperative to realize the full meaning of the above principle. We should make it clear to ourselves. When we have properly understood it we must make it clear to our potential enemies that we shall abide by it. I am sure that they understand it well anyway but they would like to see us give it up, and they are trying their best to call on any ally they can get to move us according to their desire.

It is unfortunate enough that in past conflicts such as in the Korean war we had to pit our *own* soldiers against Russia's cheapest allies, the North Koreans and Chinese. So we were under a double disadvantage: instead of using satellites of our own (which we don't have) we had to fight in great numbers; also, we were fighting at an enormous distance from our homeland. Instead of using even our most powerful conventional weapons we restricted ourselves to the types possessed by a technologically inferior, numerically superior, enemy. Such a situation spelled nothing good, and events have borne this out. Historians in the future will use the Korean experience as an example of strategic-military mistakes many times compounded. If one or the other difficulty could not be avoided we did not have to accept *all* of the enemy's conditions!

If we drop this artificial restriction it becomes quite clear that nuclear weapons will have to be used in limited wars regardless of where they occur, provided they produce a decision in our favor and are the technically best-suited means of defeating the enemy. They make it impossible for the enemy to concentrate great masses of men effectively. He would merely be wasting them, even beyond the wide limits which the Chinese might find acceptable. The development of small-yield, high-precision nuclear weapons makes it possible for us to compensate to a large extent for our drawbacks of great distance and small numbers of fighting men which we can muster in a short time. In the types of conflicts we must anticipate, time will be very precious, at least at the beginning. Here too there will be no periods of long, slow build-up as in large-scale wars of the past, though these future wars may last a long time. This means that our forces must combine power and great mobility. They can have power, though being small in number, by virtue of the small-yield nuclear weapons which have been developed already (though not all are operational) and which can be further diversified. They can have mobility if we will finally buckle down and develop new types of air lift for troops held in ready state in the United States and in crucial parts of the world where we still have possessions or friends.

The support of these forces from the sea imposes a great strain on the Navy. It is here where seaplanes and small aircraft carriers, especially if equipped with vertical-take-off planes, can still play a great role. The submarine can also be developed for landing operations such as, for example, towing submerged barges (which is at any rate a cheap and efficient way of transporting cargo, even though still largely neglected).

The Navy will also be called upon to conduct operations in closest connection with the troops on land, since missile ships can provide the kind of artillery support which otherwise could be established only with difficulty through landing of heavy guns. So-called "terminal guidance" can give the forces on the land control over the ultimate destination of missiles fired from several hundred miles at sea, and each shot can be placed at their tactical disposal. This can be extended to any distance and to any kind of missile. The complications and advantages from such operations are at the present time unforeseeable. The analysis of weapons systems is a difficult matter and requires many talented people. This particular scheme is exceptionally far-reaching with many implications and should therefore be examined most thoroughly.

The Spectrum of Nuclear Weapons

In this study many kinds of nuclear weapons have been mentioned; sometimes the distinction was made according to their "yield" or power, which is measured in tons of TNT. A "blockbuster" in the last world war contained about one ton of TNT. The fission A-bomb used on Hiroshima yielded about 20,000 tons (or 20 kilotons); hydrogen or fusion bombs can be made arbitrarily large in yield, but of course not at the same time arbitrarily small in size and weight.

There are two points that deserve specific attention: *first,* we have succeeded in making weapons (not just "bombs") smaller and smaller in their overall weight and dimensions, and *second,* we have also been able to reduce their yield concomitantly. Thus for the same weight of the weapon we can get a larger yield than we could some years ago, or we can get a small yield at low weight. This is the frequently mentioned "miniaturization" of nuclear weapons. The exact dimensions involved are naturally kept secret; but what is known to the public suffices for us to state many important implications of this development. What has happened is not entirely surprising, since man always learns how to make things better and that means often "smaller" (think of clocks, watches, radios, motors, etc.). Surprising has been the speed of the progress. This is partly due to the fact that very much energy has been devoted to the effort, which in turn can be explained by the enormous military importance of being able to develop a widely spread set of nuclear weapons.

Much of this is very recent. For example, President Eisenhower only a few months ago disclosed that there is under development a bazooka-type weapon, fired by one man, which can deliver a portable nuclear charge. In 1945 the first nuclear weapon could be lifted only by a specially fitted large plane. Naturally the yields of these two weapons differ; but this merely emphasizes the two above-mentioned tendencies toward miniaturization. Let no one, however, believe that this new weapon actually "exists" in the strict sense that hundreds or thousands are in the hands of the Army and the Marines, properly deployed with them. It exists on drawing boards, in models and perhaps prototypes, and it exists no doubt on beautiful cardboard pictures used to brief the President. Our lead times for production being what they are, much water will still run down the Potomac before this weapon is where it should and could be at this very moment.

This nuclear "bazooka" is only one of several specialized nuclear weapons of small dimensions and low yield. It is these that deserve attention in regard to limited engagements. No one can doubt that their use would have completely transformed the fighting in Korea. The very small ones were not available then, but larger ones were, and according to age-old military experience it would be nothing short of foolish not to use them in similar instances in the future. To obtain the equivalent effect from heavy artillery, many vehicles, men and rounds would have to be landed and transported. These nuclear "bazookas" would be ideal against tanks, emplacements, etc.

There are, of course, targets where other specialized weapons would be needed. If they don't exist they can be constructed. If the need for them is shown they can be made. This applies unquestionably to so-called "clean" weapons, i.e., such that reduce lingering radiation to negligible amounts.

Even the military often do not pay enough attention to the fact that the great variability of atomic weapons exists. The Army has accused the Air Force of being hypnotized by the large bombs. The Air Force maintains that the scarce nuclear material should not be wasted for many small weapons (which are necessarily "inefficient" because of their lavish use of scarce fissionable material), because the Air Force would be able to "do the job" with their big weapons, etc. Both these arguments are faulty and beside the point. Each of these weapons has a particular function.

The largest bombs of the Air Force are most likely completely useless in limited-war situations. *But they were never meant for such use.* The vastly smaller disaster of a limited war happens only because the existence and deliverability of these large weapons specifically designed for retaliation work successfully as a deterrent preventing the ultimate catastrophe. It is therefore completely false to say, as one often hears, that we have the wrong kind of weapons, that there is no point to the "big bang." It is true, however, that we are badly prepared in terms of smaller weapons for limited wars in distant countries. This is largely due to the fact that we have not recognized their increasing role and their special needs.

Even in limited war there are targets of large dimensions, for example, a harbor. Now the very troublesome problem arises whether there is an upper limit to the yield of nuclear weapons that one can admit and still keep the war "limited." Some authors have given arbitrary numbers, for example, 400 kilotons. But there is no way for a commander to distinguish, except by delicate instruments, whether the enemy has used 350 kilotons or 400 or 450 kilotons. One can well imagine what recriminations are likely to be made and how the difficulties of negotiation would be multiplied. Besides, one would have to know about the target in order to make a reasonable statement. A well-defined, fortified harbor may conceivably require many kilotons, and the target may be entirely within the confines of a "limited war." Neither may the use of a large weapon upset the limited political aims of the type discussed earlier. On the other hand even a one-kiloton weapon may be absolutely taboo if used against an open city in a territory where one wishes to keep or enlist the support of the local population. Such dual behavior is completely compatible.

I do not think that anyone is able today to state with confidence what is permissible and what is not. We do not know how the local enemy, his allies, and ultimately Russia would react. We do not know how we would react ourselves.

The central question connected with the nuclear weapons in limited war is this: Do they have an inherent property which would cause the limited war to go beyond all bounds if they are used? The answer to this question must consist of two parts, one technological, the other political:

Technologically and militarily it is easier than it has ever been in history to expand hostilities when nuclear weapons are available. If small nuclear weapons are used at first, large ones can be introduced immediately thereafter. Their compactness makes the problem of delivery to the scene of battle negligible. It is thus trivially easy to step up the intensity of the battle or to carry it to any desired extended area. Naturally the temptation to introduce ever bigger and more powerful weapons will be enormous, especially when their supply is large as we must assume it to be. The extension may even be unwanted, accidental—a new possibility previously not encountered in limited-war operations. Formerly a change in intensity required lengthy preparations, more mobilization and concentration of forces. There was time to think, to negotiate, to reconsider. This precious time interval is now lost forever. The weapons are ready, their delivery at any desired spot is no longer a major problem and in the near future will be none at all.

Politically there has been no improvement whatsoever in our ability to think through complicated issues. We are still moving at the same slow speed and are still using the same old, by now trivial, concepts in analyzing international political relations. In fact, the situation has worsened, precisely because of the above-mentioned speed-up of the deliverability of vastly more powerful weapons.

This is the fundamental reason why nobody can state with any assurance whether it is possible to keep a war limited once nuclear weapons are used, while it is virtually certain that they will be employed whenever it is militarily advantageous. And they are advantageous practically everywhere, thanks to the coverage of the whole spectrum of nuclear possibilities already achieved.

The cardinal point once more is to realize that the deterrent against a thermonuclear exchange between Russia and the United States must work absolutely, be completely convincing to both sides and that opinions or motivations are not the basis for planning:

Only the capabilities of the hostile opponents count and nothing else.

There are enormous advantages in using nuclear weapons first and the temptation to do so must also be attributed to the enemy. Consequently there cannot be put into the field an army which does not have this capability itself and is prepared to see the enemy use it.

A further point is this: The public discussion of nuclear weapons and their effects is seldom specific. The secrecy that has surrounded atomic weapons for so long, and in many ways still does, has detracted from sober and cool analysis which is possible even on the basis of published facts. So the curious situation prevails that the public on the one hand has no conception of the absolute terror which a massive thermonuclear attack with multimegaton weapons would represent, nor of the comparatively innocuous character of the small weapons whose pinpointing effects are trifling compared with the firestorms that destroyed large cities and were accepted without the blinking of an eye during the last war.

It is one thing to try to prevent war altogether or at least to make impossible the big holocaust where hundreds and perhaps thousands of multi-megaton bombs are dropped on each of the warring countries. It is another thing to try to deprive us of the use of *any* and all nuclear weapons, especially the small ones. These would make all the difference in limited conflicts—and they would make the conflicts less likely.

The idea that *any* atomic weapon, *any* atomic explosion is a disaster of a magnitude that the world cannot stand, that it spells the beginning of the end of the earth, that it poisons the atmosphere for future generations is, of course, unmitigated nonsense. It is, however, carefully nurtured by Communist propaganda, which completely neglects the fact that Russia develops, builds and possesses these same weapons and avoids mention of Russia's continued testing of exceptionally "dirty" (radioactive) devices. Some well-meaning people in the Western world, not knowing the published facts and not desiring to know them, join in the Communistic chorus. The result is that they do not differentiate between the various kinds of nuclear weapons. They throw them all into one pot. It is as if they were to insist that no policeman should ever carry and use a revolver because 16-inch naval guns are so devastating! Yet these same people (among them many church groups) would not be heard from if, at a great cost of life to us in a Korea-type war, we were again to use fire or phosphor bombs and literally burn enemy soldiers out of their caves. They were not heard from when, in attacks on whole cities, tens of thousands of civilians were "conventionally" burned to death. If weapons are immoral then *all* weapons are immoral.

This is a difficult situation nevertheless. The propaganda against nuclear weapons is subtle and clearly well organized. It is supported by the spontaneous reaction of vaguely informed people rightly fearful of the unknown. But this country must not be duped into accepting a policy that will unquestion-

ably mean the gradual loss of the whole free Western world
to the Communist Moloch.

Logistics

The Berlin air lift, the Korean war and other recent conflicts of
limited nature brought logistics once again to the fore. In a
thermonuclear exchange the logistic operations are essentially
restricted to the preparations made *before* its occurrence.
While the exchange goes on precious little can be done. Only
the weapons in being count, not the productive capability; the
deployment of the moment and the immediately possible local
logistic operations are of the essence. This situation is different
for limited wars fought at great distances from home.

It is well known that the number of artillery rounds fired by
United States troops during the Korean war exceeded those of
World War II. This gives an idea of the size of the supply
operation that made this feat possible. Since the tendency for
munitions requirements to go up almost exponentially would
surely remain in a future conflict using so-called "conventional"
arms we get an idea of the magnitude of the logistic task. The
difficulties are practically insurmountable and the risk would
be enormous. The enemy merely would have to switch to nuclear weapons in order to make pointless the high concentrations which logistic operations of these dimensions would necessarily produce.

The use of nuclear weapons with smaller numbers of specially trained men creates a complete transformation of the
problem of supply. The big one that stands out as unsolved,
however, is that of fuel since even a small force with great fire
power, in order to be highly mobile, would need to consume
great quantities. Present fuel is bulky and inefficient to transport. Therefore fundamentally new ideas about fuels are as
valuable as they are hard to come by. Science may yet make a
discovery in this area; it would further emphasize the role of
mobility.

One of the great contributions of American ingenuity made

during World War II was precisely in the field of logistics. It is still not sufficiently recognized since the glamour attached to other phases of combat is so much greater. Yet most of these actions could never have happened without the mobile logistic support which gave to our naval landing operations a freedom never before believed possible.

Since the last war speed has increased significantly for air transport, while at sea and on land there is no change. This is another reason why the speediest form of delivery of men and weapons for actual combat must be sought, leaving for the slow forms of transportation the movement of masses such as may be necessary for later occupation, supply of defended civilians, etc. The planning of these different, interlocking activities is difficult and offers interesting, though not insurmountable, scientific tasks.

"Police" Actions and Conventional Weapons

The need for possible use of nuclear weapons in limited wars does not explicitly exclude so-called "conventional" weapons, meaning essentially those using ordinary chemical explosives. Guns, rifles, machine guns, etc., may yet have a role to play. If street mobs have to be dispersed, water from fire hydrants may be still better. If a particular city has to be occupied even the smallest nuclear weapons may be too big for the task. On the other hand the small nuclear weapons of the above-mentioned bazooka type give an entirely new dimension to guerrilla warfare and sabotage. There are unquestionably many operations which involve man-to-man combat, or individual tanks against tanks. But the point is that these are subsidiary engagements and will hardly ever again have a decisive influence on the outcome of such struggles as a Korean war.

The question arises in whether the Army and the Marine Corps ought to have a "dual capability," i. e., be so organized that they carry *both* types of weapons. There is a case to be made for this. No one will argue that there should be only nuclear equipment. But it is not easy to find the right mixture of the two types. Where a nuclear weapon is superior—for example as an anti-tank weapon—it should be used, also because of the immense logistical simplification this entails. Where the conventional one is superior or irreplaceable it should be retained, i. e., mostly in the area of small arms. If this principle is observed, a possible integration of two types of weapons results, as has often been the case in war history. It is, however, highly objectionable to propose—as influential circles in the Army do—that even in expeditionary forces both kinds of weapon be carried where each can do the *same* job. In other words, one would have conventional artillery and nuclear bazookas, although the latter are at least the equivalent of the former. This violates reason, is expensive, clumsy and, above all, produces an inner conflict of strategy to which I have already referred: *Nuclear weapons require dispersion; conventional weapons demand concentration.*

This conflict cannot be resolved by one's own choice; its outcome depends on the enemy's action, notably, of course, on his ability also to use nuclear weapons. If he uses them then we are compelled to disperse, and we have no power if we are thinking in terms of conventional weapons only. If he does not use them, then we can and do have the desired superiority if we are using nuclear weapons. So whichever way we turn the matter it is necessary for us to be prepared with nuclear weapons and the "dual capability" in the same units is ineffective. The proposals to equip the identical division force in this manner are the result of insufficient efforts to think the matter through.

There is greatest need and urgency to make detailed studies of combat situations in which the full range of possibilities is explored. War games played on large-scale electronic computers, available to each of the two players must consider such cases as these: both sides employ small nuclear weapons, one side tries to possess a "dual capability," one side has a long transportation line and is deprived of air cover, airfields, etc. Studies of this sort are difficult, very time-consuming and require an intimate interplay between scientists and military men. While many are undoubtedly being made, there is the uncomfortable feeling that they are neither extensive enough nor on a sufficiently high scientific level. Or else the studies exist, are excellent, but have no influence upon the policy makers. Otherwise one would by now have abstracted in the Department of Defense the semblance of a badly needed doctrine for limited war. It is still lacking. Instead we are being offered rather vague ideas about "dual capability" and an optimistic belief that the battlefield can be controlled by the techniques learned in the last war, with lots of motorization, complicated communication systems and virtually inexhaustible, undisturbed supply lines.

Negotiated Limited War

We have seen how the exceedingly complex problem of the limitation of war is made more difficult than ever by the appearance of nuclear weapons which have never before been used in limited situations. Yet I believe that one fundamental point remains unchanged. That is the limitation of aims to something radically below the threat to the enemy's very existence. If this is understood, the possibility of negotiations at an early stage of the fighting permits the opponents to carry the limitation as far as possible. This limitation gives the enemy a chance to withdraw from the fight without even losing face, and it makes it possible for the winning side to stop pressing for the full advantage of victory in a subsidiary battlefield.

A strong indication that war is being limited by the enemy is the very manner of its occurrence: By starting on a small scale, geographically limited, involving only a small part of the enemy's forces, he has deprived himself of the overwhelming advantage of massive surprise attack. Thus, if the enemy wishes to attack the homeland and to threaten our very existence, he would be ill-advised to give that much of a signal and to invite our countermeasures. Therefore, in the limited start is contained the sign of the desire to keep the conflict within the narrow bounds.

Our best hope is, of course, that no wars whatever will occur any more. But this is so unlikely that no country can plan for it. Our next best hope is that any conflict, once arising, will be quickly contained by the fact that the world is split into two almost matched camps. That is, no matter who fights whom, how trivial the initial cause of the quarrel may be, fundamentally and eventually both superpowers are involved or will project themselves into the conflict. War actions may occur, but no matter how big they become they will be overshadowed by the portent of the fight between the superpowers involving their homelands. If these are completely threatened by each other—they are, and will remain so, since there is no defense against the saturation attacks of which each is capable—then, and only then, will strong efforts be made to contain the local fringe-war for fear that it might spread to the respective "Zones of Interior."

There is no guarantee that such containment *will* occur. But there definitely is no hope unless the big deterrent is complete, effective and fully convincing. Each side must see the dangers to itself arising from an expansion of the conflict. Putting it differently, both sides must understand that, though they are at war, they have some common interests left. These they must emphasize while at war, and make as large and important as possible.

7 Technology and Strategy: The War of the Laboratories

The Locus of the Current War

Rarely does the public get a glimpse of the tremendous struggle that is going on in the world for scientific and technological supremacy. From time to time a spectacular event occurs such as Sputnik, or the unexpectedly early Russian achievement of the atom bomb and later of the hydrogen bomb. Then the public is somewhat aroused, perhaps vaguely disturbed or even a little fearful. But soon the television peace settles down again over the country. Confident that everything is in good order, housewives return to washing machines, driers, dishwashers, and beauty parlors while their husbands drive in gaudy cars to fine factories and handsomely decorated offices. Their children of all ages go on visiting the schools and colleges where their dear little minds are carefully wrapped in cotton by undemanding educators so that they may later be ready for the soft life.

Behind this scene, in the great laboratories of the Department of Defense and the Atomic Energy Commission and among the many scientists working there, a totally different, often grim, mood prevails. In those establishments not only does one struggle with scientific and technological problems of hitherto unimagined complexity to which new ones are added constantly, but this work is carried on under the shadow of an adversary whose tremendous strides forward during the last years make an increasing impression of urgency on the scientific world. Yet only few of those who are conscious of and thoroughly informed about the true situation are occasionally given the opportunity to say an important word on how the research and weapons development should be conducted. Even fewer have an influence at the highest levels upon determining their strategic implications. Yet it is precisely here where the most difficult and important decisions have to be made. These decisions are so difficult to arrive at that the usual, common-sense, almost offhand methods of government do not any longer apply. Whether we like it or not, the shadow of modern, ever-changing technology is thrown over the process of governing people, especially when there is the deep-rooted conflict with the Communistic world.

There are two widespread beliefs current throughout the country which help prevent our making a greater effort:

(a) we are technologically more advanced than any other country;

(b) technological changes and improvements always work to our advantage.

Both beliefs are false.

To prove the falsity of these two statements in detail would require a great effort and much more space than is at our disposal. Regarding the *first* some illustrations may suffice: French electronics is at least as good as ours and in many ways far more advanced than ours; British jet engines surpass most of ours by a wide margin; Japanese optics is better than German, which in turn is better than ours; Swiss pharmaceutical products, Belgian color film, Swiss watches, British bicycles, German cameras are an easy match for the best we have to offer; Danish Diesel engines are unsurpassed anywhere in the world. The area of technological achievement where foreign developments are at least as good is of course much larger. If we look at military equipment there is ample evidence that British planes equal ours, the Belgian infantry rifle is superior to our Army's, the French artillery is superior to any we can muster.

Let us include Russia in the picture: it produces greater thrust for rockets than any other country; excellent radar equipment, in many respects surpassing ours; tanks that have no match in propulsion, armor or fire power anywhere; jet planes that are at least the equals of ours; fighter planes that in Korea outperformed those we could at first muster against them; electronic computers that are at par with our best. And this list could be lengthened.

American technological superiority exists but in two different directions: we are *on the average* better, and we can produce great quantities of good products after standardization has been achieved. Even this superiority is sometimes less the result of ingenuity than of the ample supply of raw materials which so far has permitted essentially wasteful production and consumption habits. One may say further that while other countries excel technologically in a few lines over the United States, this country is *on the average* or in the aggregate superior to all of them (though even in this sense the case is debatable regarding Switzerland). Clearly we too have technological superiority to show—but not in missiles; perhaps in nuclear weapons (But who can know the facts here and in Russia? Has anyone actually dismantled nuclear weapons of Russian origin and compared them with ours?), and probably in nuclear reactors.

We should contemplate these facts soberly in order to come to a proper understanding of our position. These facts will make it clear that in our great struggle *we are not simply sitting on top of the world*. Too many of our leaders tell us this too often. Repetition does not make it true. We are at best on a broad

plateau peopled by many nations. To be sure, I am not referring to total brute strength or aggregate wealth. In both of these
we now outdo any other nation. I am talking about the state of
accomplished technology.

The *second* point, that technological *changes* always work in
our favor, is equally false. This is a singularly complicated
matter but it can be made clear from a few illustrations: When
nuclear weapons were invented they seemed to give us the advantage. This proved not to be so. We are far more vulnerable
to them than Russia is because of the high concentration of our
population in cities. The ballistic missile is another case in
point. This advance-delivery system exposes us more than Russia, which has a vastly greater area in which to hide her capability. The Polaris-type submarine with a 1000- to 1500-mile
missile range threatens us more (for the same reason) than
we threaten Russia by the same device. Nuclear power gives
other countries a greater advantage in providing cheaper energy than it does us. And so we could go on.

The important observation to be made is, of course, that it is
impossible to predict with confidence whether or not changes
will work in our favor. These examples show that there have
been significant technological changes which are not advantageous to us either in a military or, necessarily, in an economic
sense. These facts alone disprove the validity of the general
statement that technological development is always to our advantage. Of course, tomorrow a discovery may be made in this
country which completely changes the whole picture by giving
us supremacy. We do not know. We would be foolish to count
on it. But we must not exclude the possibility. If it happens it
would be only through research, the deep, basic scientific probing of the world around us. If such discoveries are made elsewhere we must strive to the utmost to exploit them quickly—
if they become available to us—lest we actually fall behind in
this most tremendous struggle in the history of mankind.

All this teaches us one lesson: No technological change of
any significance whatever, i.e., a change involving a new scien-

tific step forward, is a matter of indifference to any of the great nations. Or, to put it differently, every technological change disturbs *all* advanced nations. It does not matter where it is made. Naturally, it will also affect underdeveloped countries, but that is not of great consequence now. There the effects are more indirect while here we are concerned only with the precarious balance between the two antagonistic blocs, a balance which will not last for decades.

To give some illustrations: The invention of railroads affected the countries that introduced them, but this did not constitute an immediate menace to neighbors or distant lands. Motorcars helped the growth of the nations that developed them, but again, for others they were at most a minor disturbance. However, the airplane was different, since it reached so easily beyond narrow borders and has grown so quickly into an aggressive tool of war. Nuclear energy is a vast step in this development; rockets by necessity infringe on the living space of other countries. Future achievements, notably the possible control of climates, finally will touch every nation on earth. These are effects that differ profoundly from the mere demands made by industrial nations upon the resources of the world. They are full of ominous portent.

In times of peace and when there were ample sources of raw materials all over the world for the advanced countries, and so long as the underdeveloped countries did not vehemently press for growth, there was no disadvantage in the spread of industrialization. On the contrary, the more technology advanced and the more intimate the contacts among nations became, the more trade flourished and wealth grew. This is quite different now when everything centers around the power each bloc can command.

Technological Change and Strategic Experience

A strategy is a feasible plan of action. From among all strategies the "best," or "optimal," has to be selected. This would not be too difficult, if there were only a small number of strategies and if there were no interference. Unfortunately both nature and the enemy interfere. Nature, although not hostile, is capricious: bad weather sets in, accidents of all sorts happen, etc. But nature's actions can be treated and counteracted statistically. That is to say, one can take care of such events in the conventional manner of insurance: by improvement of design, by increase in number of machines and men used, etc.

It is different with the opponent: his intentions are clearly opposed to ours, and his plans aim at nullifying ours; he too wants to pick his optimal strategy. The plans interfere with each other, and the problem of what is "best" for each is consequently a deep one. It cannot be solved by merely using the common-sense approach of military academies. This is the domain of the mathematical theory of games of strategy, which has clarified the conceptual problem of decision making, established the necessary theorems and shown the methods for selecting and computing the optimal strategies, i.e., those strategies which are the best possible courses of action no matter what actions the enemy may be able to undertake.

The feasibility of a plan, which makes it a strategy, depends on the given state of technology. With many difficulties, learning from the experience of many costly wars, military men have been able over the years, or rather centuries, of fairly stable technology to abstract certain rules, learn definite patterns (e.g., of deployment of troops and of fleets) and develop teachable routines. This process of learning was possible because the changes in technology were slow and gradual. From arrow to crossbow, from wooden ship to iron ship, from sail to steam, the transition took decades and centuries, if not longer. During each slow and gradual transition, experience could be gained for all. It became apparent eventually that what was proper for one technology would not work for another. This process of learning was a painful one. History is replete with poignant illustrations where those who would not learn quickly enough were beaten down.

All learning is time-consuming, especially if one has first to discover what has to be learned! The military are in a particularly difficult position. They need tradition, firm rules, convincing proofs from experience in order to handle large and complicated organizations. Mistakes they make may affect the survival of the nation. So it is little wonder to find conservativism and a reluctance to deal with radically changed weapons, especially when these may require significant breaks with traditionally proven behavior.

Weapons technology has never before in history changed as frequently and with each change as profoundly as now. A ballistic missile with a nuclear warhead, even though a ballistic device, is a vastly different instrument than what the biggest gun ever was. A Polaris submarine force has little to do with conventional submarine warfare. Biological and meteorological warfare looming on the horizon defies all notions of usual military operations, and power of the magnitude of nuclear explosions was never before contemplated in military doctrines.

The crucial point in the present situation, made earlier in this study, is that *there exists no operational experience with any of the new weapons.* It is in regard to these weapons precisely that even the strategic ideas most recently gained from combat experience have lost their meaning.

In previous wars, not excluding Korea, where nothing but conventional weapons was used, there was always time to learn. During combat itself adaptation was possible, selection of targets, understanding of the enemy's peculiarities, preferences and idiosyncrasies. More important, the best officers could be gradually found. Battles lost eliminated one general and brought a better one to the fore. Battles won confirmed the man in command. In long wars entire sets of generals were consumed until the victorious man emerged. The price of learning was not merely taxpayer's money but the blood of soldiers sacrificed to gradually discovered incompetence. There seemed to be no other way of learning.

No new method has been found for discovering the best general in peacetime. It is rare even for stationary weapons technology that the ultimately victorious general is the same who was in command at the beginning of hostilities. However, in the present situation *if we have the big thermonuclear exchange lasting a few days (or weeks at most), there is no time for learning.* Just as the weapons in existence, nay, the ready weapons deployed and surviving the surprise, are all that we have, it is the (surviving) commanders *now* on the spot, the war plans *now* in existence, at this very moment, on which everything depends. Our existence depends on what we have thought and done up to that moment. One shudders when one surveys the scene and is forced to think that what there is should really be the best that there could be. It must be so since otherwise the entire system of determining strategy is wrong. This we are reluctant to believe and certainly cannot prove because in order to do so we would have to describe the better system. Who can do this? It cannot be done intuitively.

In a limited war there is a difference. Although the use of nuclear weapons would be new, the weapons might be small and their use spread out over time; the war itself would, as likely as not, last long enough so that some faults in the initial plans could be corrected in a more conventional manner and at the conventional cost in blood and tears. However, the shorter and the more violent the war, the more it matters what has been done and thought before its outbreak.

The speed with which more and more complex weapon systems are being introduced places a particularly heavy burden on the analysis of their uses. A new weapon arises because some physical discovery or invention has been made, based on either old or newly discovered laws of nature. It is hardly ever constructed because of a preconceived strategic notion. Thus, new weapons disturb existing notions of strategy. This has never been more evident than now. What some of the strategic implications are was the subject of the preceding chapters.

The real problem is, of course, whether this interplay between technological change and strategic employment is brought to the highest possible level in our or any other military establishment. There is good reason to doubt this. Information about Russian efforts is scant, but this lack of information is poor comfort, since it is no proof that the efforts are not being made.

The technological changes associated with atomic energy overshadow all others by their very obvious power and spectacular character. But at a different level, shrouded in at least the same secrecy, are the developments in the chemical and biological fields. Not only poison gas comes to mind, but other agents that might transform warfare more profoundly than the nuclear weapons would. It may, for example, soon be possible to introduce secretly into a country chemical agents that would not destroy life but would temporarily destroy the will power of the population, and in particular of the leaders of the country. This is neither impossible to imagine, nor difficult to execute in the near future. Perhaps it is already being done at present. Perhaps it would be a good idea to feed tranquilizers to all the participants of international conferences in order to produce agreements. It would be interesting if that were done secretly by one side only. Then the country receiving such treatment might surrender without realizing what it does.

Chemical and biological warfare can be both deadly and gentle, according to choice and the development of the art.[1] The latter is progressing fast and as a consequence the unfortunate men of state some day will have to make decisions which will make those needed today appear simple. It is little wonder that even the mention of chemical and biological warfare is almost taboo. This reticence will not last very long. The Russians will take care of this too: their published material shows the great effort they are making in this area, and we know how little they release for publication! The life sciences have long been their specialty. And let us not forget that unseen biological agents are even more elusive than radioactive fall-out.

[1] One hates to use the noble word "art" in connection with warfare, killing and destruction. The fact that it is customary to do so is an indication of the intellectual fascination these things have for the human race!

There are no convenient Geiger counters to tell us when an infestation of a country, or region, or perhaps a government committee has occurred.

Strategic thinking requires the conception and development of rigorous, that is to say, ultimately mathematical, methods. Too few military men seem to appreciate what new types of problems they are confronting and what new talents they need.

The questions of the best strategic and tactical use of modern devices are indeed exceptionally difficult. I have attended countless discussions of these problems at all levels and have been impressed by the earnest search for the correct answers and the seriousness of purpose displayed by the widely different participants, military and civilian. If one attends meetings of physicists and mathematicians it does not take long to find out where the limit of human knowledge is at present in those fields, who the best minds are and what is the most powerful thinking that can be brought to bear on those topics. If one meets with social scientists, difficulties already begin to arise. Identification of the best is more difficult. But if one enters the area of strategy one is quickly at sea and wonders time and again whether what is said and written is truly the best the country can produce. One goes from meeting to meeting, from document to document, hoping to find assurance, hoping to be able to identify the "best," the "most powerful" thoughts. There is no assurance, there is only the lingering fear that our efforts are not great enough, not sustained, that perhaps the problems are even beyond our capacity of proper formulation and subsequent solution.

It is in this spirit, incidentally, that the modest attempts made in this book have to be discounted.

Weapons Intelligence

The complexity of modern weapons appears to rise exponentially. Each new device overshadows the other in the difficulties of its design, production and handling. The amount of knowledge that goes into the making of weapons is truly impressive. It has to be matched by those who use them. I am now not referring to their strategic implications, but only to their use under prescribed conditions set by the strategic plans. This means that the weapons demand military personnel who are their equal. The advancing technological level requires therefore more and more intelligence of the user. A sword, a bow and arrow, a rifle and even a machine gun can be used by comparative morons; intelligence helps, however, and, as always, gives a better chance of survival. A naval gun and a submarine torpedo are useless unless they are in the hands of properly trained people. So it goes up the scale until we reach the very latest devices. Since we now cannot talk any longer of individual weapons, we must consider entire weapons systems with their complex interdependencies, all set into a scene now encompassing the entire world and soon, possibly, outer space. Correspondingly, the demands made by the weapons on the weapon users have gone up exponentially. They have risen to a point where most officers have become laymen vis-à-vis the weapons placed in their hands. They are virtually required to be applied scientists or they have to abdicate making military decisions.

What is a general with ordinary training and experience to say when it comes to deciding whether one kind of propulsion system for rockets is "better" than another, or how anti-missile-missiles are to be deployed, or at which rate they are to be fired? Clearly the answers are either the outcome of long scientific studies, as in the first case, or they are obtained from lengthy computations with their results built into the system's behavior, the general being only a stand-by, as in the second case.

Most people are, of course, laymen vis-à-vis the things they use: How many understand the television set or the chemistry of the explosion motor of the automobile? The point is, obviously, that it does not matter whether they do or not: there is always a service man waiting around the corner, and what owners do with these instruments affects few. Not so with a modern weapon.

The need for greater scientific understanding affects not only the use of modern weapons but also the speed with which new weapons and devices can be developed. If military officers have a thorough scientific training there can be a great speed-up. A modern weapon can often be used by more than one service; for example, a missile can be put on board ship or be used on land. As it is, however, if one service develops it, the other cannot get hold of it easily because of interservice rivalry. But, more important, in order to bring a weapon into the development phase a laboratory, say of the Atomic Energy Commission, may require tests which only the Air Force can carry out. Instead of being able to go directly to a field command which could do a simple experiment, the laboratory personnel must climb endless ladders of hierarchy to get permission. If there were in those hierarchies enough scientifically trained officers, swift action might be expected. Or better still, they would see to it that a proper mechanism of easy communication were set up once and for all. This is not a trivial matter. There have been instances where considerable amounts of money had to be wasted, not to mention the unnecessary loss of precious time.

What this problem leads to is the demand for much more flexibility wherever new weapons are being developed, a greater flow of information and speedier action than can now be obtained. This may not seem very important, but it is a situation where a scientific approach to the problem, with great freedom allotted to the individual weapons laboratories, would produce a great change. In order to get this change for the better a scientific spirit must prevail where now administrative protocol reigns supreme.

The demand that many high officers be scientists is not unreasonable. Some have, indeed, learned so much that they do qualify even though they do not hold formal degrees. But it is a grave deficiency of our defense effort that we do not have many, in fact have only absurdly few, officers who hold Doctor's degrees in science. Again the situation is different in Russia. There the number of scientifically trained officers is very much larger, and everyone knows what rigorous demands the Russian schools and universities make before granting degrees. A statistic showing how few American officers, especially of high rank, have formal scientific training of an advanced kind would be a shocking revelation.

Scientific training of high caliber for officers would also help to improve the working relationship between the military and the scientific world. Relations are not bad by any means but a vast improvement is possible and necessary, particularly in regard to contract research.

Basic Scientific Research and Weapons Development

So much has lately been said about the need for basic research that I shall add only very little though this topic is nearest to my own interests. There are some points that are neglected in the current discussion. They have to do with the universities and will be taken up later in this chapter.

The fundamental fact about the relation of support for basic research and the military balance with the opponent is this:

No matter how much effort is put into basic research, this never directly threatens the opponent.

Even the greatest possible support of basic research does not provoke the enemy to attack, while a crash program in, say, missiles or bombs may very well do so. This was encountered in the discussion of shelters. More important even, no matter how much basic research is being promoted in one country, this does not lead to increased armament in the other. If we augment our arms the other side by necessity has to do something similar in the armament field. But it would be utterly foolish to try to match a greatly stepped up program in basic research by making more bombs or tanks. It can lead only to more basic research all around. The result will be applications to the benefit of mankind. These may eventually outweigh the applications to military art although the primary motive for supporting basic research will have been the hope of discovering new methods to make the country safe against the threats it faces.

By basic research we mean in the classical sense the activities directed toward the discovery of new facts and laws of nature irrespective of possible applications. There usually are practical applications, however. Some come quickly, others are delayed for decades. Some are for peaceful purposes, others bear on military matters or make new, never-before-thought-of military operations possible (e.g., the use of fall-out for denying territory to the enemy was not possible before the discovery of radioactivity). But nothing can be programed, ordered, contracted for. It would have been ludicrous, as has been remarked, to charge a physicist, before 1900, to discover Einstein's fundamental equation $E = mc^2$. There would not even have been a way to talk about this because nothing existed that could be put into words. The very concepts of the theory of relativity were lacking. It is equally absurd today to give such orders, although this has not dawned on all inside or outside of government who sponsor research, even basic research.

The support of basic research demands complete freedom for the scientists to push in any direction they choose. The better the individuals are, the less can anyone tell them what they should do. There must be no regimentation, no idea that working in offices from eight to five, with telephones ringing, reports to be read, progress reports to be written, is the proper expression of scientific work. A good scientist will find his own style, and if teams form they too will establish their own modes of work.

Few scientists work alone. The theorists can do this, but their work is dependent on the results the experimenters produce while, in turn, they show the latter new avenues for experimental investigations. The experimenters are far more numerous than the theorists, and since much of the experimenter's work requires funds vastly in excess of the support of his own person, there is here the difficulty of determining whom to support. It is now well known how costly research, especially in physics, has become. The tremendous installations for discovering the properties of matter may require instruments which individually cost one hundred to two hundred million dollars to build (more than the endowment of a University like Princeton) and corresponding amounts to run. If dollar funds were much larger than they actually are, there would still be the problem of whom to support, since such installations need workers with scarce specialized talent which could be used also by other basic research efforts. There is thus ample opportunity and need for administrative decisions. The dilemma cannot be overcome because only rarely are administrators able to understand the needs of those who make the demands. Fortunately, in some important cases where much research is involved, as in atomic energy, it is the laboratories which *de facto* run the show rather than the Commissioners. For this we have to be thankful. Of course, there are from time to time singular exceptions among them; it suffices to name John von Neumann.

The support of some fields is easy. Pure mathematics needs only the financing of good brains. It is fortunately easy to discover, even among the very young, what a good brain is, since mathematical aptitude shows early and is very specific, perhaps even more so than that for music. No costly machines are needed, no teams; only an occasional conference and an outlet for publications. In all the pure mathematics thus generated there will invariably be new results which suddenly and in unexpected places and instances will find dramatic, practical application. This is where the pay-off lies from a practical point of view.

In basic research such notions as "duplication," "concentration," etc., simply do not apply. The more fundamental the work is, the less is it possible to think in these terms. Would it have been wise to instruct Isaac Newton not to work on the mathematical method he later called "fluxions" (now known as "calculus") or on gravity, because that would be "duplication of effort" since others at his time were already working in these fields?

There are crucial times in science when virtually everyone in a given area is working on precisely the same problem. One of them may then succeed in solving it. An element of wholesome competition exists, but deeper is the motivation from scientific curiosity and the desire to share in the excitement of the act of discovery. Those on the outside can have only a faint idea of the tremendous stimulus that causes scientists to make the great efforts needed for such accomplishment. This is the most precious and delicate thing to preserve.

Since it now is not only respectable but even fashionable to support "research" there has been an upgrading of activities: what was formerly engineering is now "development research," former development work is now plain "research" and applied research work is frequently called "basic research." This shift in terminology would be innocuous were it not that the dollar expenditures for all these, deliberately put together, give a false, vastly exaggerated picture of the extent to which research[2] truly deserving this name is supported by government and industry. The true figures are not nearly as large as the alleged six billion dollars per year seem to indicate. Even that number ought to be corrected for the loss in purchasing power, especially in making historical statements about the alleged great rise of scientific support. No one can tell with certainty how much is really being spent on basic, completely unfettered, scientific work. We can only be sure that it is not enough, and we know for certain that the support is not stable.

Indeed, one of the saddest circumstances of the past which, I am sure, will be repeated in the future, has been that the finan-

---

[2] An unfortunate word! "Exploration" or "Search" would be right. But "Re"-search smacks too much of dusty scholarship, of the old tomes of past ages gone over once more to uncover some obscure occurrence or thought, only leading to an additional cherished footnote in a Ph.D. thesis.

cial support of basic research has been so very uncertain. The moment savings have to be made somewhere and budget cuts are in order, it is basic research that suffers most. The reasons are well known. The activity is least understood, the scientists form no pressure groups, there is no clear "practical" use of their work, "nothing to show." These are bad reasons. It is high time scientists made a better case for themselves and their work. Indeed it is a worthy problem to discover a social, political mechanism for the support of basic research that will not be at the mercy of the frequent ups and downs of government budgets and national incomes! This end will certainly not be reached by agreeing to the primitive proposal to make research expenditures of the Department of Defense a fixed percentage of the military budget.

There ought to be a constant searching of souls among the sponsors of basic research, especially in the Defense Department. One agency, more than any other in the government (and perhaps even outside it), has understood how to support research with the maximum of freedom accorded the scientists. That is the Office of Naval Research, an institution which also has understood that continuing, steady support is imperative.

Money given to scientists must be steady and free. The scientists must be able to decide what to do with it, without having to ask for permission to buy this or that piece of equipment, to carry on this or that experiment in any way that seems most suitable. Estimates of the amounts of money, unrestricted in this sense, now available in government laboratories are absurdly low, probably less than $20,000,000 per year. In the total defense outlay for Research and Development this is a tiny percentage, perhaps 1/10 of one percent. Even if the true amount were three times larger, it would still be negligible. Naturally the scientists should have to account for the way they spend the money; but the crucial point is that *they must be allowed to justify after the event, not before.* And, most important, the justification must be to *scientists,* not merely to contracting officers who, if at all able to judge on *scientific grounds* the need or lack of need of an experiment and the manner of its execution, are too far removed from the spot and the crucial moment in time to assist properly.

It is very hard to get this vital point across. But its significance has been demonstrated ever so many times. Indeed, during the most spectacular advances in applying science to the defense effort this condition was fulfilled. During the last war the National Defense Research Council functioned this way, and the Manhattan Project, especially its great Los Alamos Laboratory, could never have succeeded otherwise. No one advocates reckless spending, or incomplete accounting procedures. It is the freedom to decide, on scientific grounds, how available money should be spent that is of overriding importance. To the layman on the outside this may appear to be a minor issue, or a suspicious one. Yet there is, I am sure, no other procedure in the field of research by which a bigger pay-off could be obtained.

It is almost distasteful to have to point once more to Russia. What we did with greatest success during the last war the Russians have learned from us. They practice our former principles while we have lost sight of them. This fact was demonstrated by the steady and massive support Russian science received from the state even during the Stalinist period. Science in Russia is largely independent of political upheavals. A few words referring to Marx, communism or the "imperialist aggressors," sometimes written at the opening or closing of a scientific paper, is all that was and is demanded. The rest is solid, often first-class, scientific work.

Apparently there exists a pact in Russia whereby the politicians leave the scientists alone provided they are willing to pay this small price. As a consequence work on rockets, rocket fuels, nuclear propulsion, etc., that necessarily had to precede the first Sputnik and later the very big ones, has gone on steadily over the many years. Unquestionably in Russia scientists have obtained ample funds and directed their own work. In the United States they have been less well-placed in both respects. Everyone knows the consequences. We leave the programs to administrators and military men who have no scientific training. We turn programs on, off, on again. And for many crucial years we were blessed with Charles E. Wilson, who did not care to know "why the grass turns green"—the man who is reported to have said that "basic research was when you did not know what you were doing." Add to these observations the fact that this was also the period of Senator McCarthy, the loyalty oaths, and the time of the foolish and distasteful Oppenheimer persecution. Inflation, furthermore, whittled away the purchasing power of the already negligible funds spent on basic research. Indeed, a sorry picture.

And so we have reached the fearful point of danger where world leadership in science may pass on to Russia. This is a mortal peril because scientific supremacy would then be in a hostile camp. It would be used against us militarily and industrially. Important scientific discoveries would not even be disclosed to us.

It is a historical fact that the seats of power and of learning were never separated for long.

The No-Sayers

The management of research in the Department of Defense has been bedeviled by the existence of numerous offices empowered to review proposals, and to send them from review to review. Yet hardly any of these agents could or would say yes. Projects have been constantly passed on from one office, committee, board to still another and it has always been difficult to pry them loose from the vicious circle. Many good officials caught in this process have become exasperated and by their often direct, nonconventional acts have saved proposals from an eternal travel among the no-sayers.

The new Director of Research and Engineering of the Department of Defense now has power to break this deadlock. But the organization is so immense that he cannot physically become acquainted with all he should know. Therefore he will have to change the system itself, and this can only mean the removal of countless unnecessary review actions. He will have to change the no-sayers into potential yes-sayers, i.e., give them authority and responsibility also to accept instead of merely passing on.

There is, however, one form of saying "No" which is not practiced enough. That is the abolition of projects—mostly in the development stage—which have aborted or have been superseded by newer, better developments. As a rule these are hard decisions. Aircraft carriers are an instance; so are destroyers. Tanks are still being produced which are technically inadequate; they have gasoline instead of Diesel engines, and they may never get to a place of action. The Nike-Zeus missile is continued though it cannot cope with the attacker against which it is to defend.

These are large projects on which hundreds of millions of dollars have been spent. So what is more natural than to spend some more money, thereby hoping to make the project a success after all? Besides, this is a practice followed by many businessmen, in particular by banks, and is known as "throwing good money after bad." Here it is even worse: not only is money involved but, much more important, scarce engineering and science resources are tied up which would be better employed in vital, living projects with a future. The difficulties of turning projects off permanently and completely are compounded by inevitable political pressures to keep them going for reasons totally unconnected with defense, such as possible local unemployment and the like.

The concentration of research in the Defense Department superficially appears logical from many points of view. But it harbors extraordinary dangers. If the incumbent is not first-class, he can produce havoc. As is often the case, the first, excellent man who holds office may be followed by others far less capable. Suppose Mr. Charles E. Wilson had had a subservient director: Wilson would have been able to destroy many basic research projects which formerly he could not have reached, because of the diffuse organization, the comparatively independent life of the research programs in the three military services, the defective information flow. A deep problem of organization is to build a system that is virtually independent of the particular qualities of the people who pass through it. A good organization ought to be what has been asserted jokingly of the Navy: designed by genius so that it could be run successfully by idiots.

However great the role of the Defense Department may be in respect to basic research, it can only initiate, support and finance. The fundamental work is done elsewhere, not even in government laboratories, which are always predominantly concerned with applications. The progress of basic science must still come from our universities, where the principal work should go on and where, self-perpetuating, the conditions for the future are continuously recreated.

But what of our universities?

The Universities: Mainstay of Our Future Power?

Placing a question mark here is a saddening necessity. There ought to be no doubt.

Perhaps we could survive a war tomorrow fought with what we have on hand at this very moment and with the ideas now in the heads of the leaders. But there is certainly no question that the preservation of peace and our existence as a free society over the long run is impossible, if we fall behind the enemy intellectually and technologically. Our ability to produce, after long preparation, standardized weapons becoming obsolete by the time they are deployed in quantity counts for little in the long run. Our power of creative thinking translated into new tools and fresh actions will determine whether we are to survive. Nothing can be said about how creative the nation will be in the future; this is unknown and unpredictable. But one can examine the conditions and the framework within which the creative process is supposed to take place. Some conditions are definitely more conducive for creative thinking, others less. This assertion is possible in spite of some exceptional cases to the contrary, i.e., great thoughts were sometimes produced under the most adverse circumstances.

The launching of Sputnik I suddenly focused much attention on education in the United States. Perhaps more has been written and said about its various aspects within one year than within a decade previously. We are therefore well-informed about the financial needs, the shortage of teachers (due to poor pay and the population increase), the lack and deficiency of science and language teaching in most high schools, the backwardness of only mildly motivated students of all ages in their knowledge even of reading. We have heard about the intensity of work at the school levels in other countries, including Russia, and about the great number of students in that country already surpassing the number of graduates in science and engineering in the United States. We have also heard about the intensive motivation of the students in Russia, their adoration of science and technology. Their dream for the future may strike many of us as a dreary technocracy built into the framework of communistic ideology. Though these are not our ideals, the motivation is there.

One illustration may show the difference between the two countries in regard to the interest in science. A well-known, highly technical book on quantum mechanics, one of the most difficult parts of mathematical physics, recently published in this country sold 2400 copies; this is considered a good sale. Of these, probably ⅓ or more went abroad, as is the case with many scientific works. This book appeared in an unauthorized, pirated Russian translation and sold 28,000 copies—all of them, of course, within Russia. This throws as sharp a light on the growing disparity regarding the intensity of the scientific effort in the two nations as one may wish to obtain. Not that the Russians were dependent on this book and had nothing to match. On the contrary, some of the best textbooks on theoretical physics are by Russian authors, such as Bogolyubov, and are fortunately available in English translations.

Yearly book production in different countries gives an interesting picture. The United Nations shows for 1954 (the last year for which comprehensive figures are available) that the Soviet Union then published over 50,000 titles, Japan 20,000, Great Britain 19,000, Western Germany 16,000, India 14,500, finally the United States 12,000 titles. The Netherlands, with a population about ⅛ that of the United States, published 7,000 titles. The definition of what a book is, or a pamphlet, certainly differs from one country to another; therefore, these statistics are not strictly comparable. And while the question of quality remains unanswered, this information is, nevertheless, sobering. There is here a certain measure of the intensity of intellectual life and effort in various countries that should make us sit up and think.[3]

At present scientific leadership is still in the Western world, but it is being challenged. This may be a deep, historical process which we cannot stem; it may be only a temporary retardation. A flowering of the arts and sciences in one region has been repeatedly followed by a decline, a new center of learning springing up elsewhere. Or great migrations of talent have occurred. After the bloom of Greece came the dominance of Rome. The great period of the Renaissance in Italy was followed by an even greater surge of the sciences in the West and North of Europe. Before our eyes American scientific life has reached heights for which there seemed to be little likelihood even fifty years ago.

Unquestionably, with the growth of population in the world, improved communications and rising standards of living, scientific activity will develop where there was none before. Recently a rather difficult paper in mathematical economics was published by an author from the Sudan; in remote parts of Russia,

[3] In April, 1959 the *Ladies' Home Journal* published an article which gives a detailed account of a family living on $200,000.00 annual income. There appear budget items for club dues $2,091.00, for servants $4,183.00, for extra help at parties $1,000.00, and for books—not $6,000.00, nor $600.00, but $60.00. Let us hope that this case is as singular as is the high income.

which thirty years ago were still mostly illiterate, great universities arise.

It may be safely assumed that the distribution of intelligence is rather uniform throughout mankind. Given the pressure exercised by technology spreading to every corner of the earth, it is only to be expected that much dormant talent will come alive. It is, therefore, by no means certain where the intellectual centers will be, even in the near future. We may experience great surprises. Once a center exists, if it stays alive by growing, it will be a force toward which more intellect will tend. But this is a delicate affair: a great center can be destroyed in short time but it takes years of cultivation to develop.

Therefore the strongest support of the activities of the mind, comprising the natural and social sciences, as well as the arts, is mandatory if we wish to survive with our institutions intact or modified, in the course of time, only in a sense acceptable to us. This is a continuing task of such magnitude that we must never rest. It is not accomplished by appropriating more money, giving scientists a dinner at the White House, setting up foundations, admitting more students, necessary as all these things are. There must be a change of mood, a new orientation, a wholly fresh dedication. The President, Congress, government agencies all can do something to improve conditions; but this is not where the real problem lies. It rests squarely with the universities themselves, and there primarily with the faculties, helped by a few, all too few, enlightened administrations.

The universities must provide a new leadership and take the initiative. No one else can. There will have to be much soul searching and a pushing back of mushrooming administrations. The scholars and scientists themselves will have to run the universities where they do not do it already—and there are precious few where they do to even a very limited extent. Teaching will have to be raised to higher levels. Colleges and universities must stop wasting precious time now lost during the first two years when they teach much of what should have been taught at the high-school level. They will have to make far greater intellectual demands on the students. Also standards have to be raised for admission to the teaching profession.

The changes universities need will not come overnight. But if they do not start soon the center of gravity will fall elsewhere —first in special new laboratories, in new institutes divorced from teaching. Eventually it will go outside the country. It will do so because these laboratories and institutes are *consumers* of talent and genius. They do not *produce and develop* it, no matter how many "job-training" courses they and industry may have. To regenerate there must be the great schools, the great centers of learning where nothing else matters but the discovery of the new and the preservation of previous works of the mind.

We have done much lately in this country to endanger the intellectual future: from the arrogant anti-intellectualism so widespread among the public, via the low economic and social standing of the teaching profession, to the actual persecutions of those who dare to differ from the conformist patterns set by the uninformed multitude.

It is not enough to provide money. The milieu in which the sciences and arts will flourish is infinitely more important, since once they start flourishing money always comes forth. But it is difficult to create the right milieu. I believe that in the extensive discussions about science and education in America which have taken place since Sputnik I this point has been neglected. The fact is that the universities, which should provide the ideal milieu, do not do so, and no one else can. They have not evolved an organization conducive to unfettered growth of intellectual life. This is the really serious matter.

American university organization is antiquated. The universities and colleges are the last strongholds of the feudalism of past ages. They are not truly democratic institutions, though they wish to support democracy. They are not good representatives of the "republic of scholars" which should make up a university. Trustees, themselves not elected but co-opted by other trustees previously co-opted, appoint a president. The trustees rarely number among themselves scholars or scientists and are, for the most part, only vaguely aware of the creative process in scientific discovery and invention. The appointed president in turn appoints the deans, who appoint the chairmen of departments, and so on down the scale. The professors are not looked upon as independent scholars; they make up the "personnel," the "teaching staff," as they are disdainfully referred to. They have individual "superiors" above them, which is not the case in Europe. There the rector, duly elected from the ranks of the professors, is *primus inter pares* for a year or two. He is almost invariably a man of the highest scientific and scholarly accomplishments. Each dean is similarly elected for equally short temporary office. In this country the appointments to these offices often run for decades. Few business corporations are organized in this manner and if they were they could not succeed.

I do not think that there exists one single major university in this country that counts among its trustees, regents, overseers, or whatever the names of these bodies may be, a substantial group of periodically elected members of the faculty. Most boards have not one single member of their own faculty among them—not even co-opted. Many do not have men on the board with more than the lowest academic degrees. Yet these undoubtedly well-meaning and devoted men decide on the curriculum where often even the titles of the courses are unintelligible to them. (If they act only *pro forma,* why go through these motions at all?)

These superiors, notably the ever-multiplying deans, are too frequently not eminent, active scholars themselves, but by a lively interchange of honorary Doctors' degrees with their counterparts in other institutions they try to attain the appearance of special authority. Yet on these men depend advancement and puny increases in normally measly salaries. Thus, professors tend to conform to the ideals of an essentially nonscientific, nonscholarly body of administrators maintained above them, even in regard to education policies. Too few act as freely and independently as must be expected of scholars and men of science. There is a saddening inability and unwillingness to speak one's mind, lest one's opinions be interpreted as a criticism of the administration. How sad to see professors submissive to administrations, which should be nothing but their instruments and conveniences in the education process.[4]

Scientists are continuously exposed to the severest scientific criticism, even from their youngest students. On this they thrive. Most administrators, on the other hand, whether in business or government, are prone to reject and resent criticism. There unfortunately exists no generally accepted criterion to determine the objectivity of criticism of administrators. Therefore, it tends to undermine that kind of authority. It is invariably taken to be a reflection on the administrator's ability or integrity. Criticism need be nothing of the sort.

This unholy setup beclouds the atmosphere at our universities, wonderful and promising as they are in so many other respects. How can they talk convincingly about democracy when they are lacking some of the essentials of democratic institutions! How can the mind explore freely in all directions if these unseen but mighty barriers exist? How can "liberal education" be provided by essentially illiberal institutions? The mood on the university campus is tepid, placid, genteel. Apart from the usual spring follies of a few students one hardly hears a whisper of a "great debate." There is little fermentation; there is little evidence that the youth of our day, or many of their professors, are aware of the terrible danger which faces this country and the world.

[4] *The New York Times Magazine,* October 12, 1958, carries an article, "A. B. = 'Academic Bureaucracy,' " which describes, sometimes whimsically, but in general correctly, the ridiculous growth of academic bureaucracy which imposes a heavy, time-consuming and exceedingly expensive burden on colleges and universities. The most interesting, nay, devastating, feature of the article is that the author, "a professor who has spent years in leading universities," wishes to remain *anonymous!*

Many American professors complain, however, that their German colleagues did not stand up more forcefully against Hitler. True; but do they not see a difference? McCarthy had no storm troopers, executioners, and concentration camps, and trustees can *at most* dismiss.

The pressure for conformity and acceptance of authority is the very opposite of what the creative mind needs. True, there are highly creative people who will not be stopped by anything, but these exceptions are rare. Creativity would be more common if the milieu in which the young minds grow were more favorable. And once the badly needed fiercely intellectual atmosphere is there, new minds will always be attracted.

What has all this to do with weapons for America? With our strategy? With our survival?

Everything.

One fact is certain regarding our future: If we are spared the great disaster of a thermonuclear exchange we are challenged in other areas, none more important then the realm of the mind. Only our scientists or scholars can discover the new facts of nature which may give us security either by new weapons, new defensive devices, or even better, by fundamentally new ideas which make war totally unacceptable and impossible as a means of settling differences among nations. Our political and social thinkers will have to come forward with ideas about the peaceful organization of the world allowing for the new facts of the conduct and danger of war. Some of these ideas will have to be radically new and unconventional since present thinking does not carry very far.

The war of intellects between the Western and the Communistic worlds will unquestionably encompass more and more fields. It is now sharpest in all fields bearing on weapons technology. Even there, we are not doing all we could. Our future power can flow only from the universities and the laboratories they feed. There is no other source.

As said before, there has been very much talk about the needs of American education. It has centered about the high schools, and some gratifying first steps have been taken here. But it is disappointing to have to record the lack of response regarding the universities. Where are the truly great gifts from foundations, industry, the rich? Has there been an outpouring since Sputnik? Have the governing classes understood that more is at stake than a few percent more or less in taxes? Have the universities themselves interpreted their new, unique and overriding role for the future of the nation? Isolated voices are heard from time to time, but taken all together, the universities have not shown the awareness of their mission.

The supreme talent in this nation is not attracted to science and scholarship. It has gone into law, business, medicine, perhaps into practical politics. Thus it has brought about the tremendous growth of the country and given it the material wealth and power that amazes the whole world. This does not mean that every businessman or lawyer—not even every hundredth or thousandth—is a genius or simply exceptionally intelligent. It merely means that many of the first-rate minds have been attracted to those activities with the inevitable consequence of raising the whole level. In other countries the great talents have devoted themselves to science, the arts, perhaps to the military profession. This complicated social process cannot be changed in a free country without destroying the very freedom of choice we wish to preserve. Therefore, we must demonstrate by example the unique importance of fine, original minds for the survival of the nation. In a Communistic country there is no need for advertising agents or corporation lawyers, and none for economists such as the present writer. For our survival economists are possibly also less important than physicists, mathematicians, chemists—or even poets, if you wish.

The True Boss of Government Research

Funds and talents are limited, but of problems there is no end. So compromises are made. Not every scientific project can be carried out. We do not assign people to projects, we try to interest them by showing them the problems and the opportunities. Better still, they themselves come forward and make proposals, sometimes so tremendous as the search for controlled power from thermonuclear reactions. Some work is basic, some applied, some turns quickly into development. Some work succeeds, other work is abandoned; some requires vastly greater support than had at first been dreamed of. Everything is in a continuous state of flux and adjustments have to be made constantly. Entirely new, completely unforeseen, fields open up, especially when basic research begins to pay off.

There is no super-mind that could direct all these many efforts; there is no one who understands the merits of all enterprises and could weigh the importance of one against the other. From thousands of pieces the whole program is somehow put together, appropriations are obtained from the Congress, more compromises are made. There simply is no other way. But, as stated before, there is the possibility of leaving to the laboratories, to the directors of large programs much more freedom than usually has been the case.

Some agencies are pretty good as far as granting freedom is concerned. In most cases there is tight control, notably from the Defense Department. There has to be a justification for almost every pencil bought. Or, it is even prescribed which pencil should be bought and the manufacturer is told how to make the pencil. The total effect is loss of time and administrative expenses which have been estimated to exceed the actual research dollar by a factor of three or more. Thus the money that reaches the laboratories, the people who do the thinking and experimenting, is only a tiny fraction of the impressive billions of dollars proudly quoted. Obviously the amount reaching the researchers has to be smaller than the total appropriation; how much smaller is difficult to say. It is safe to say that the research appropriation should be better than it is—not a very helpful statement. To make it more precise a thorough investigation of the overhead costs should be made. This is clearly a task for Congress. If made, such an investigation would uncover all the usual absurdities, and after a lot of paper had been used to record them and to protest against them, the old routine would go on as before. The reason would be that behind this complicated and quite unsatisfactory process, in the background, stands the real ruler of government-sponsored research: the *Bureau of the Budget*.

Here is the true source of power. When the mountain has labored and brought forth the approval of a research proposal, when everything has been done to fit it into the existing budgets of the services, the Bureau of the Budget steps in to question the decision, perhaps to make a new one. We do want control over the way our money is spent by the government. There are countless ways of avoiding waste, and the tighter the control the better. But here we have purely fiscal interference in scientific plans that is as senseless as it is wasteful. When it has been figured out carefully that a certain test, for example, a weapons test, cannot be made for less than, say $1,000,000 or $2,000,000 the Bureau may let this figure pass, or cut it to $700,000 or $874.325. If the figure stays cut, the result is that the necessary measurements cannot be made at all, or are imperfect and have to be made again some other time, in the aggregate costing more money while precious time is being wasted. This does not happen once; it happens again and again. Throughout the entire research and development program one can find thousands of repetitions.

It is one thing to set fiscal limits to scientific enterprises. It is another to interfere in the design of scientific experiments and explorations. The controllers of the Department of Defense and the Bureau of the Budget should determine the general fiscal framework within which research and development are to be carried out, according to Congressional appropriations. But both must stop interfering in highly technical scientific matters totally outside their understanding and competence.

The outsider may have great difficulty in realizing the seriousness of this situation. But it is no exaggeration to say that a revision of current practices would intensify the scientific effort of the country more than anything short of the appearance of a new Manhattan Project.

Observations like these have been made time and again. The situation is well understood by many people, some in powerful positions. Yet nothing changes. If anything, the power of the Bureau of the Budget increases. It has far superseded the Treasury in importance for the fiscal-budgetary processes of the

United States. This may be all to the good. But fiscal meddling in scientific programs will be definitely detrimental to the well-being of the country if it continues.

Will this change? Who is to make the change? The Bureau of the Budget has no motivation to do so. The task is the President's.

8   Economic Power and Burden

> ". . . luxuries have become necessities, necessities have become luxuries."
>
> —SENATOR J. WILLIAM FULBRIGHT

American and Russian Power

We have assumed that the two antagonists have at this moment enough nuclear power at hand in deliverable form so that they could destroy each other, possibly many times over. This is a particularly unpleasant form of a stalemate but, given certain conditions, which were examined in previous chapters, the hostile countries may be deterred from using their force. But this is not a stable system because there may be independent changes on either side which can upset the precarious balance. These may be (a) technological innovations affecting offense or defense, making the preparations of the other party obsolete; (b) inability of one power to maintain the existing system because of its costs or economic inability to change the system simultaneously with the other country even though a new technology becomes available to both; (c) collapse of spirit, i.e., lack of staying power on the part of one power, although the other conditions are fulfilled.

In this chapter we shall deal briefly with some economic aspects of defense. Mountains of paper exist dealing with problems in this area; yet there are some points which need restatement and further clarification. Their examination often runs along very conventional lines and is too frequently separated from a simultaneous understanding of the fundamental strategic considerations.

The first point that has to be made absolutely clear is that the economy and the economic well-being of the people are *not* the dominating concern. Overshadowing everything is the safety and survival of country and nation. If a *minimum requirement* of a military establishment and minimum instrumentation of policy can be found, then these are the least the economy of the country has to produce. They may exceed its capability. Even in that case surrender is not the alternative; other considerations appear, such as reliance on alliances, on world opinion, on restraint of the enemy, etc. If these were meaningless, no small, peace-loving country could ever have survived in world history. Not many would, if they were entirely alone, not shielded by much bigger powers whose own interests demanded that the smaller countries be protected. A large defenseless country, on the other hand, offers an open invitation to be taken over; it cannot count on protection from many small ones.

The minimum requirement should be exceeded by a safety factor. A rich country will tend to make it large.

The determination of the minimum requirement is an exceedingly difficult task. It is the responsibility of the President, the National Security Council and the Joint Chiefs of Staff. Whatever ideas are generated among them depend on the simultaneous process going on in Russia, where in turn a dependency on our plans exists. Clearly no side can proceed without consideration of the other side's plans and capabilities. This interplay corresponds exactly to a game of strategy where no player is in control of all factors on which the outcome depends since some are under the control of the opposing player.

It may happen that there is a *uniquely* best way of playing this game. It is then possible openly to announce the policy. Whatever the opponent does cannot affect the validity of the decision—always excepting discrete changes in technology. This is an exceptional condition and does not apply to the present conflict. Here the need for secrecy enters, since discovery of the other party's measures, which he will also keep secret as far as possible, would be of the greatest value. Thus we have to make decisions about the minimum defense requirements without being fully informed and in face of the fact that our opponent will try to nullify our efforts by his own decisions.

The scientific problem of decision making in the face of this type of uncertainty is fascinating. It transcends the ordinary type of uncertainty that can be taken care of by insurance. You cannot insure yourself against Russian political and military decisions as you can against fire and hurricanes. I doubt that the most modern mathematical devices which are now available to analyze precisely such situations have ever been used in arriving at proper decisions. If they had been, this information would have transpired. There is, therefore, room for possibly significant improvement in our national decision-making process. The usual phrases about the "calculated risk" have behind them exactly nothing. They do not stem from a proven scientific method. But it will not be a simple matter to supplant the policies based on such vague notions.

Let us assume that one has arrived at some estimate of minimum defense requirements. In order to be evaluated it has to be put into relation to our own economic power and to that of Russia. We should also compare the Western bloc and the Eastern, including especially China. Furthermore, that power is not stationary; each country has a potential of further development. It has given an indication of that potential by its past performance.

There is no objective way to measure the "economic power" of different countries as, for example, the United States and Russia. In particular, "money" is no measure, not even for one single country, let alone for comparing several widely different countries over long periods of time. So we have to rely on common-sense argumentation, extended by the knowledge which is summarized in economic theory and derives from the study of past experience.

A clear indication of economic power is the ability of a country to produce the things it wants in proper quantity and quality over a desired length of time. The latter condition has to be added since a country may not be capable of a sustained effort of a given nature. We should also add that certainly in former times the ability to turn quickly from one kind of production to another mattered. For example, production of civilian consumers' goods could be dropped or curtailed to be replaced by production of war materials. This change is possible only if the consumers' goods are deemed plentiful and/or unnecessary, at least for some length of time. If we are thinking about a sudden thermonuclear exchange this ability, formerly one of the principal sources of strength of the United States, is of little consequence.

The conventionally measured "standard of living" gives a fair idea of differences in wealth and income of various countries, over time. There are many difficulties with the notion, arising from changing technologies, variations in tastes and desires, variations in products made, in their quality, geography, falsification of records in terms of money if inflations occurred, etc. All of these can here be neglected. Even at their best, the standard of living indexes are, however, only superficial indicators. They hide precisely what matters most for our purposes —the existence of "power."

A country may decide—by means of monetary and tax policy, or if organized like Russia, by means of direct central planning—to keep a lower standard of living than it can afford. Instead it may plow back into the production process large parts of the annual product. It may insist on a high rate of investment, thereby broadening the basis for later consumers' goods production. It may do this for many years. It will then be well equipped with capital goods while in terms of consumers' goods its "standard of living" has not risen as fast as that of others pursuing a different policy and perhaps starting from a different level in the first place. But eventually it will not only catch up with these but surpass them.

Thus rates of growth should be compared. But, of course, not the growth of the standard of living narrowly restricted to consumers' goods, both durable and perishable. Instead the investment volume, the production of capital goods, is what matters.

This would still not give the true picture of power. A country may invest in industries which will ultimately produce consumers' goods and nothing else; for example, it may build automobile factories. Or it may build factories that are to turn out tanks, warships, nuclear weapons. In both cases steel is used, manpower; engineers are tied down. But the effects in regard to power are entirely different.

Thus, when we hear that the fast-rising Russian steel production is now 55 million tons per year, while ours fluctuates between 70 and 110 million tons per year, and Great Britain's is about 20 million tons, this may mean very different things; depending on whether the steel is consumed in pleasure motorcars, use of steel for new factories for consumers' goods, use of steel for war goods and for expansion of factories capable of making these. The usual, simple comparisons of steel output hide all this information. They are far too global; they must be broken down. We can do this somewhat for the United States and the NATO countries, but the needed Russian figures are, as usual, lacking. On the basis of general information, however, we know that the percentage devoted there to military production is vastly greater than anywhere in the Western world. Furthermore, there is every reason to believe that the *absolute* quantity of steel so used is greater than in the West. We are completely mislead when we comfort ourselves in the light of the figures giving *total* steel production. Or, we are scared less than we should be when we see how the total Russian steel output begins to creep up to our level. The use of the steel gives the significance to this information. While they make weapons and expand general production facilities we use it largely for motorcars, buildings, even furniture. What a difference in regard to augmenting a country's power!

The same could be said for electric power, for oil production, the output of engineers and scientists. In the latter case Russia is already overtaking us in absolute numbers. But besides that, many more of her engineers and scientists work (perhaps even more intensively, certainly longer hours) in defense establishments, while too many of ours construct new models of washing machines, refrigerators, cars, television sets and what have you. Nothing, absolutely nothing of the latter improves our power, our chance of survival, relative to that of Russia. What does it matter that their buildings are not as modern as ours, that their restaurants are simple, that they live in crowded conditions, that their hotels are primitive? But these are what the travelers see and report on, unaware that behind all this, kept out of their sight, a mighty engine is throbbing, working toward further expansion of the whole economy and providing ever-increasing power for the military.

Instead of comparing standard-of-living indexes—themselves of shaky construction—we should compute *indexes of economic power,* taking all the above considerations into account. They would be numbers expressing the use of resources for future expansion of the whole economy, the particular growth rate of industries important for defense, the rate of use of materials by the military effort, etc. In the light of these figures the fact that even the overall rate of growth of the Russian economy has outstripped that of the United States for several years would assume a new importance. Their rate of growth is very likely near 7% per year, while the United States economy grows only at about 2% yearly. An economy growing at the first rate should double in a little over ten years while the other needs over thirty-five years to do so.

This incompletely grasped fact is even more ominous if we were to compare the two power indexes. The diversity would show up still more. We are still on top—no doubt about that;

but not for long! And we could surpass Russia in economic power any moment we chose to do so. But we have made no such decision. On the contrary, we bask in the glory of the outpouring of consumers' goods and starve our military in some absolutely essential fields—not to mention civil defense!

The growth of the Russian economy and of Russia's military power is not the consequence of an innate superiority of their people or an expression of a system operating flawlessly at the highest rate of efficiency. There is every indication of blundering, of waste, of an accumulation of errors and mistakes. No evidence exists of a superiority in their way of organizing life. There is simply a difference in orientation and evaluation. They make up for the shortcomings of their system by intensive, long, hard work and by depriving the common man of things he seems no longer to want to forgo as readily as he did a few years ago. Still, the fact is that Russia's power rises rapidly.

Yet there is no particular problem here: there is only the question of our own behavior, of our estimation of the present and the future danger. I believe that this is a more troublesome situation than if there were a big, unsolved problem before us. Then we would make an effort to solve it.

We can state with almost general validity a new law of government and administration: *those situations deteriorate fastest where it is most obvious what should be done.* In this case what we need to do is to place a greater burden on our economy in order to secure the type of military strength we need most: the Oceanic System of a mobile dispersed retaliatory force, a vigorous advance in scientific effort, a strong but diversified limited-war capability, the sub-economy and fall-out shelters.

Just as we saw that one-sided discontinuous steps in the nuclear capability of the two big contestants are exceedingly dangerous, so too we see that the same applies in the economic-industrial power area. We are doing exactly nothing to appraise the very long-run tendencies. We believe that we see the situation properly by looking at the items in which we excel, and we take comfort that the distance between us and Russia is still enormous, say, in the number of motorcars, washing machines, television sets. The trouble is, however, that in this context they are trivia, and as such don't matter.

The Limit to the Burden

How large a burden can be imposed upon the economy in order to make us "safe," if safe we can be? Can one objectively, scientifically, determine how large the military budget should be, or what its upper bounds are? If 38 or 40 billion dollars is appropriated, is that too little or too much from the point of view of the economy? Or could we even go to 75 billion if the government should decide that only for this amount could we provide a military defense setup that we "need." How are these amounts to be divided among the different weapons systems and military forces?

These are terribly difficult problems. They go to the heart of economic decision making: how to allocate scarce resources among competing wants in such a manner that an optimum allocation results, i.e., one which cannot be improved if the circumstances do not change. Here the problem is one of many stages: how much to divert from civilian uses for consumption and development; how much of that diverted part to allocate to future rather than current production and maintenance of war materials; how much to produce of every single major weapon; how much of our facilities, both military and economic, to make available to our allies, real or potential. All this in the face of simultaneous decisions of the opponent which in general remain unknown to us.

If someone should think that this set of problems can now be solved *in the concrete case,* he has either an unwarranted confidence in what present economic science can accomplish, or an unjustifiably low opinion of what a scientific standard requires. I am not even talking about precision versus approximation. I am simply stating that one cannot treat these questions with the commonly used theories only. They involve essentially political decisions to be made on the basis of some scientific knowledge combined with a great deal of political expediency. Both are based on very imperfectly known facts. This is an unpleasant mixture of ingredients and it is little wonder that no one is satisfied with the outcome. But more, much more, can be done in order to obtain a better result and a clearer understanding of the process involved. Here are some misconceptions:

For example: (1) *Inflation is no measure.* It would be nice, if we could define the limit of the burden as that point where "inflation" is produced by arms production. Everyone seems to know what inflation is and how it is to be measured. But there exist some twenty-seven different definitions of the phenomenon; and its measurement by the cost-of-living index—or any other such device—is correspondingly arbitrary. This uncertainty quite aside, the crucial observation is that inflations have very different origins, many of them having nothing whatever to do with armaments. They can arise from credit expansions on the stock market, from government deficits, from international influences, etc. Thus, if an armament program is being undertaken and inflationary pressures appear, it is by no means certain that the latter are the consequences of the former. There may be an entirely different reason for the inflation. If, therefore, the inflationary symptoms were interpreted as indicating the limit beyond which the arms effort could not be pushed, a false conclusion would be drawn.

Consequently, the appearance of inflation is not necessarily conclusive. Of course, many inflations—the worst indeed—have been associated with war; but not so many with peacetime armament programs. But even if they were it would still have to be shown why an inflation should be avoided at all costs—one of these costs being precisely the failure of the arms program on which may hinge the very survival of the nation. Those who maintain that an inflation is the worst fate that can ever happen to a country—and there are many who talk in this manner—have not thought deeply. They have certainly not tried to imagine what war with Russia would mean, or peaceful surrender. The miseries of inflation are a pale shadow of either disaster.

Indeed, a determined government may very well *use* inflation against a recalcitrant population as a powerful instrument in order to get its programs carried out! This is not a nice way of governing, but it is effective, even powerful. It is also a dangerous policy, since inflation can easily get out of control. But one should not exclude the possibility that it might be tried in times of crisis, especially when the people are not willing to accept other, better measures, such as increased taxation.

(2) The *objections of the taxpayer* also do not determine the limit to the burden. Yet these are often taken as a sign of when to stop diverting resources to the armament effort. In some countries the objections become stronger at an earlier point than in others. In Russia, if there are any at all, they are not listened to. This is one reason why the Communists can push their efforts so much farther than we do. Naturally, there is some limit here too; taxes could conceivably be imposed so that they would gravely interfere with the very working of the economy. But as for the frequently heard statements that they do so already in this country, that they "stifle the initiative," that as a consequence there is not enough "venture capital"—for all this there is no shade of proof. There are only assertions. Different circles and income groups raise different objections. Those who make the most noise are not necessarily the ones who are most worth listening to.

Or let us look at (3) the *percentage of the national product* absorbed by the military effort. We spend about 8 to 9%—a trifling, easily borne amount, considering the magnitude of our product. During the war we were up to perhaps 40% and survived economically without having greater trouble than some trivial rationing. We do not know what the corresponding figure is now in Russia, but it is certainly much higher than ours, probably 30%, though the country is poorer and the diversion from civilian goods production weighs more heavily upon the people.

It may seem that this percentage gives a good measure. But this is not so, for the simple reason that the figures are very unreliable. True, they are used as if they were significant up to a

1% variation. The fact is, however, that they cannot be trusted to even 5 to 10% variation. Consequently it is very hard to state with assurance what diversion of product to armament has occurred previously and whether the present percentage indicates the best we can do. We get only a rough idea of what the facts are and what they were. But no matter how we look at them, they never tell us definitely the point beyond which we cannot go.

The true limit of the burden is the willingness of the people to carry it.

The defense we need is the defense we can afford.

These statements explain why so much has been accomplished under certain circumstances, why some nations have surprised the world by carrying on during wars in seemingly hopeless situations, why reconstruction succeeded where it seemed impossible that vigorous economic life could ever arise again. If countries fight for a cause—as the people see it— they are willing *and thereby able* to go to much greater lengths in depriving themselves of the immediate in order to obtain the fruits of the future.

Neither in the last world wars nor in the Korean war was the United States in a situation in which a really critical effort was demanded of the people. So great was the power of this country that a tremendous Army and Navy could be raised and a great outpouring of arms and equipment could occur without really depriving the people of very many conveniences. There is no experience to show how the American people would behave if great sacrifices were demanded for a long time. I doubt that they would act differently from others. But it would be necessary to tell them why sacrifices are needed and to prove that they would lead to the intended goal. At present very little is being done to communicate this information and as a consequence the resistance to more sacrifice—if such it can be called —is considerable.

The current, widespread belief that any increase in our defense budget must by necessity lead to an unbalanced budget and "hence" to inflation is completely wrong. To begin with, a government deficit does not necessarily mean inflation, especially not when the deficit is covered by the sale of government securities to savers, and not even when they are sold to banks even though the banks may expand credit in order to buy the securities, provided unemployment exists and idle resources are available. There will be unpleasant shifts in demand and relocation difficulties, but no general inflation. The main point is, of course, that most deficits can be avoided by the simple expedient of increasing taxes and reducing other expenditure (for example, farm subsidies and veterans' benefits). The amounts of additional spending needed for defense are so modest at any rate that inflation need not happen because we need not allow it to happen. Inflations are not natural disasters like hurricanes; they are man-made and they can be controlled, checked and even prevented.

This country worries about the limits to the military budget, whether we can "stand," or "support," a 2%, 5% or 10% expansion of this item at a time when there may be three to four million unemployed. This is such grotesque reasoning that it would be foolish to add even one word. Always remember that for one billion dollars more per year we can keep a very large part of SAC in the air. What this means in added safety was amply discussed in earlier chapters. And we do not have to wait years for new products to do this. We can start doing it tomorrow. To get some perspective on the cost of this item: We spend per annum about three quarters of this amount for new swimming pools!

Such is the situation today. In the near future, perhaps less than two decades away, the picture will have changed profoundly. By that time China—unless ruined by overpopulation —may have emerged as a great industrial power, perhaps as far along as Russia is now, and Russia, of course, will be at a power level matching, if not far exceeding, that of the United States. China may be manufacturing nuclear weapons and long-range ballistic missiles. This prospect opens up entirely new vistas of alliances, classical political procedures, and expansions of conflicts on a new scale. But by that time we may also have made war truly impossible or we may have destroyed ourselves.

The "Military Worth"

When a business has to decide which allocation of its scarce funds is better than another one, it can compare expected costs with expected sales and profits. All are expressed in dollars, in other words, by numbers. Without such numbers it would be very difficult to calculate. How could one be sure where the advantages and disadvantages were unless one could calculate for the multitude of items and their combinations? What would a "profit" or "loss" mean? Businessmen would be in a great dilemma; they would gingerly try to feel their way through the almost countless possibilities. They would soon discover that they sometimes had committed gross errors and sometimes had astonishing windfalls. They would be very uncomfortable in this numberless world of theirs, and each one, and all of them together, would quickly try to design a substitute. But they would hardly hit soon on our present price system, which incorporates the vast amounts of information (gratis!) that a businessman and producer needs in the complex world of today.

The military man has nothing of this sort at his disposal. There is no method of giving a numerical expression to the "military worth" of different weapons systems, of deploying forces here instead of there, of producing x rather than y units of one weapon versus z rather than w units of another. And remember that there are at present at least a thousand systems to choose from! Yet the choices have to be made and men and resources are limited. To make things even worse, the weapons systems have not been tried, they cannot be tried, their effects are only estimated for the future, prospects are not certain, and therefore their assumed values are not certain either.

Calculation is very difficult in such situations. How superficial all this talk is about "calculated risk" when the most elementary factors that have to go into a calculation are unknown and numbers are nonexistent.

So what we find today is a curious mixture of dollar-money accounting, usually down to the last penny, of "costs" of weapons systems, these costs to be pitted against their "worth" in the overall strategic pattern of the country, a worth the Department of Defense is not able to express in generally acceptable numbers. As a result, the Congress and the people (not to mention the Bureau of the Budget!) look hypnotized at the monetary figures alone and are completely at sea when it comes to the real assessment, i.e., the value of the weapons systems for the defense of the country.

It is not known whether Russia possesses a method with which to avoid this dilemma. They face it too, and besides there is a strict parallel between this problem and the one of a centrally directed socialistic economy where the market prices are essentially phony. If they have no better method, their difficulties are—for once—at least as great as ours. We may suspect, however, that they let the military-strategic wants come first and care very little about conventional "costs," real and imagined.

It is much to be regretted that the research efforts of the Defense Department have not been directed more energetically toward remedying this situation. It is a tall order to ask mathematicians and economists to produce a convincing scale for comparing and measuring the military worth of disparate weapons systems. Perhaps no amount of support or pressure could have produced the desired scale on which so much depends. But the attempt should have been made with much vigor. Of course, it took many generations until a method for assigning a number to "utility" was devised although much attention was given to that notion, which is so fundamental in economics. The measurement of temperature too did not come overnight. Nevertheless one now can gain from having made such elusive things as "utility" or temperature numerical. These results were possible only because of much abstract thinking. The same kind of intellectual effort might pay off handsomely for determining "military worth." To develop a method would be more important than to introduce some further, purely technological, advance in some weapons system. It would improve the use of all of them.

The reader may wonder whether the difficulties described above are really serious and whether an abstract method could accomplish so much. Let him imagine himself—whatever his business—in a world without numbers, or in a world where there existed only a few of the numbers with which he now deals daily. No more need be said.

Strategic Requirements

One might think that other conditions for procuring the strategically needed material are better fulfilled. But this is not so, in spite of some valiant efforts in various directions, for example, to develop a good inventory system—a truly formidable problem where much progress has been made.

In World War II requirement committees were set up and the needed stuff was produced as directed. Priorities were assigned, then fought over, and modified when new needs appeared. There was much obvious and much hidden waste. There was "waste" of a different kind: It occurred when great masses of material accumulated on some Pacific island but the changes in strategic plans were so swift that these depots were completely by-passed, the battle having moved on to other areas in the victorious sweep of the war. This was hardly waste in a conventional sense: Although material was produced and placed where finally it was not needed, the lack of need was due to improved, unforeseeable but hoped-for fortunes of war.

We could now have new requirement committees making the ultimate decision as to how much should be produced and in what order. But we are not in that kind of war situation and need a more orderly procedure. Yet without having solved the question of determining the military worth of the various alternatives no convincing, rational choice can be made. Only the usual vague, intuitive appeals to strategic needs, etc., are possible. This is a thoroughly unsatisfactory situation.

We cannot remedy it now. But there are other troubles, each one almost as serious, and all put together give rise to the fact that we do not procure as efficiently, swiftly and cheaply as we could. Two points shall be briefly mentioned. A full discussion would fill volumes.

The *first point* is that as far as procurement techniques are concerned, there exists here no deep scientific problem. Common sense, properly applied, can produce enormous advantages. Procurement procedures are fantastically complicated, ridiculously detailed and cumbersome. Specifications are written where they are pointless, where the paper they are put on is worth more than the object specified. Instructions are given to manufacturers that hamstring them, leaving little or no room for spontaneous and competitive improvements of either product or method of production.

This is an area where gross, i.e., substantial, benefits can be easily derived. Needed is drastic action—sharp cutting of red tape, a transfer of responsibility to producers, a removal of large numbers of contract officers from factories and their employment in strictly military positions, relieving the chronic manpower shortage there. Manufacturers would have more freedom to produce, and waiting time would be cut down.

All this has, of course, been said many times; but nothing happens although there are no reasonable counterarguments. There is merely inertia. I have shown above how the obvious things do not get done. Here is a good illustration. Yet the Secretary of Defense has the power to remedy the situation. A grave trouble is, however, that the large industrial corporations do not offer a good example themselves. They too have ensnarled themselves in tremendous amounts of red tape. Though they complain about the particular brand used by the military they have become brothers under the skin in that respect.

The real problem is not to discover *what* should be done, but to discover *how* it is to be done. The action will never originate within the system. It has to be imposed upon it. No doubt Congress could produce the needed effect.

The *second point* is that a *new budgeting procedure* is needed. This becomes daily more apparent and has been occasionally recognized.

There is a need to budgeting over longer periods than one fiscal year, and to get away from the historically conditioned partitions of defense money into three major parts corresponding to the services. Though two separate conditions, they are closely related.

The yearly budget is artificial from many points of view. There is no objection to choosing the year as the accounting time unit where the type of expenditure is of an essentially recurrent nature. This applies, for example to the feeding and clothing of the military forces, to their schooling and training, etc. For these activities one could choose almost any other arbitrary time interval, but the year has become the convention.

It is totally different for research and development work. Here the time periods needed to accomplish anything worth while are invariably much longer than a year; often they run to five years or more, in research perhaps to decades. In order to plan properly, capital must be available for time intervals corresponding to the type of commitment made.

A greater spacing of time between budgets would also have beneficial influences upon the work done. At present most military men spend half the year making up the budget for the next year. During this time they are completely distracted from their real tasks of preparing, developing, modifying war plans, searching and testing new weapons systems, carrying out military exercises or just plain thinking. The higher the officers, the more they are being abused by the perpetual needs of making up, defending and modifying budgets. This is a shameful waste of rare and specialized talent.

The disadvantage with yearly budgets is also that too often programs are turned on, turned off. This "on again—off again" business is poison for all research and development work. It is also exceedingly expensive. Much of the present waste is due to precisely this circumstance.

Budgeting over longer periods, of course, somewhat reduces the power of various controllers and of the Bureau of the Budget. But this would be all to the good, since their continuous interference with scientific and technological programs in this area introduces entirely arbitrary, random elements into the decision process. Stability is wanted, not capriciousness.

The idea of budgeting for periods longer than one year is, of course, not new. It is much advocated for fiscal measures of a countercyclical nature in order to combat depressions of business. It is also practiced in industry. In some enlightened government agencies, such as the Office of Naval Research, basic research support is, whenever possible, put on a "continuing basis," assuring funds for more than one year ahead. What has been done there with much success and to the benefit of scientific work ought to become a practice extending over large parts of the military budget. Here is a great task for Congress.

The other condition necessary in budgeting procedure is a different apportionment of defense money. The last reform of the Department of Defense contained elements of a suitable idea, but it has already been dropped. It was to assign to the Secretary of Defense the power to shift funds among the services according to strategic and technological needs. This placed great, perhaps too great, power in the hands of one man and it jeopardized prerogatives of the Congress.

A better proposal is one made recently.[1] It envisages the establishment of a budget for our Strategic Force, which would comprise SAC, the Polaris force, and other components. The Strategic Force would be budgeted as one, rather than via the military services separately, with the resulting inevitable wrangles about "equitable" shares, etc. Congress would determine how much should be spent on the retaliatory, deterrent force as a whole. Should technological development de-emphasize SAC

---

[1] *Report of the Underseas Warfare Advisory Panel* (cf. footnote, p. 92).

and lift the Polaris concept, this shift would mean an internal compensation within the main amount. We would get greater flexibility which is badly needed. At present the construction costs of more Polaris submarines are simply charged against the Navy's shipbuilding budget, where this item really does not belong.

This proposal is sound from every angle. It uses strategic, functional concepts rather than historical, traditional ones which once upon their time were also strategic-functional but which technology has made obsolete. Beyond this we have to have a single Strategic Command under which all our retaliatory capabilities are combined.

It is easy to see that the two notions, i.e., of different budget periods and functional budgeting, can be and, indeed, should be combined. The ensuing improvements could be startling.

Lead Time and Productivity

An enormous, cumbersome machine finally grinds out, with incredible delays, a minute product. If we strip the picture of all embellishments we find that we have little: few ships, few planes, few soldiers, few missiles, but tremendous pipe lines, very much fixed, dead equipment, an administrative machinery that should be able to handle five to ten times as much as it is called on to take care of. Our total military budget is large by any standard. (It is, of course, not nearly large enough in terms of the threat to which we are exposed and in terms of what we can afford in order to meet it.) But one cannot suppress the feeling that what we get out of it in ready fighting strength is substantially below the possible.

How could it be that Russia, so much poorer than we are, has numerical superiority in almost everything: hundreds more submarines, thousands more tanks, millions more soldiers, more guns, more planes, more missiles? The complete Russian military budget is difficult to determine, but it cannot be much larger than ours. So the answer is that either the Russian product is inferior, hence cheaper, or that their productivity is greater than ours. There is no evidence of the former. What is the evidence of the latter?

The measurement of productivity is a very difficult, tricky matter. There is no generally accepted method for it in economic science. There are so many twists and turns in trying to determine productivity that almost any statement can be supported. But remaining very conservative, the following observations are in order:

Russian "lead time," i.e., the time elapsing between the design and actual production of a military item, such as a bomber or missile, is definitely and substantially shorter than lead time in the United States. This fact is well known and has often been commented upon. The differences in time are often astonishing. Yet the products themselves are, *in their functions,* not greatly at variance. Russian bombers, having had a lead time of only 3 years compare well with the corresponding American planes, for which lead time was 6 or more years. This is a measure of productivity of a particular sort, but fitted to the present occasion.

It is necessary to explain the disparity and to take steps to abolish it. There are three obvious reasons for the difference:

(a) Russian working hours are much longer than ours. At the same time we worry increasingly about the problems our own leisure imposes upon our society. It would be a shocking revelation to most to see how few offices (from the Pentagon down), factories and laboratories are in operation even on Saturdays, let alone 24 hours a day, 7 days a week. Our military industry is run as if we were in deep peace and certain forever to stay there, not in a deadly race for superiority or at least equality. It has been confirmed repeatedly, though very reluctantly, by high authorities that a "missile gap" exists with Russia, i.e., that our production rate is much lower than theirs and that they had an earlier start. Yet our only working Intercontinental Ballistic Missile, the "Atlas," is being produced in only a single shift; it would be trivially simple to double output within three months' time. The major projects on which work around the clock is going on can probably be enumerated on the fingers of one hand—in spite of the fact that we are critically short in some decisive equipment.

(b) Much of our equipment is fancy and gadget-ridden and therefore more difficult and expensive to produce. There would be no objection to having finer and more ample instrumentation, greater conveniences for crews, etc., if it were clearly demonstrated that these advantages outweigh decisively the delays in getting good production runs. There is no attempt made to give such proofs.

(c) Our equipment is not stabilized early. That is to say, we start the production of a complicated piece of equipment, say a bombing plane, and keep on modifying its design during the production run. The B-52, for example, was not stabilized until 267 planes had been subjected to such interferences! One does not have to be an expert in mass-production techniques to see that this means delays and expense. Again, who proves that the modifications are vital, or even desirable? That they are worth the trouble they cause? The modifications are usually the outcome of the fantastic bureaucratic superstructure which has to justify its existence by frequent interference right down to the last steps on the conveyor belts.

A significant part of "lead time" might be called "contract time," the period that elapses between the decision of the Department of Defense to acquire a particular device and the actual completion of the contract. This period often covers an entire year. It is not an easy thing to write a contract for a new missile or submarine but the inordinate length of time required to write the necessary papers is largely due to the insistence on far too much detail, on too many, often absurd, regulations on how to produce and on review requirements by the potential "no-sayers" we met in the last chapter. Any industrialist producing under defense contracts could write volumes showing how production could be speeded up were he given more freedom.

All this can be changed. There is no particular problem here.

There is certainly no situation which awaits the prior solution of a deep scientific problem. All that is needed is the recognition of the facts and the determination to introduce proper modifications into the current practices. The responsibility lies squarely with the Department of Defense and industry.

It is likely that the present organization of procurement will not do the job. A very probing reform is needed. A Ministry of Supply in the British manner may very well be required. It is regrettable that the 1958 reform of the Department of Defense has not even produced an adequate discussion of these matters.

I believe it is safe to say that Russian military industry is not inherently more productive. It is simply ruthlessly run, and Russians work longer hours at lower pay. They produce efficient war engines without luxuries. They produce them quickly in ample quantities.

Why spell out the lessons to be drawn from this observation?

The Vulnerability of the Integrated Economy

A large, modern assembly plant for motorcars in this country, a plant in which several thousand men go to work at the moment the conveyors are set into motion, will open in the morning with only enough material at the gate to last for twenty minutes or half an hour in feeding the conveyors. Just as precisely timed as the interplay of the different conveyors within the immense building is the interplay of this plant with others, miles away, whence the parts and raw materials come. The ability to start the production run every morning on so low a margin is truly impressive. It shows how superbly organized these factories are and it speaks eloquently of the confidence the managers have that no time will be wasted and no losses be suffered.

Some of our military logistic systems are similarly set up. From distant countries orders for esoteric spare parts needed to keep incredibly complex weapons systems going arrive at some center. The parts are recorded on cards or tape, which are fed to electronic machines which locate the storage place of the parts, perhaps in a different region of the country. They can then be shipped together with additional replacement parts ordered, as the case may be, from the same overseas base. The military have made a tremendous step forward over the last years in keeping better inventory levels and dispatching needed items faster than before. The tasks they face are unique and transcend in complexity anything even the largest business corporations in the country have to cope with. This is true when considering merely the number of items involved; it is even more impressive when one recalls that the whole enterprise is beset with the difficulties of not being able to determine easily the "military worth" of the operations, while business can calculate comfortably with dollars and cents.

Integrated systems of this kind demand stability. They need it as far as the volume of transactions is concerned: it makes no sense to organize for mass production unless you really have masses of the same goods to produce. They need it as far as mechanization is concerned: A great sameness of operations is the prerequisite for mechanizing highly complex, interlocking transactions.

These systems are highly efficient, but they are very vulnerable. A mass production organization undergoes violent fluctuations if the output demand falls off and it is highly inflexible if a more than superficial change in the product becomes necessary. This is why the motorcar industry can change the shape of fenders and the placement of the headlights from year to year, but needs many years to bring out a new design. "Lead time" is high. Random disturbances are also hard to absorb. A few inches of snow interfere easily with the interlocking of factories running on low inventory of raw materials because traffic will be fouled up. Should one of the factories in a chain be knocked out by strike or sabotage, the others will immediately suffer. The logistic system of the military works under the same type of handicap. There different centers are so closely related to each other that the destruction of one can mean the complete paralysis of others.

Planners of military logistics are in a curious dilemma: on

the one hand they must design a setup and procedures that are as economical as possible. This need pushes them toward an IBM card-calculator type of arrangement that will work efficiently if peace prevails and no part of the system fails. On the other hand the logistic support is critical for war, in which case parts of it will certainly be destroyed, with the consequence that the whole system will be gravely affected, if not wholly inoperative. If, instead, one had built a less perfect, less advanced system, probably a more expensive one, carrying larger stocks, with each center fairly autonomous, the destruction of one of these centers would not lead to a swift and violent disturbance of the others.

This dilemma is, of course, only a particular instance of the basic difficulty in military planning: if there is no war, all military preparation is wasteful, and if there is a war, no matter how much one has prepared, it is never enough.

At present, however, the American economy is organized exclusively for peace, though we produce war goods. Our production organization takes not the slightest consideration of the fact that a war may disrupt it severely. It is not even protected against sabotage, for which, as was shown before, a new dimension has become possible. A high degree of integration makes a country far more vulnerable than a more primitive economy. A part of China or India could be taken by an enemy without greatly affecting the rest of the country. But if the West coast of the United States were occupied we would practically lose our ability to produce planes and missiles. This type of occupation in war is, of course, not likely, but if destruction from the air is considered, then it is another matter.

The interconnection of all parts of an economy is the result of the application of a highly developed technology in a country that believes it will remain at peace, or rather, a country that expects never to see war at home. The military logistics system should not make this assumption, no matter what is done by the economy in which it is embedded. Therefore, we ought to rethink the logistic system which has been set up during the last few years in a form mainly to suit the ideal of minimizing costs while shortchanging the military purpose which it is to serve.

The American economy, not being centrally planned, has come naturally to this high, efficient and dangerous degree of integration of all its parts. It is continuously making itself more vulnerable to all forms of attack which we have to contemplate. We would have to change our conception of economic organization basically in order to reduce this danger. It would also be very expensive to do. Therefore, other forms of protection have to be found.

Russia is in a different position. The more she intends to produce consumers' goods to be sold at markets where people want to buy, exercising free choice, the more she will approach the Western conditions. Though Russia is moving somewhat in that direction, her investment activities are strictly controlled and the placement of her industries is strongly influenced by strategic considerations—an element totally lacking in the United States. The consequence is that the Russian economy is made up of several island-regions each one of which is geographically well separated from the other and quite self-contained. For this reason, assuming even a very severe attack on Russia, short of total annihilation, that country has at present a better chance for recovery and comeback than the United States possesses, coming under the same kind of attack.

It has been explained above, p. 125, how by constructing a "sub-economy" we can substantially improve our recovery ability in the event of total attack. The system would naturally also work for more limited cases.

Economic Warfare

The nuclear stalemate shifts pressure toward limited wars. If Russia finds us a match in that respect too, the pressure is once more shifted to economic, political and ideological warfare. In these areas we should excel.

Economic warfare is not a clearly circumscribed activity. The first act is to keep our own economy going, to demonstrate to the world that our own system really works, does not suffer too great ups and downs and does not live at the expense of others through exploitation.

We have accomplished this superbly. With only trifling interruptions our economy has grown and continues to support a fast-rising population on the average at increasing levels of real income. There has been an unprecedented stream of gifts to other countries, first to help them overcome the ravages of World War II, later to help them grow and participate in the new possibilities offered by the technological revolution of our age.

These acts are determined by a variety of motives. The desire to help, irrespective of any other reason, has been very strong. Later there appeared the political need not to let Western countries turn to Communism or be swallowed up in the Eastern bloc, because in their weakness they would no longer have had the will to resist incorporation. Here aid of a more specific kind, often coupled with military assistance, became necessary. Then there is the part of the world not so directly involved in the military picture, composed of South America, Africa, India, Southeast Asia and others. These countries are struggling to raise themselves economically. The decision regarding which economic system to adopt is in many cases not yet made. They are watching the economic performance of the Western and the Communistic bloc and will be inclined to accept the system that in their eyes performs better and appears suited to their particular conditions. The choice made will necessarily afterward bring political, cultural and ideological affinity. Consequently, the two antagonistic blocs are increasingly concerned about that large part of the world where new centers of power are bound to form.

Some of these offers of economic aid and military assistance relate to the immediate present, others involve a more distant future. In the latter case, when the United States believes a slow and not very spectacular build-up of economic systems is necessary, sometimes the patience of the underdeveloped countries is taxed. They are then prone to turn to a type of support that is eye-catching though perhaps less effective in the long run. As always, events of the future are discounted in the minds of men when compared with the needs of the day.

The United States' help to the Western European countries has frequently been concerned with the redressing of their balances of payments, with stabilizing their currencies. This was a sound procedure for highly developed nations. But the balance of payments is not something foremost in the mind of the man in the street. He is only indirectly affected by its vicissitudes and he does not understand its workings. Nevertheless it was the right thing to do to remove deficiencies through complicated monetary operations with full confidence that the benefits of an orderly monetary and credit system would finally filter through to everybody. Eventually the people would associate the improvement in economic conditions with American aid. This policy requires confidence on our part in the basic stability of the advanced society we are helping by these means. Such confidence was justified as far as Great Britain, France, Italy, Holland and other Western European Countries are concerned; it also worked well with Japan, the Philippines, and other Asian countries.

It is a different matter, however, to help less developed countries, say Korea, Indochina, Indonesia, Egypt, and Libya. There it is necessary to convince the common man that help is being rendered by using demonstrable methods. The construction of a dam or an irrigation system may be less important for the country than a basic reform of the agricultural administration. But the latter is an abstract procedure whose benefits and disadvantages are scattered over time and among many people. It is not a plastic act, cheering up the people, inspiring them to emulate the free enterprise system. The conspicuous Assuan dam, on the other hand, will speak eloquently to the uneducated fellah of help given by Russia, though it may only have been of partial advantage, or even the least important thing to do. But there it is: a monument of a "friendly" government's assistance.

We have not used this technique to our advantage. Where we have built conspicuous installations, they were military, such as the air bases in Morocco which are now lost to us after hundreds of millions of dollars have been sunk in them. These bases associate us once more with "the bomb," contribute nothing permanent to the well-being of that country, and are useless for us at any rate because of political change. Our assistance program has not explored the psychological impact of our operations. Consequently, we have not obtained the benefits that we could have. There is still time to proceed differently, because the need for our foreign economic operations is not diminished. On the contrary, the sharp increase of Russian economic assistance and infiltration places a new emphasis on this area of our conflict with the Communistic world.

There is a strange parallel with the strictly military position: For too long a time we were hypnotized by the Air Force's desire to have us produce bigger and bigger bombs, i.e., of larger and larger megaton yield. We neglected inexcusably the possibilities of making small-yield weapons on which our flexibility largely depends. In the meantime Russia developed a high ability to wage limited war which we could not match. This produced the Korean debacle, a war which we fought under the most unfavorable conditions.

Similarly, we make large grants to existing, often tottering, unpopular governments instead of contributing individual, specific installations and benefits directly visible and lasting before the eyes of the citizens even after the government has fallen. Such acts need not be costly. This is one of the reasons why Russia, with her much more limited economic ability, has chosen them. We can counter easily and effectively if only we put our mind to the problem. This is one area where we can do much better and vastly more than Russia. But the imagination is lacking, the drive, the intimate knowledge of the countries in question—or at least that knowledge does not get through to those who have the final power of making selections and deciding on programs. By stepping up this type of visible economic assistance we can not only accomplish economic aid but also impose a strain on Russia she will have difficulty in meeting.

Here we therefore come upon another aspect of economic warfare: Not only is it a question of gaining the political and possibly military support of other parts of the world, but also it becomes a question of how to impede the hostile use of the economic power of the enemy. We have given little thought to this problem, perhaps because we do not like to wage this type of warfare, perhaps because we see in economic activity essentially a means of peaceful intercourse among nations, benefiting all.

This sentiment is nice and laudable. Yet we do manufacture hydrogen bombs and missiles and so forth because Russia does. So why should there be compunction about economic warfare of the more technical kind which impedes the expansion of Russia's power abroad or even limits her weapons capability at home? Ultimately all boils down to the allocation of effort and resources. These are typically economic decisions of feasibility.

Comparing the United States alone with the Soviet Union the first is at a disadvantage because of the growing dependency on imports of vital raw materials such as oil, copper, manganese, zinc, etc. Where those materials cannot be substituted for by domestic production or synthetics made from plentiful though inferior resources, we are vulnerable. Our dependency on the free world increases steadily either in the quantities of materials already imported or because new ones appear on the list. Russia, on the other hand, is so large, and still so little developed relative to her immense resources that she can shut herself off from the rest of the world and still grow at almost any rate she chooses. Her development and her arms production will, of course, be speeded up the more freely she can import machines, machine tools, raw materials that are difficult to

mine (for example, industrial diamonds), and can pay for them
in the conventional way by goods she has in plenty (furs, tim-
ber, manganese, gold, etc.). But this exchange of materials will
only govern speed and ease of growth, not touch on survival at
an existing level of welfare.

If we consider the Western world as a whole and not the
United States alone, the situation is not only comparable to that
of the Soviet Union, but better. But there is a political problem
of whether the Western world will continue to coöperate and to
accept the leadership of the United States. Russia does not have
that problem.

Increasingly the access of the West to resources is being
challenged, partly because of Russian political interference taking the form of "economic" intervention in underdeveloped areas.
The Western aim must therefore be to keep Russian influence
away and to secure the underdeveloped areas, to prevent them
from becoming Communist outposts. This is generally well
understood, but the methods by which we proceed are sometimes little suited to the exigencies of the individual case.

There is one point worth particular consideration: Apart
from the moral horror that stops us from starting a war of aggression—or even prevention, should it be possible—it is the
loss we would suffer that deters us. We have much to lose—
not only people, but cities, treasures, wealth. What would remain would be pulled down to low levels, and our present
standard of living would not be reached again by the survivors
for generations, if ever. *Unquestionably our wealth is a deterrent for ourselves.* A poor country, if in possession of the necessary destructive power and the capability to deliver it, is less
deterred to use it. It may even have the illusion that, like a robber, it could gain from an attack on a rich country. But quite
apart from this, the expected loss will govern behavior, the loss
surely incurred from retaliation by the opponent. The loss can
be made greater either by more effective retaliation or by the
increase in the value of what is bound to be destroyed. Should
an enemy country think little of losing millions of its people, its

cities, its treasure, an increase in that valuation would immediately increase our own retaliatory power without any change on our side having taken place. We can do exactly nothing to influence the way the Russian government values the lives of her people. But what about her wealth?

There are unmistakable signs that the Russian people are craving a higher standard of living. They respond quickly to any improvement offered. The stronger the people press for more and more consumers' goods, better housing, transportation, motorcars and all the other material amenities of life, the greater are the losses they would suffer in war. Not that the individual Russian is warlike. He may be this as little as is his American counterpart. But the individual Russian has very little influence upon government; nevertheless, there exists a rudimentary process of policy determination, based to a certain extent on public opinion, and the Russian government itself may come to judge the price of attack higher when the country is rich than when it is poor. Granted, this will be a slow process. But it is one that can do no harm.

So we come to the conclusion that the increase in economic well-being of the masses in Russia, a better supply of consumers' goods of their free choice, especially of durable ones, can only be to our advantage. Perhaps methods can be found to strengthen the awakening movement in Russia which demands greater consideration in this respect. The desire for the enjoyment of life and the pursuit of happiness is unquestionably strong among the common men in Russia. It can only work in our favor.

Note that this is not the standard argument that a greater production of consumers' goods would decrease Russia's ability to make weapons. I assume nothing of this sort. It is unnecessary since we started at any rate from the assumption of nuclear parity and know that Russia is strong in limited-war capability. Rather I think that the valuation of their own possessions would go up and that this would necessarily work to everyone's advantage. The danger to the world comes from the have-nots who are in the grips of a strong ideology and who can lay their hands on powerful weapons, perhaps given to them. It does not rest with those who are satiated.

Long-Run Prospects

Suppose that, happily, there is no thermonuclear exchange over the next twenty to thirty years. What are this country's prospects?

A war would certainly destroy our way of life, perhaps destroy us altogether. Does peace mean nothing else but a bright future, ever-climbing national incomes, growth, happiness? Does it mean safety?

Only a fool would predict the future. But there are now trends and tendencies whose reversal would require almost miracles.

Within sixty years world population will double—a horrible prospect. Even if birth control is widely introduced the future number will not fall much below that figure. The positions of both the United States and the Soviet Union relative to world population, particularly that of China, will be much lower than they are now. All countries will make greater claims on the world's resources. Our dependency on others will increase, unless we gain independence through scientific progress allowing us to find and exploit domestically available resources.

Already now the difference in wealth between rich and poor countries is widening at a truly alarming rate. It will continue to grow. If that were a domestic phenomenon relating to income classes, we would know that this condition could not last. It never has. We would witness mass revolutions. There is no reason to expect that such conditions can endure among nations, especially now, when the high information flow brings a fair picture of living conditions in the rich countries to the poor ones. As long as the rich hold on to their devastatingly powerful weapons the poor cannot move. But if the rich countries fight each other (but not so much as to extinguish also the poor bystanders) the poor countries will remain in poverty for an indefinite future, possibly to rise in a more distant time and form new centers of civilization quite different from ours. Even if they do not fight each other, they will experience unimaginable trouble from the great masses of the poor. And if the rich countries promote the welfare of the poor ones, they may be reducing the basis for their own wealth unless new resources are discovered at a much greater rate than now. Or basic scientific discoveries have to be made to enable the world to support the great masses of humanity and eventually to stabilize population growth.

Nations now hostile to each other may well discover that they do have common ground to stand on. As yet there are not many signs of moves in that direction.

9 The Security Process:
Information, Intelligence and
Secrecy

What Facts Are Given?

At all levels of decision making, facts have to be known. If they are lacking, efforts must be made to obtain them. Often they are very expensive. Sometimes these efforts fail. Then assumptions must be made. If possible, facts should be quantitative; they should be precise, reliable. They should be available in time for study and evaluation. There should not be more facts than the decision maker can handle. He should not be swamped by irrelevant details. And he should understand the facts he gets.

The world is vastly more complex than ever before and there are therefore infinitely more facts than ever before. No one could wish to know them all even if they were available, which, of course, they never are. But usually we want to know more than we actually do. Often it is difficult to state what it is we want to know or to know more about. Frequently it is impossible to do so before the sequence of events has occurred.

From the facts we know we draw inferences. Some are about other facts not known to us, others are for the purpose of making decisions. Many of these inferences will be faulty. How easy (and dull) it would be to live in this world if there were no such mistakes! How naïve the widespread belief among those who clamor for more defense information that the people would necessarily draw the right conclusions from an enlarged body of published fact!

Just consider how much has been published about the effects of nuclear weapons, about fall-out, Russian strength, our defective educational system, our backwardness in missiles, the preposterous delays in nuclear propulsion for aircraft, and so on. But have the "right" conclusions been drawn? By the people? By the Joint Chiefs of Staff, who draw one conclusion when speaking jointly, others when speaking separately? By Congress? What are the right conclusions?

The American public is better informed than that of any other country in the world, or at least that tiny fraction that reads the *New York Times* and the *Congressional Record* and wades through thousands of pages of testimony before Congressional committees. Correctly speaking, therefore, more news and evidence are available here to those who *seek* it than anywhere else in the world. In particular there is a tremendous outpouring of defense information originating from the services, industry and Congress. There is nothing remotely like it in Russia. If it were really vital for the country as a whole to possess this information, as is often explicitly asserted, and certainly tacitly implied by its disseminators, we should be much better off than we are compared with Russia, where that information is lacking to the general public. So either it is not vital for the public at large to get all the defense information made available, or they do not care for it, or they do not draw the proper conclusions. If they did, there would be an insistence on measures that would definitely improve our military and political position.

Behind the vast masses of published material there exists a

tremendous body of secret information. It is certainly enormous, considering that every few years tens of thousands of documents are declassified, for example by the Atomic Energy Commission. But there still are literally miles and miles of filing cabinets holding secret papers.

For the public this information does not exist unless it is betrayed or simply duplicates what the public knows anyway, or at least can know, if it follows the legitimately published reports and news items relating to defense matters. About a possible betrayal there will be more to say: it cannot affect very much quantitatively, but might concern important matters. It has often been stated—and simply horrid examples have been given—that very often perfectly well-known facts of common life or science have been classified as "secret" (quite recently, for example, the dates of the greatest proximity of earth and moon, which were probably known to the ancient Babylonians).

In general there is no telling how such things happen; how could the rules governing military and atomic secrets produce such errors? But considering merely the masses of paper stamped "confidential," "secret" and "top secret," one must wonder whether so voluminous a body of knowledge outside our common knowledge can possibly exist. This is virtually impossible. The presumption is, therefore, that much of the secret material is not worth being called "secret" but contains well-known data, trivialities, or at least is totally antiquated.[1] This conclusion, far from irrelevant, merely points up the wasted expense of handling and securing classified documents.

A bad secrecy policy affects the progress of our defense measures and concerns the safety of the country. There has to be secrecy of all sorts. The problem is how much and where,

---

[1] For example, a careful, objective and strictly historical study of the Pearl Harbor attack and its antecedents is not being released for publication. Its author belongs to a government-supported institution and the manuscript is thus in the clutches of an interminable, capricious clearance process.

how long it should last, and who should have access to the various kinds of secret matter.

The total information about defense matters consists of a public and a secret part. The public discussion can use only the public part and does not know how much it is neglecting by not knowing the other part. The presumption is warranted, however, that there is not much difference between the two as far as the basic, overall conditions of our defense situation are concerned. Indeed, there should be a much greater difference. But here is our dilemma.

The Dilemma of Public Information

In a democratic country, where money is appropriated in a highly specific manner for government purposes by the duly elected Congress or Parliament, the people want to know where their money is going and Congress wants to know as much as possible about the needs for and purposes of the monies they are to vote. The people could show confidence in Congress without insisting that full detail about all appropriations be made public. Congress itself could appropriate without knowing all details, as, for example, is the case with some funds voted for the Atomic Energy Commission and with all funds going to the Central Intelligence Agency, where even the total is not published. But when it comes to the whole defense budget such a procedure is clearly incompatible with a democratic process. Even Russia publishes a defense budget of sorts, although it is known that large chunks of weapons expenditure and practically all monies spent for atomic purposes are hidden in a variety of innocuous other accounts.

The people also want to be reassured that we have modern weapons in quantity, are keeping up with the latest technology, and are at least as advanced as the enemy. Therefore, they have to be given evidence—through publicity, shows, parades, which are intended to inspire confidence.

Often, however, there is a struggle: to introduce new arms,

to remove obsolete weapons and discard outmoded ideas—all a never-ending process. To get action on these it is often good to go before the general public; but this may require the disclosure of a great deal of technical information which should better be kept under cover. Yet without public pressure, built up from a modicum of understanding, action to reform the services, to equip them with new weapons, to organize new services, may not be taken, to the detriment of the country.

The information the public wants and, more rarely, needs, is also information given to the enemy. There it does not stay with the public but goes straight to the experts among the military, the technicians and industrialists. So what is given out is given to the enemy. Does that make much difference?

There are only two possibilities regarding the value of information flowing to an opponent or enemy. The situation is again strictly identical with that in games of strategy: In chess the entire information is on the board before each player. Both are completely informed; there is nothing a spy for one side could do to ingratiate himself with the other side. In poker the situation is different: each player knows only his own cards and would like to know those of the others as well as their plans. Any information he could conceivably get about them would be valuable. A spy would therefore be able to command a price for such information.

It is often stated that a politico-military conflict of the type here considered is "a giant chess game." This statement is quite misleading. It misses the crucial point that this giant game is far more complicated than chess by virtue of the different conditions pertaining to the state of information of the antagonists about each other. Our game of life and death corresponds better to a poker game than to anything else. As in poker, there is present a strong element of bluffing, which is the attempt to spread wrong information, from time to time intermixed with true information. This is intended to make it difficult for the opponent to distinguish true from false and thereby to improve one's own position. Although the Russians are presented to us as excellent chess players—which they are —they excel far more in the military-political poker game in which we are involved with them. We, on the other hand, behave almost invariably with extraordinary naïveté.

Since it is a poker game, not a chess game we are playing, it follows that we have a great and positive interest in keeping information to ourselves. It is always more difficult to *obtain* information; it is easier not to pass it on. This is a fundamental matter and should be of greatest concern to us. It is necessary to think very hard and to take a cold view of the situation which is beclouded by a great deal of confused argumentation.

The dilemma in regard to making information public is this: If we give out freely much military and technological information we are helping the enemy. He can form a more accurate picture of our present capabilities and our plans for the future (e.g., from contracts awarded to industry). This is of great value to him. But some people argue that we also benefit from this general dissemination of such news: our industries are stimulated to produce better weapons and devices, to produce them more cheaply, to initiate research on their own, etc. Our society is so complex that no one can foresee what value a particular piece of defense information, spread via the ordinary media of communication, may have for an ingenious mind in industry or science. It may be very great. The connection between the communicated piece of information and a new factor introduced as a result of it may be rather remote and tenuous. But without the stimulus coming from some news release the new idea or proposal might never have come about.

Such a development is uncertain. It can only be shown after the event and then it is of a doubtful character. I know of not one striking case that could be mentioned. Although the defense information released to the public may or may not prove to be of benefit to us the value of this information to the enemy is *certainly* great, no matter what it is, as long as he can sift the true from the false. This statement applies to peace and war unequivocally. In judging whether a particular piece of information should be released an estimate has to be made as to whether it is of greater value to our own effort or to the opponent, the enemy.

This estimate is not easy to make. It may not be possible to make a convincing case one way or the other in most concrete instances. But the effort ought to be made, and procedures and techniques could be worked out which would improve our lack of knowledge in this field.

Instead of proceeding in an orderly, rational manner we have a chaotic situation from which the enemy can benefit in a manner unheard of in history. There never has been a country which has by neglect of vital principles worked so much for the benefits of an implacable enemy. It is nothing short of grotesque for a country to possess espionage laws under which occasionally an agent or spy is convicted when at the same time the government of the country and the military services hand out on a silver platter information thousands of times more valuable than any network of spies could uncover.

Russian Information Policy

Russia has always been secretive, even under the old czarist regime. This is an old story and I shall waste no words on it.

Today, as in the days of Stalin, Russia plays her cards close to the chest. She knows the value of information and is not willing to distribute it gratis. Her military services do not hand out even a tiny fraction of the military information that ours so gladly part with, always urged on and on by special information officers, frequently on leave from the advertising agencies of Madison Avenue.

Russia has the same problem we have, namely, to show their own people that there exist power and progress, that the government does everything possible to secure the defense of the country and that the military are well equipped and organized. They solve the dilemma by occasional parades through the streets of Moscow, which are then shown on films all over the country. It is then that the Soviet citizens briefly see the latest weapons rolling by and get a quick glimpse of supersonic planes swishing overhead. These carefully arranged shows are about the only occasions when foreigners can observe the new devices for a brief moment.

There is no publicity hunger as in the United States. Certainly, Russians also are vain, craving for recognition (to wit: the many medals!), but publicity is dangerous for political reasons and because of the deadly form of rivalry under the Communistic system.

Russia does not tell us anything unless it is by virtue of a careful design. There is always a purpose behind the disclosure of information: to impress, to threaten, or to persuade a potential friend. Indeed, even when military action occurred in which Russian forces were involved, not even then were their latest weapons or devices—or even their best troops—used. The Russo-Finnish war is a classic case. It produced among the neutral Swedes as well as in Hitler's mind the idea that the Nazi Army could cut through Russia "as a knife through butter." This was the result of planned, costly deception. This was bluffing on a grand scale and in the classic manner. It paid off.

A very recent example of a different kind is this: At the Geneva Atoms for Peace Conference of 1958 the United States made a fine showing of its peaceful achievements in the nuclear field. But then the Russians revealed, in the form of a movie, a 100,000 kilowatt nuclear power plant, far bigger than any the United States has in operation. It came as a complete surprise. The world was told only at a moment selected by Russia for maximum impact.

We may have an exaggerated conception of Russian power. Or we may underestimate it. At any rate from the *published* accounts little can be concluded, far less than one can conclude about our own abilities on the basis of the information we provide freely all over the landscape.

Could a Russian private citizen sit down and write a book corresponding to this one, strictly on the basis of published, freely accessible material, giving the same kind and amount of information about his country as this does about ours? Even if he could write it, could it be published? The answers are obvious.

To sum up. Russia places a high value on military, defense and industrial information and therefore does not part with it unless a definite purpose is served. On the other hand she utilizes freely and extensively all that is publicly available from this country. The gap between the two states of information is enormous and to our detriment.

The Great Information Giveaway

The stream of news about our national defense is broad and swift-moving. An unending sequence of bulletins and news releases keeps the newspapers happy. We hand out practically everything: the precise number of planes ordered, with details about types, the places of their construction, the makers and the types of engines used. We release news about virtually every defense contract signed, or even better, we tell before they are signed who gets the letters of intent. We mention each ship when keel is laid, we show photos of the public ceremonies when it is launched. We keep "secret" planes in places where they can be inspected and photographed at leisure from outside the restricted enclosures. Missiles labeled "top secret" are virtually dissected for the public before they are launched in tests. All bases of the Strategic Air Command are known; future missile bases are widely advertised, sometimes with statements of the number of units they will contain. So, for example, the Air Force in May 1958 announced (!) that the 5th Missile Base for the Titan Missile would be placed twenty miles from Denver, near an already existing Air Force Base. (Incidentally, how clever to concentrate all, so as to make a more important and more convenient target!) Or, on November 21, 1958, the *New York Times* published on its front page a photograph of an Air Defense Base under construction on Long Island—another release by the Air Force. The article states the number of Bomarc Missiles made by Boeing that will be placed there; that they will have nuclear warheads; that the nuclear components will be stored on the site, etc.—all supplemented by a map, showing also the vicinity of other Air Force installations. It is even shown that the control building will be so-and-so-many feet (given to four digits!) away from the firing site. This information should make it that much easier for the Russians to "zero in" on the crucial part of the establishment. Has Russia ever published anything even remotely similar about a single one of their own installations? Would our military commanders welcome such information?

One West coast missile manufacturer even advertises in the newspapers precisely how many missiles of all types he has produced (the advertisement costs perhaps charged to a government contract?). The Navy and Air Force repeatedly report on the precise amounts invested in the new superfuels, on the progress the new factories make, where they are located and when they start production. We tell precisely which factories make what progress in solid fuels. The moment a new radar is introduced a press release appears. And so it goes on and on.

When a new discovery is made which does not necessarily have an immediate military application, we should be careful to look beyond the obvious. We should ask ourselves whether a release of the discovery is warranted or whether it might have implications for military use in the future. A clear case—one may even say of obvious implications—was the invention of the transistor. This wonderful instrument replaces bulky electronic tubes, uses small fractions of the electric power the latter need, requires no warm-up period, and has made possible a formerly undreamed of miniaturization of devices so far using electronic tubes. When the transistor was discovered in 1948 we promptly informed the whole world. Suppose we had kept it for ourselves for two or three years? We could have taken a great step forward compared to Russia, which by virtue of our disclosure was immediately placed by us in the same position in which we were ourselves. Sputnik might not have been possible in 1957 nor the highly developed guidance systems for Russian missiles. Two or three years can be crucial in the present circumstances and American industry would not have lost anything. Was it really so important for pocket radios with transistors to appear on the market when they did, instead of a few years later? What would we have lost? Not the development of the transistor. There would only have been a different diffusion of the new device in industry. It would first have gone to the military for the benefit of national defense rather than to broadcasting controlled by advertising agencies.

There seem to be no national secrets. There is only this insatiable craving to tell "all about it," all the time, as soon as possible, to everybody. But who is "everybody" and why should he know?

There is first of all Russia. I am sure that this reckless throwing away of information of the highest value is counted by the Russians as one of the wonders of the world. They must find it harder to explain than, say, the origin of life. They can see in it only another sign of the decay of the capitalistic Western world.

There are others who benefit: the companies who produce the weapons and devices; the speculators who are looking for quick profits on the stock market; the people who produce, process and print the mountains of paper containing the information. All is, of course, completely legitimate under the information system. It is the latter which is rotten. It produces a complicity with the Russian interests among all parties concerned, although to those parties the publication of technical information will hardly appear in this light; when the truth is realized, however, it may prove embarrassing if they think farther than their pocketbooks.

It is argued that the liberal spreading of information is helpful to the defense process itself. It arouses interest, brings new minds into the picture, stimulates competition, speeds up everything, leads to the invention of new weapons and devices. These are nothing but assertions. There is no proof. There is a counterindication, a hard fact discussed in the previous chapter:

lead time in the United States is longer than in the Soviet Union and Russian military equipment is not inferior; sometimes in crucial instances it is superior to ours.

It is also stated that the democratic way of life requires government in full view of the people, that they have a right to know all about our defense, that thereby they are able to make the right decisions, which have their ultimate roots in the people. This is another slogan behind which almost anything can be defended. There is, again, no proof that the amount and kind of information here under discussion is really needed. There has been a particular body of information, that one about the effects of nuclear weapons, also previously mentioned (p. 55) which has had no impact whatsoever precisely where it should have made itself felt. I am, of course, referring to civil defense. The people were told the basic facts, but they have shut their eyes to them, and if they have drawn any conclusions they were either wrong or defeatist.

Democracy can very well flourish without the Department of Defense announcing every single major contract for new weapons, giving detailed information about the placement of missile bases and so on.

One of the most fallacious arguments that constantly recurs but gains nothing from repetition is this: There is no point in withholding information from Russia "since she would get it at any rate." That may very well be true, but the point is that Russia would get this information often much later than she does now, and this time delay can be of great value, especially when the race is so close. If information is not passed on freely this does not mean that all of it should be classified, i.e., kept secret. It merely means that we make it harder for the enemy to find out facts he can find out about. He has to make an effort where now he needs to make none. He has to sift, to evaluate, to distinguish true from false. He has to maintain a larger network of agents in this country with the likelihood of easier detection, of defection and the certainty of greater cost to him. In short, we would behave more rationally.

Perhaps the outstanding example of the American belief that the people must immediately be told as much as possible is the famous Smyth Report of 1945. This brilliantly written document is perhaps the most organized premature disclosure ever made by this country. It gave in great detail a picture of the Manhattan Project, which produced the first atomic bombs. It described the techniques of uranium diffusion, the production methods; it gave a clear idea of difficulties encountered and showed how they were ingeniously overcome. Photographs were attached giving a good idea of the dimensions of the plants. It did not tell how the bomb was constructed, but it gave practically all relevant information up to that point.

Here again we gave away information of tremendous value to the Russians, who were then already concerned with their own plans. One can easily imagine what the disclosures of the Smyth Report must have meant to the Russians. If we had been less communicative the Russians would have had great trouble finding out what we told them. Yet the news of the first Russian atomic explosion in 1949 came as a shock. Why?

Where Russia does not get invaluable news handed out gratis, she can easily secure other information at little cost by the purchase of prototypes of machines, devices, latest developments, etc. This is precisely what Japan did before the last war. It is well known how much the art of copying was developed in that country and how much Japan benefited. We know that many Russian products are near copies of ours. The United States is not the only sinner. A few years ago England sold one hundred jet engines to Russia, for no particular reason. Russian jet planes could not have been developed as rapidly had it not been for this unique gift. What a difference between having to develop an entire new industry from scratch and being given a large sample of the final product with which to experiment freely!

Let anyone who defends our present policy of distributing technological and defense information freely and indiscriminately answer the following question:

In what instances has the Western world, the United States in particular, freely received information and prototypes from Russia such that we know precisely the nature of their defense products and the size of their programs? In which cases have our own efforts profited from such information?

There are, of course, no such cases. We give, but receive nothing.

I have no illusion that there will be a profound change. The interests working for continuing, even broadening, the present policy are powerful. Some are ideologically motivated; others have a piously hidden pecuniary basis.

If there is no change in our policy the lopsidedness of the information flow will continue since there is not the slightest chance that Russia will become as communicative as we are. The United States, and with it the whole Western world, will stay at a permanent disadvantage. This disadvantage must never be forgotten in any appraisal of the basic conditions under which our defense efforts take place.

"We Have . . ."

So far we have been concerned only with the spreading of *correct* information which the people allegedly need. But there is also a great deal of misinformation being handed out. It is the result of miscomprehension, enthusiasm, vivid imagination rather than an attempt at willfully misleading the public or the enemy. Its sources are governmental as well as journalistic and political. When the government is involved there is always a suspicion of wanting to paint a comforting picture.

Much of this misinformation is in the form of false conclusions drawn from possibly correct facts. One of the worst forms is statements to the effect that "we have" a certain weapon, device or installation when at best a few of them exist, and only vastly larger numbers would have any operational meaning. Take, for example, the President's announcement in 1958 of a nuclear charge fired from a bazooka-type weapon. "We have" this thing. But do we? Is it already produced in numbers large enough so that our forces are right now equipped, trained and can be deployed in strength in an emergency, especially of the limited-war type? Nothing of this sort is the case. Therefore we do not "have" this highly desirable weapon. It has merely been shown to be feasible, and before the condition is reached when we can talk about this weapon in an operationally meaningful way a fearfully long time will elapse. So what is accomplished by this announcement? The people are lulled into a feeling of security, into believing that if our troops had to go to battle tomorrow they would have at their disposal the most modern small nuclear weapon this country has been able to design. Instead their equipment would not differ much, perhaps in most cases not at all, from the equipment used in the last world war.

What is described above is not a singular instance. "We have" (always) numerous weapons and devices in that state of development. That is natural. As old ones go out of use, new ones enter gradually. But this process of birth is constantly being misrepresented. From conception to birth takes some time, as we well know, and the baby is not born a full-fledged man! When we are in possession of a few individual nuclear-powered submarines we do not "have" a nuclear submarine *force*, since only about ⅓ are ever at station. That amounts now to about 1 or 2 submarines and what "force" does that represent? Yet this is the way we hear government officials talk about the "fact" that we do have the nuclear-powered craft and the Russians do not have it (are we sure?). But they do *de facto* have some 500 conventional submarines and we do *de facto* have fewer than one third of these! One wonders whether this is a deliberate misleading of the common people, who cannot always have all pertinent facts before their eyes and cannot know operational practices and limitations, or whether it is an equally regrettable sign of the sloppiness of our thinking.

In this manner there is a perpetual *Schönmalerei,* a constant painting in bright colors and pleasant hues. What is said may not always be downright false but it is misleading, overoptimistic, wishful thinking. This kind of behavior should be radically eliminated when we are discussing national defense.

Intelligence

Since we get nothing gratis from Russia we have to try to get the information by concerted effort. The Central Intelligence Agency is the principal form this effort takes. It is shrouded in deep secrecy. This is as it should be, at least for part of its activity. But by far the largest share of its work is the analysis of news and facts from publicly available sources, the putting together of a great jigsaw puzzle that never remains quite the same. This work could be done openly and could come under public scrutiny. It requires many people well versed in thousands of different branches of human knowledge, familiar with foreign countries, languages, sciences. Therefore the staff of the Central Intelligence Agency is large and its budget would be impressive if it were known.

Then there is the work of secret agents, performing the kind of services the public is more likely to think of when the Central Intelligence Agency is mentioned. Nothing can be and nothing should ever be said in public about this part of the Agency's work. If there is one point in the government's operations where complete secrecy is needed it is here. There must be confidence in the ability of the persons directing this work. How well they do it will be seen from the results: If important events in the making are reported to the President, the National Security Council and other vitally concerned offices before they become publicly known and if this occurs frequently then we may assume that we are well served. If the Agency misses frequently in that regard it may either be objectively impossible to get the information or the Agency is at fault.

No one on the outside can judge with confidence. Even those on the inside will find it exceedingly difficult to set criteria to measure or even estimate performance. It is the problem of "military worth" once again, many times compounded. Once more: The businessman does not know how easy everything is for him since he has numbers to deal with. There certainly are none here. Even if all were known, the notions of "cost," "investment" and "pay-off" would remain exceedingly vague. The dollars spent are no measure at all. There is no doubt that if methods for scaling, estimation of effort, etc., could be developed great help could be derived from them. One hopes that thinking in this area will be stimulated by the research organizations in the government.

Our intelligence services, however, do need scrutiny and supervision. There must be a challenge to the Central Intelligence Agency other than the necessarily vague, spotty and *ad hoc* demands made by the users. These are primarily the National Security Council, the Department of Defense and the State Department. None of them has a comprehensive view of the Agency. As in basic research, none can know in advance what he should know, where he should look. It is therefore necessary to set up a Congressional committee similar to the Joint Congressional Committee on Atomic Energy. There, too, deep secrets have to be dealt with, but there has never been an indiscretion, let alone a betrayal of secrets, from members of its Subcommittee on Military Applications, where the most sensitive matters are discussed freely. It is justifiable to conclude that a supervisory committee for the Central Intelligence Agency would also work free of trouble. Great care would have to be taken in selecting the membership of this committee and to provide for severe sanctions should indiscretions ever occur.

A grave problem is presented by the question of to whom the information should be distributed. The dilemma is, of course, that a wide distribution might disclose the areas of special interest to the Central Intelligence Agency and thereby endanger secret sources; but if the Central Intelligence Agency reports are held too closely they might as well never have been made at all. The Central Intelligence Agency cannot judge to whom in the defense establishment what pieces of information are of value. This is particularly true of scientific-technological information, which should get the widest possible circulation in government laboratories but does not. It would be easy to devise methods for safeguarding the legitimate interests of the Central Intelligence Agency and yet make better use of the mountains of data assembled. It is almost as great a problem and effort to use and interpret the latter as to gather and organize them. In the scientific field this job cannot be done within the Central Intelligence Agency. The information has to get quickly into the hands of the actively working scientist. He alone can judge its meaning. He alone can select what is "interesting."

Since only the various branches that use information can determine their own needs it follows that demands for information must also originate in part from the outside. The military know, as a rule, the general categories of information they are seeking. But they cannot know what specific information to ask for, such as information about unknown new devices. It is still less easy for the other parts of the government to estimate what information will be of value before they see it. But on the other hand it is virtually impossible for the Central Intelligence Agency internally to determine in what areas the most vital scientific information might lie. The interplay of the agency with the scientific community and the defense laboratories is completely unsatisfactory. What is needed is closer communication between departments and Agency to improve information distribution.

Although it is unquestionably the task of the Central Intelligence Agency "merely" to gather information and to process it properly and not to be otherwise involved in policy making, there is here a fundamental difficulty. Everyone knows that possessing facts exercises a strong influence in decision making. "Letting the facts speak," while allegedly not influencing the decisions of others is a well-established procedure for using influence. If one is fortunate enough to have many facts at one's disposal from which to choose freely, or a quasi-monopoly, the possibility of influencing becomes even stronger. In the area of foreign policy the Central Intelligence Agency thus willy-nilly is a positive factor, in an indirect way, it is true, but in an important one. This policy-making power is even further removed from Congressional control than the State Department, which is another reason why the Congressional committee suggested above would have a function transcending a mere technical control. The possibility always exists that Central Intelligence Agency officials may develop policy ideas of their own and wish to give them expression by putting one fact ahead of another. But even when such a deliberate policy does not exist can there be an "objective" selection from, and condensation of, countless numbers of data, far too many to be considered in their entirety? Is not all fact gathering implicitly evaluation—keeping some, throwing away others? The point is to understand the implications of fact gathering in general so that, in the concrete case, we realize that the Central Intelligence Agency also is a policy-making organ of the government.

Programing for Intelligence

By far the largest part of intelligence work has nothing to do with secret agents, spies, tapped wires, beautiful women, meetings in the dark, etc. It is primarily a task of collecting known facts and making correct inferences from them. This sounds simple; but in reality that is what much of science is for.

Consequently, scientific methods must be brought to bear on our intelligence efforts, new methods must be developed, search for new methods must be instigated. The Central Intelligence Agency—as well as the corresponding agencies of the military services—should therefore be staffed with highly competent scientists capable of developing new procedures continually. The difficulties of attracting first-rate people to intelligence work and keeping them at it are great, mostly because of the familiar conflict between the scientists' need for communication and publication and some requirements of secrecy even in this area. Perhaps new techniques can be found to compensate for the disadvantages of working in secret; obviously much better pay should be offered.

Even in the military services officers engaged in intelligence work are often being discriminated against in their careers; they are looked down upon by line officers and advance less easily. Yet where would the others be in preparation or combat if not for good intelligence reports! It is easy for the services to change this situation. While there unquestionably are many highly capable and devoted persons serving, there is also evidence that the general intellectual level should be much higher. In the past there have been indications that the intellectual capacities of CIA personnel often mattered less than their social status. As long as students, freshly recruited for the Central Intelligence Agency, came from so-called "good families," preferably with Ivy League background, they could compensate for poor academic records. This has become almost a bitter joke at many universities and, coupled with the low salaries paid, has naturally increased the difficulties of bringing first-rate intellects into intelligence work, even temporarily. A scrutiny of Central Intelligence Agency personnel according to their intellectual achievements is clearly indicated and possible; it would in no way endanger the operations.

The inadequacies of some personnel may partly account for the low level of information that prevails throughout the country about Russia and many other parts of the world. Even publicly available information is sometimes omitted or poorly interpreted. Thus there had been unnecessary surprise after surprise: the atomic bomb, the hydrogen bomb, the first satellite, the first nuclear-propelled surface ship, nuclear-propelled aircraft, and there will perhaps be others by the time these lines appear in print. Our entire approach to foreign countries is still unbelievably naïve, in spite of increased travel and exchange of people both ways. But that is a topic about which more will be said in the next chapter.

A good illustration of how publicly available information

from Russia is overlooked is offered by Sputnik. The Director of the Institute of Scientific and Technical Information of the USSR Academy of Sciences has demonstrated to the satisfaction of some American scientists how information about the satellite had been published long before the October 1957 launching. It is in such matters that our own information and intelligence services break down. Either there were no reports made, or they were not understood, or not appreciated. More likely, if made, they were kept top secret. This would not be surprising at all: it has happened frequently in the military services that openly published Russian articles have been translated and classified as secret! The excuse—if that is any— is that not to do so would disclose our interest in the subject matter. As if we should not be interested in *anything* coming out of Russia! Especially when it comes from the military or from the USSR Academy of Sciences!

The many instances where public data were either not used or poorly interpreted or where the general approach to a foreign country is suspect have the following consequence: they make us doubtful whether the analysis of secret data, going on in secret and never challenged by any other part of the government or by independent supervisors, is of the quality to be demanded. The outsider cannot state anything with assurance; he can only raise the question. This is not so in the Department of Defense and in the services: There exist numerous supervisory bodies and committees composed of knowledgeable people who have access to all the information that exists and enters into the decisions. It is only the general public, not having access to secret data, that is in a quandary because it can never know whether the picture it forms of the state national defense omits essentials. *Some* people within the defense organization can know the facts and these people are constantly under scrutiny by others from outside who also know them. Not so with our intelligence establishment.

We do not know, therefore, how advanced scientifically are the methods used by the intelligence services in coping with their difficult tasks, or whether new devices are being developed. There exist techniques, for example, in mathematical economics, which would lend themselves to interpretation of existing data and to the formulation of new questions to be asked of data as yet unknown. These techniques would be important to the intelligence services in programing actively for new information instead of accepting data only as they accrue by themselves or by accident. Other techniques could be thought of and possibly entirely new ideas might occur. These do not happen by themselves. A strongly scientific spirit has to be brought to bear on this work. Perhaps this is already being done. But in the public mind there will always remain a big question mark.

Secrecy for Security

Our vast giveaway of information is coupled with the existence of varying degrees of "classified" data, controlled by strict security regulations. There are at least two major systems in operation at the same time. One is determined and operated by the Department of Defense, the other by the Atomic Energy Commission. The regulations are detailed, painstaking and fill many large volumes. Thousands of security officers watch over the systems and the classified materials. They have a great deal of power and a heavy responsibility. They are conscientious; if they stick to the letter of the law it is for their own protection and often also for that of the persons who have access to classified information. Their authority extends to the *form* and handling of the data and papers; they have no primary function regarding the *content* of secret documents. The decision as to whether a piece of information or equipment is to be classified requires a special authority given to certain individuals or bodies. Likewise "declassification" of a document demands an act by a specially empowered person or group of persons.

There are several stages of classification: confidential, secret, top secret. In addition there are higher degrees, which restrict access even for persons who have been given "clearance." There is, for example, the "need to know"; i.e., a person, even though cleared, will not have access to some information unless someone else establishes that he has a particular reason to learn about the data in question. (More will be said about this device.) The White House requires its own clearances; so does the Central Intelligence Agency; and the Atomic Energy Commission, under law, has its own realm of clearances and regulations. So what the system accomplishes is the partitioning of the whole body of classified information into many smaller or larger parts, with special barriers set up sometimes.[2] Few people have access to everything; some clearances are given to tens of thousands, for example, to industrial workers. But what the latter learn are only small segments of even one single field.

Whether a particular clearance should be granted a given individual requires a search for information about him. It is made by special agents, by the FBI, as the law may provide. This is expensive and time-consuming, but there would be no other way. The material itself requires special handling, safes, guards, records, etc. I know of no estimate of the total costs to government and industry; but it must be staggering. Other than the money costs are the delays the system imposes on communications, the frustrations, the irritations, and the general decrease in efficiency, which is unavoidable. I have already commented above that a prime problem is to determine what should be classified. Now I shall not raise this issue again

[2] It still sometimes happens that papers and memoranda written by persons holding a certain clearance are classified so high that they, the authors, no longer have access to them. A particular incident of 1957 is that of an eminent scientist, a member of the National Academy of Sciences, who worked frequently on a vital problem at a certain base. When he appeared there he was conducted to his room, locked in and allowed to work. Sometimes he appeared in uniform, as reserve officer. Then he did not need to be conducted, but was forbidden to enter his workroom and to see his own papers. The obvious end is the loss of the services of this scientist to the defense program.

but rather ask how the system of classification works and how one can live with it.

Indiscretion and Betrayal

First is the question of how tight the system is, how closely it guards the secrets it administers. This is an exceedingly difficult problem. The information that becomes known to the public from time to time about the obvious penetrations into it by spies is only one measure of how well the system works. More important are other breakdowns, such as indiscretions, deliberate violations by journalists and other writers who come into possession of secret material, by members of Congress, by military men, e.g., for purposes of advancing the interests of one service over those of another. "Secrets" that become known to large numbers of people are exceedingly difficult to guard. Someone will always talk. Men talk because they want to look important, they become careless, they come under the influence of drink, etc. Some may defect; but this is apparently a remote possibility.

Second is the question of the internal efficiency of the system. Granting the need for a security system, is ours the best we can design? Are there any pressing reforms which would improve its functioning and reduce the headaches of all who have to live with it? Is any one studying methods for change and improvement?

I shall comment on both questions together.

The saddest comment to be made is that our security system is not very tight. Secrets are not closely held. An exception is the weapons secrets in the possession of the Atomic Energy Commission and its technical laboratories. It is, however, here where the most notable defection occurred (Fuchs) and where —as a natural consequence of the tightness and the presumptive importance of the secrets—the efforts of spies have been greatest.

The lack of tightness is to some extent due to the tremendous volume of secret material. There are very many points where classified matters touch on matters that are common knowledge. In those cases it is often difficult for a person possessing secret information to distinguish clearly whether a particular item is secret or not. The inside and the outside information is frequently very similar, the secret part being perhaps only a small detail, a novelty, a modification of a well-known device. If, on the other hand, the secret matter concerns a nuclear weapon, a torpedo, poison gas or an infrared search device, the distinction from everyday objects and knowledge is pretty obvious. It is then easier to keep secret things secret and for the men who have to deal with them to hold them distinct in their minds. On the other hand, many of the secret things are supremely curious, interesting, fascinating (sometimes in a morbid sense). This makes for a desire to talk about them; it produces enthusiasm in the act of discovery and in the phase of development. It suffices to refer to the Manhattan Project, which developed the first chain reaction, produced plutonium, the first man-made element, and finally the atomic bomb. There security was tight but excitement was running high. This constituted an element of danger for involuntary disclosure.

Besides the great quantity of secret matter that should remain classified there is much material that is unnecessarily classified. It is nothing short of annoying to see matters of public knowledge classified. The cleared personnel are then always in a quandary: technically they are not to discuss such things in public; perhaps they even have to deny ever having heard of them although it may merely be a matter of education whether they have or not. Always remember the ancient Babylonians already referred to above! Not to mention Galileo or Newton, let alone the latest textbook of physics. A simple use of pencil and paper for making trivial computations often results in the immediate determination of some "secret" matter.

The frequent classification of patently nonsecret material, of outright trivialities and absurdities, has a bad influence on the morale of the persons subjected to security regulations. A spirit of rebellion is produced, a negative attitude is generated toward *all* security regulations and toward the officials administering them. This is undesirable and leads to constant conflicts.

The inclusion of such material in the body secret is often done in order to be on the safe side. "In case of doubt, mark the document secret" seems to be a maxim too frequently adhered to. The fact that this decision produces delays, costs money, prevents valuable criticism, makes unnecessary trouble, is usually of no concern to the person empowered to classify documents. A much stricter limitation of such powers is indicated in order to separate the chaff from the wheat. This will improve control where it is needed and make it more meaningful.

The worst feature of our present system is the occurrence of many indiscretions or outright betrayals of secrets. The offenders go unpunished provided they are placed high enough or are journalists and publicists from whom publicity benefits, so dear to this civilization, can perhaps be derived in the future. Many cases have become known. Others occur but cannot be discussed, because this would indicate that some indiscretions are indeed indiscretions and do cover a vital matter. A disclosure would only give added weight to the fact that a breach of confidence has occurred and heighten the interest. In many instances the Russians would immediately know what has happened and see the importance of an unauthorized disclosure. In such cases the government should take severe steps and prosecute right away, using the full power of the laws. No particular problem is present when the indiscretions are made by government officials since internal disciplinary procedures are available. It is difficult with Congressmen, who cannot easily be touched and who are treated gingerly anyway, especially in view of the appropriation power of Congress. It is particularly dismaying to see disclosures made by high-ranking general officers while what they disclose remains still classified for all others involved in the particular secret. Sometimes there may be an element of strategy involved in such disclosures—then normally referred to as "high" strategy, whatever that may mean. This is a benevolent interpretation which need not correspond to the facts. But it can always be given as an excuse and then becomes irrefutable since the outsider can never know what the true motivation may have been.

A cherished activity of many periodicals devoted to particular services or weapons is as follows: Staffed by knowledgeable people, they gather many small, stray items of information, sense the existence of secret matter, and being in the possession of a great deal of background information, are able to ask such pertinent questions that even denials can become affirmations. Thus they often get hold of, or come exceedingly close to, carefully guarded secrets. This material they then publish, believing it to be their duty to do so. All the while they may be able truthfully to say that they have not seen classified documents and have not engaged in spying. Yet the net effect is precisely this. We can be sure that these periodicals are most carefully scrutinized in Russia. For the price of an annual subscription they have performed services which Russian Intelligence otherwise might have to pay for dearly or never get at all.

It is interesting to note that the same journalists who print secret material insist strongly upon protection of their own secrets: they would rather go to prison than disclose their sources. And businessmen who assert that the economy could not progress far enough and fast enough without the widest possible spread of information are masters in withholding it so long as their own enterprises and pocketbooks are concerned.

The information disclosed by periodicals is *not* the giveaway information discussed above. These are added gifts made to Russia. Since it cannot be proved that the giveaway information really contributes to our defense effort it is even more difficult to see how this country could possibly benefit from such additional disclosures.

Occurrences of this type are hardly ever noticed where the Atomic Energy Commission and its weapons laboratories are concerned. Security is much stricter and a sound tradition for anonymity has been established over the years. But once closely held atomic information about weapons passes, as it must, to the military, secret matter is downgraded, not necessarily because of a downgrading of the classification but because of the looser manner of handling. Also many more people have access to it, and so the seemingly inevitable process is set into motion. Secrets, a few years ago among the most jealously guarded, can now be read in newspapers—without ever having been formally declassified. In most cases it would be physically impossible to trace the course of dissemination back to the sources. But it should be possible to apply higher standards now and in the future.

An illustration is offered by the following: On March 19, 1959 the *New York Times* deemed it necessary to publish on its front page, with big streamer headlines, a report on three nuclear high-altitude explosions of 1958, until then kept strictly secret. These explosions formed part of project "Argus," concerned with a study of the earth's magnetic field and the question of whether the effects of such shots would hinder or advance a possible defense against ballistic missiles. It is not necessary to go into further details to show the extremely important nature of the problems involved. The publication of this information by the newspaper caused a world-wide sensation and produced, as was to be expected, often fantastic interpretations, including one, in particular, that now effective defense against missiles was assured, when, if anything, the contrary has been shown. The *New York Times* argued that it had the "right" and "duty" to publish its account, their contention being, for example, that "several thousand people had been involved" in carrying out the operations and that the Russians "would learn about them anyway" (the old arguments; see above!). The fact is, of course, that the weapons laboratories of the Atomic Energy Commission employ thousands of people, but the secrets are kept. The Russians learn about them only as and if they rediscover, through great efforts of their own, and probably much, much later, what in this case of flagrant violation of the secrets of the nation they were presented with by the first newspaper in the country.

There is no doubt that our security system needs great improvements. It is not difficult to point out what should be done immediately to make it work better. The preceding remarks contain more than one lesson. It is another matter to find a different system that works inherently better and does not produce the degeneracy which every known system has exhibited, here or elsewhere. There is also one particular realm where it is difficult to incorporate secrecy; that is the field of scientific activity.

Scientists and Secrecy

In the long run science is doomed if it is to be pursued in secrecy. The two are incompatible. This is not because of some psychological peculiarity or abnormality of scientists, but is a consequence of the inner structure of science as such. What is known will be forgotten unless it is publicly known and remains knowable. No significant additions to our knowledge will be made unless they are incorporated into the broadest framework of knowledge already in our possession. They will not even occur except by the inspiration coming from the problems known to everyone in a given field.

Secrecy thus interferes with the process of preserving and developing science. At best secrecy is possible in the short run; in the long run all nations working in the same area reach approximately the same state of knowledge, especially in the field of basic research. This is due to the fact that the laws of nature are everywhere the same, talent is randomly distributed among men of all races and existing knowledge or lack of it poses the same problems everywhere. There are differences inasmuch as some experimental work has become so expensive that only large and wealthy nations can investigate certain fields. However, costly experiments are not restricted to the United States. No matter how much they may cost, Russia too can afford to build the same machines and make the same experiments. She may even build better and more costly apparatus or make more expensive experiments. Other, smaller countries can do so by combining their efforts, as they are actually doing.

Secrecy is accomplished by compartmentalization and by keeping people from going freely from one compartment to any other. In science one has to do precisely this all the time. Some of the most important advances have come from crossing over from one science to another until a new one arises from the combination. Here is, therefore, the basic trouble, the fundamental difference.

Besides the classification of data into various categories there has been established—especially for "top secret" matter—an additional criterion: the "need to know." It does not, in general, suffice to possess a top secret clearance in order to see a top secret document; someone has to establish that the person in question actually needs to know the contents of a given document so highly classified.

On the surface this regulation seems reasonable and it is an added precaution. The number of people becoming acquainted with highly sensitive matter is held down. There are many cases where this works out well. Suppose a new torpedo has been invented: there is no need for people to know about its principles, except for those who make and use torpedoes. This becomes a somewhat dubious restriction, however, if the question turns up whether this torpedo is better than, say, a new air-to-water missile. Then a need to know develops that may not have been foreseen. And how should the Air Force man working on his bomb ever find out that there is such a thing as this new torpedo? Or how should the torpedo inventor know that he should compare it with an aerial bomb for which he has no "need to know"? These difficulties are overcome somewhat because committees exist bringing together individuals from different services or branches of one service, and information slowly spreads. But it is an uncertain process, working often with incredible delays, in which chance plays a great role. It works only because many who participate in this system make their own interpretations of the rules governing the "need to know."

Closely connected with this "need to know" is another device sometimes employed: documents are marked off "For Air Force Eyes Only" (or whatever service it might be). This restricts the information to Air Force personnel holding the respective security clearance. Now there may conceivably be affairs happening in one service that it would not be nice to let the others know about—little rivalries, perhaps disciplinary matters, etc. But if such a restriction is ever placed on (classified) information about weapons, test results, scientific data, thus withholding them from other services, this defeats unification of our military effort in a decisive way. Unfortunately such pernicious practices exist. They should be rigorously eliminated, however painful it may be for one service to let the other discover that a particular weapon is a disappointment, that a test has gone against a sacred strategic idea, or that one service may have stumbled on a weapon or device which would really advance another service—a horrible thought.

The "need to know" restriction is sound when applied to strategic plans, target selection, origin of intelligence information and similar areas. But the moment scientific activity is involved, the need to know loses all meaning. It then becomes one of the greatest of all impediments that can be erected against science in the defense program.

First of all, the "need to know" is frequently determined, but certainly administered, by security officers. These men have the unenviable burden of protecting security, of seeing to it that everything runs smoothly, that the secret matter is protected, and the newcomers to the system receive proper training. These duties they perform zealously, and it is due to them that no more damage occurs than actually does—unavoidable damage considering that neither the world in general nor our security system is perfect.

But these men are not scientists. The interests of the two

groups are diametrically opposed to each other. It is hard to make clear to security officers that scientists must not only not be restricted, but rather be encouraged to look at things not their immediate business, to discuss their work freely with others, to learn from scientists outside their own fields about latest ideas, developments, etc. All this free browsing, seemingly pointless, is impossible within the classified area, even for people who hold high clearances. Even scientists within the same service, nay, even within the same laboratory, are often forbidden to talk to each other about their work! Here is a basic trouble and here an immediate reform is necessary and possible without endangering security.

The proposal is, therefore, to create a new category, say a "scientific top secret" clearance, to be given to ranking scientists within the Defense establishment and the Atomic Energy Commission combined. Admission to this clearance should be made reasonably difficult, but in each major laboratory a sufficient number of scientists should hold this new clearance. These men should be given free access to all information in laboratories other than merely their own without having to show cause in each individual instance why they would like to make the contact and what specific aims they are pursuing. The point is precisely that they may have no definite purpose in going to another laboratory except the normal drive and curiosity that motivates any scientific activity. They may be expecting help for their own problems and instead may be giving help on entirely different ones. All this is practically impossible under the present system. The existing scientific committees do not fulfill this function, and the scientific consultants who are sometimes involved with more than one laboratory and more than one service are no substitute for this function.

This freedom of movement and unplanned access would have a most beneficial influence upon the general atmosphere reigning in the scientific community inside and outside of the classified areas. There would be much more feeling of participation. Much unwanted duplication would be eliminated; a great com-

petitive stimulus would be given. As a result, a quickening of
tempo, an intensification of effort would bring nothing but
benefits to national defense. There are other technical means to
strengthen these tendencies. For example, classified journals
could be issued in which a great deal of information could be
recorded and spread. Some might even be distributed to industrial contractors.

One of the main objections scientists have to working within
the defense setup is that they are prevented from publishing.
Often the decision as to what is publishable lies with the military, or more specifically, with security officers, who cannot always be good judges. Hence there are conflicts and there is
dissatisfaction. There always will be: the contradiction between
secrecy and science is too profound for them to be avoided. But
the conflicts can be reduced.

Every effort must be made to bring as many first-rate scientists as possible into the orbit of defense problems. Since the
present security system is one of the reasons why it is difficult to
secure the best talent in the country for any length of time, the
question of how to improve the security system with this particular aim in mind should be constantly before the Congress
and the Defense Department.

The fault is, however, not only with the official regulations.
Many scientists take an unreasonable view in demanding too
much freedom from secrecy. It is true that free communication
among scientists is indispensable for speedy progress of science.
However, besides looking at the interests of science one must
also look at those of defense. The former do not always clearly
outweigh those of the latter. Though it is perhaps the noblest of
man's activities, science is nothing sacred. Its interests can be
overridden on occasion. Furthermore the false conclusion is
made—already once referred to—that every scientific step forward *eo ipso,* automatically, mysteriously, helps *our* defense effort. This is not necessarily so. Because of numerous asymmetries in our relation with Russia a new discovery may benefit
that country more than ours. Or if it does benefit ours, it would

be foolish not to keep it for ourselves, at least until it is rediscovered elsewhere.

Spies

Secrecy, whether in business, politics or war automatically generates spies. In this age of science they can be relied upon as using the most refined techniques imaginable, making themselves more elusive than ever before.

A discussion of secrecy without assigning a proper place to spies is therefore incomplete. But it must remain incomplete. How can one write about spies whom one cannot know or, if one should know, could not mention in a public statement? The role of spying in the information process and for determining optimal strategies, on the other hand, can be determined in a rigorously scientific manner. Appropriate comments were made on pages 60-61 and page 228.

Although we throw mountains of valuable information away, handing it to the Russians, and although the military services obligingly supplement that part by ill-conceived news releases about matters that would better be kept strictly under cover, Russia still has need for spies. As a consequence, there undoubtedly exists a larger network of enemy agents in this country than the man in the street may assume. From time to time strong indications of its effectiveness appear. Or there is mention made in high places about the existence of spies, statements that are not just intended to fan a spy scare.

An illustration is in order: Russia has published a list of United States atomic tests. The United States Atomic Energy Commission has revealed many, but not all, test shots made (Russia, of course, makes no disclosures of comparable detail about her test program). How did the Soviet Union get the complete information? The obvious answer is from monitoring, i.e., from measurements of air pressure, fall-out, seismic shocks, etc. This has promptly been asserted. The inference and the Russian assertion are both wrong: There exists solid, massive physical evidence that no amount of measuring done by Russia within her own country, her satellites or on the open seas could have disclosed all American test shots. Thus it is clear that the evidence was obtained from spies working in the United States, who would find it easy to procure the information.

One further remark is possible and needed: The progress Russia has made in military and scientific affairs to the extent that she endangers the very existence of the United States and the whole Western world, is *not* primarily, let alone exclusively, due to successful spying. There has been some help from spies; no doubt about this. But, considering the magnitude and complexity of the task and of the Russian accomplishment, the services of spies can only have touched isolated points in the whole picture. This is particularly true for the scientific achievements. Spies could never have been of great value had there not been the fertile soil where some particular idea or discovery could be made to bear fruit. There is still too much talk in this country to the effect that spies gave Russia what she has, or that the capture of some German scientists was vital. Nothing can be farther from the truth, and it is high time that we face the facts—that the Russians are capable and powerful enough to do on their own what they have done.

Besides, let us not forget for one moment that our giveaway program relating to military and technological information is unparalleled in history and helps the Russians more than if they were to enlarge their network of agents by a thousand times.

Telling Our Strength: The Stockpile

It was shown above how the mere existence of overwhelming power poses a threat to others. If small nations nevertheless feel safe, it is because they are sometimes not interesting to the superpowers, are perhaps living with them anyway in fruitful symbiosis, or are protected by the interests of other powers. But the fact remains that a display of strength can have a strong element of threat, especially when there is no prior provocation from the other side.

From time to time, however, it has been necessary to make a

show of strength: to remind a would-be aggressor of the risks he would be assuming, especially when there was reason to believe that he underestimated the difficulties he would run into.

Such a move can preserve the peace. It can show in advance the futility of an enemy's undertaking, bringing him to reason without having to destroy him. This may, of course, be a purely temporary effect. He may be stimulated to new efforts in order to overcome the disparity. Then a new situation arises which has to be dealt with separately.

Perhaps one of the most closely guarded secrets in the United States is the "stockpile." By this is meant the composition of our nuclear weapons stockpile, i.e., how much we have of the different kinds, and also how much fissionable material is on hand and is being produced. Anybody who can help it stays away from this information. Under our present policy it is better not to know anything about it at all. Having no information is the best safeguard against giving it away. It is the only completely effective safeguard.

However, anyone can infer the existence of a tremendous stockpile from the known investments made in atomic energy and from the frequent announcements that we could devastate any other country many times over (if unopposed), and that we have tactical atomic weapons (which we would hardly construct unless we were satisfied with the supply of the more important strategic weapons).

But it is one thing for us to make such a deduction on the basis of rather vaguely known facts, all of them secondary at best. It is another for Russia to arrive at a firm conclusion that this is indeed the case. We might be bluffing. We might even fool ourselves. We might have fallen in the trap of speaking about "we have," when we possess actually, physically and properly deployed, only tiny fractions of what we should possess in order to give us the power we claim to have.

Potential aggressors have an inherent tendency to underestimate the risks they are likely to run into. This has been shown time and again in history. Though they were ultimately destroyed, they caused great suffering and wasted man's talents, treasure and time. Had Napoleon and Hitler known more about the ultimate strength of their opponents they might never have undertaken their ventures or they might have waited until they had gathered more strength, could they have done so.

We must remove this danger from the present scene. One way of contributing to this end is to show our stockpile to some highly placed Russians, preferably to members of the Presidium of the Communist Party. I assume, of course, that the stockpile of big strategic weapons is really devastatingly large, as we have been led to believe.

There is no value in merely making announcements about our strength. Nor does it make sense to threaten. Nor is it important to pass this information on to anyone except to those who make the ultimate decision—they must see for themselves. This disclosure would be something entirely different from the haphazard passing on of defense information criticized in the previous pages. It would be a deliberate strategic move in our efforts to preserve peace.

To impress firmly upon the minds of the leaders of Russia the conviction that an attack on the United States would be suicidal is one of the chief tasks of the American government. Showing them our strength is one way of achieving this aim.

10 Negotiations and Diplomacy in Nuclear Parity

"We shall have to use all imaginable tricks, maneuvers, bluffs, deceits. We shall hide the truth and use unlawful practices. So long as Capitalism and Socialism exist side by side, there can be no peace. At the end one or the other will triumph and the death song will be intoned either for the Soviet Union or World Capitalism. Until this point has been reached we shall have to use treachery and to maneuver adroitly."—LENIN

Wanted: A Science of Politics

There is no doubt in the mind of anyone living in this country that the United States wishes peace. Probably in the whole Western world few would have doubts to this effect. We are convinced that we would go to great lengths to preserve peace, even when put under pressure and when provoked by actions of our opponents, actions which would formerly have led to war. We have suffered planes shot down over international waters, have seen our ambassadors insulted by street mobs, our flag torn down and burned in the streets. We allow our chief of state and the nation to be addressed in most insulting terms, in words which not so long ago would have produced ultimatums, troop movements and fleet concentrations. This deterioration in the tone of international conversations is concomitant with the brutalization of war which we have observed for the last half century or more. Why war has become so brutal will not be studied here. What is important is that our increased insensitivity to insults and actions originating from the other side is a sign of the awareness of the great danger which countermoves and traditional behavior entail. It shows on the one hand weakness and on the other realization of consequences far worse than the insult and the offense.

A large power can, of course, absorb offenses from a small one without suffering damage thereby. This is not the problem. The crucial fact is that the large powers talk to each other in a manner formerly deemed impossible. Paradoxical as it may sound, this worsening of manners is a device invented by the big powers to lessen the danger of war. Once they resort to this, the small ones follow suit, even when talking to the big ones— the United Arab Republic is a case in point. In the latter instance it is, of course, a true example of bad manners only, not a new behavior conditioned by the fear of thermonuclear war.

This play among the big powers is part of the type of war we are engaged in now. It is dangerous in two directions: First, there is an upper limit of insult and probing we will not let be exceeded; we have not made clear where it is and we may not know it ourselves. In former times these limits were well established and formed part and parcel of the diplomatic tradition. The present new uncertainties introduce both risk and safety. They are akin to bluffing in poker and they are therefore essentially a defensive device. Second, there is the effort by the other side to widen the zone of action ever more. Thus, we are supposed to overlook outright insults, then to accept the shooting down of planes, to tolerate the one-sided abrogation of agreements, etc. All this is gradually accompanied by specific threats, the demonstrations of new weapons, etc., in order to soften up our side so that eventually less and less will matter to us. Perhaps finally we will suffer, so the other side supposes, the loss of Berlin and the Middle East, no matter what we say to the contrary at present.

This observation raises the question of how political principles, techniques of political and diplomatic behavior and the new facts of the nuclear stalemate, with its possible transition into sudden world-wide catastrophe, are related to each other. It is here that the science of politics should come to our help. But what is the state of that science?

First, we shall say nothing about the principles. We in the West are on one side, the Communistic bloc is on the other. Each side has an ideological superstructure of phrases which have different meaning even to people on the same side. The differences in the principles are now singularly vague compared with those of earlier times, when they were often pinpointed to a highly technical phrasing of a particular theological dogma. No one has a precise definition of what "communism," "free enterprise," "socialism" really should mean. Each of these has a different connotation for different people. But broadly speaking, the schism between the two blocs is effectively described in such terms, at least to the satisfaction of the governments who use them in order to cover up the real struggle for power which determines our fate. One cannot seriously expect governments to speak a language that satisfies the demands of logic. So these statements of "principles" have very little operational value. They do become important the more seriously they are taken. We have seen this above, when it was pointed out that the clinging to abstract ideas intensifies conflicts, makes them bloody and bitter, and has a tendency to prolong wars well past the points where even the broadest, most generous interpretation can assign any meaning to them.

The trouble is that it suffices for one side to stick to "high ideals," in order to make life for the other side miserable, if not impossible. This applies even to partners in the same enterprise.

Political scientists have spent much time and effort to produce a body of knowledge that is singularly unsuited to guide us in the present dilemma of our life—a body of knowledge that is a peculiar mixture of constitutional law, history and description of political institutions of all kinds, everything generously sprinkled by strong opinions and value judgments. Some maxims of behavior occur occasionally, for example, those formulated by Machiavelli. They may or may not be "good" or "respectable"; at any rate they were an attempt to formulate rules by which men can seek the attainment of their aims in political situations.

Political science does not offer a systematic body of such rules applicable to the present circumstances; it is not, as one says, "operational." Of the social sciences only economics has so far achieved a modicum of operational value. This is due to the fact that an applicable, practical economic theory has been developed to some extent. We know, for example, how to make or stop inflations, how to tax without destroying the taxed source of income and many other things. We do not yet know how to stabilize employment, how to compare tax burdens placed on different persons and how to perform other important tasks. Political science may help us to set up a workable constitution but not to know whether it will be applicable to a given country. It certainly contributes little, if anything, it would seem, to resolving the problems the world faces now, the most important of which is how to live with the thermonuclear stalemate, how to get stability and safety for all participants in the most fearful struggle the human race has ever been involved in. And it tells us nothing of how to cope with the growing unbalance in the world due to the increase in population and in the widening gap between poor and rich countries.

What negotiations are possible with the Communistic bloc involve bargaining of the most delicate and difficult nature. As on the military side of the picture, one is here also concerned with the problem of decision making under uncertainty, where the uncertainty is not of the simple, well-understood kind to be dealt with by probability theory, but is of the highly complex nature arising from the strategic moves of the opponent, who labors under the same difficulty. This is precisely where political science should make its most significant contributions. Nothing is offered, except the mathematical techniques associated with the theory of games of strategy, but to this theory political scientists, with a few exceptions, have paid virtually no attention. So far political science has not even abstracted the counsels given by Machiavelli in order to discover whether a consistent system of rules of behavior could be constructed on that basis.

So in the present dealings with the Communistic world, instead of receiving firm guidance from scientific techniques and explorations, one has to fall back on common sense and experience. But this is no common-sense situation and no one has experience with the type and extent of danger that a false move entails!

It is little wonder, then, that our greatest weakness is probably not in the military or economic sphere but in the political realm. We have not scored high, we hardly ever have the initiative, we seldom know what we want or whether what we sometimes want makes sense to ourselves and the world.

The responsibility of formulating and executing foreign policy lies with the Department of State. Short of a surprise attack on this country, the greatest danger to which it is exposed is that the State Department's actions either will precipitate war or unwillingly push us into gradual surrender. Naturally the Department's aims are quite different, but how effectively are they being pursued?

Brass Hats and Striped Pants

All measures, all thinking, every decision ultimately goes back to some people's minds. The military have carefully worked out procedures to select the leaders they entrust with their major decisions. Special schools and academies take the young officer higher and higher. Difficult examinations are required and stern selection boards must be satisfied before nomination to general officer rank is secured. The probability for a young officer ever to reach that rank is, indeed, very slim. The number of men from whom to select is impressively large. If the methods are sound, the results should be gratifying, and it should be hard to imagine that others than those actually chosen might be more qualified to become the country's top military leaders and experts.

Yet the "brass hats" are scorned, looked down upon, put under direction of civilians who seldom possess even a small modicum of the technical competence that the generals and admirals have acquired. We hear it stated, jokingly, that "war is too serious a matter to leave to the generals," a phrase that incidentally did not originate in this country but in France, which attests to the universality of this lack of estimation. There are doubts raised as to whether military officers are even normally intelligent; they are accused of the wildest excesses of red-tape stupidities and are held intellectually responsible when the fate of battle turns against them.

This is perplexing. There is a grain of truth in all the criticism: Army red tape during the war was exasperating; but so is the red tape of the big corporations even in peacetime. Not only do military men sometimes lose engagements with the enemy, but also businessmen go broke on occasion. The average intelligence of men in any walk of life is perhaps not impressive, though it is not clear what such statements mean. So all these criticisms either are trivial or otherwise miss the point. There is much to criticize. Everything could be better, if we only knew how to make it better. As to the civilian direction of the military, there is only one sound reason for it: military operations must fit into political plans and schemes. By themselves they would be meaningless. There is always something to be accomplished that reaches beyond the battlefield: submission of the enemy's government, a change of his political aims and ideas, limitation of his political-ideological goals. The military operations are only tools to accomplish this. In that sense Clemenceau's statement can be admitted. But it is senseless to interpret it as necessarily pointing up a deficiency in military minds or thinking. The military are technicians serving a higher purpose

—that is all. As a rule, they understand this relationship perfectly well.

Military matters have become so complex and so involved that the ordinary experience and training of the generals and admirals are no longer sufficient to master the problems. Hence they turn to the scientists to invent, develop, interpret new devices and, indeed, to suggest methods of their employment and even strategies. The different services have numerous advisory committees of scientists, special boards are appointed from time to time, numerous working conferences are arranged and mixed civilian-military summer study groups often work for months to produce documents which shape Air Force or Navy programs. The services have chief scientists who work in closest contact with the top command. The Joint Chiefs of Staff through their Weapons Systems Evaluation Group, the Air Force through the Rand Corporation, the Navy through its Operations Evaluation Group and the Office of Naval Research, and the Army through the Operations Research Office try to learn about the intricate and fearfully difficult matter that comes before them in constantly changing form. The interplay between the sciences and the military is not what it should be—that was discussed in Chapter 7. But it exists, is powerful, and we obviously could not live without it.

The initiative to seek contact with science and the scientists comes normally from the military men themselves. In a long association in which I had ample opportunity to watch them, I have found those maligned "brass hats" ever eager to listen to scientists, even to laymen, if only there was some chance that they might have something to contribute. More often than not their attitude is: "Here is a big problem. Can you help us?" And this is *not* restricted to the making of new bombs, better fuel, a new guidance system or what have you. It often comprises *tactical and strategic use* of the things on hand and the things only planned. In other words, these are the specific "military" matters which one might think would be jealously guarded as their own, sacred domain.

A word should be added about the devotion leading military men bring to their office. They work hard—harder than most executives in business, and just as many kill themselves giving their best in these times of "peace" as businessmen do in pursuit of money.

What about the State Department in respect to its attitude toward its tasks? How are the "striped-pants boys" doing compared with the "brass hats"?

The State Department operates far more as a closed club or shop, compared with the Defense Department, although secrecy weighs more heavily upon the latter. This is partly due to the way the individuals who are in charge are running affairs at the moment, but it is also built into the structure of the office. Furthermore, this is in the tradition of diplomacy, which has always loved secrecy, double talk, deceit and expression of lofty ideals as parts of the trade. Sociologically there has always been a peculiar selection of members of the diplomatic service. Formerly in Europe, it was a domain of aristocracy; later only money was necessary. In this country the important embassies fell to the rich of the party in power. This is true to a certain extent even now, though a new but pitifully small group of more expert and truly qualified men has begun to appear. Yet family connections, school ties and similar important qualifications are still observed. The consequences are well known: a genteel and conformist but unsuitable group sets the tone for the larger numbers of employees who only gradually succeed by making up in competence what they lack in those other more "significant" characteristics. It still happens that many of our ambassadors and hosts of their subordinates are unable to converse freely in a single foreign language, and are innocent of knowledge of the history, politics and customs of the countries they are sent to. There are others who can match any expert student in any of these fields. But they are a small minority.

The true problem lies elsewhere: What is the proper training of the diplomats on whom so very much depends? It should, of course, be in political science, which is so sadly lacking in operational value. It should include extensive language instruction as a matter of course. Diplomats should become well acquainted with science and its impact on society, with economics and history and their role in understanding interrelations among the needs of different countries. Most important, they should have a thorough acquaintance with the military problems of the country and with the weapons systems which control our lives by virtue of their mere existence in our hands as well as those of others.[1]

A comparison between military officers and the members of the Foreign Service is difficult. But one must seriously doubt that the latter would come off as well. There are far too few specialists among them while the military have many. If there exist some, they are seldom employed to best advantage. If one were to comb the State Department for men in somewhat important positions who have a reasonably good acquaintance with modern science, with mathematics, logic, the techniques of decision making, programing, game theory, probability theory, one would find few indeed. They would have no influence. There is no trace of a record that the State Department is interested in these new developments. Indeed, too often humanists, lawyers and others pride themselves on their lack of knowledge of mathematics and the sciences, while at the same time demanding that an educated man be familiar with their often unintelligible scholarship relating to the "true, living" arts. There is, therefore, no understanding of the fact that mathematics, logic and perhaps the natural sciences can contribute significantly to the problems the State Department faces.

The State Department's attitude is in that respect quite different from that of the military services. There exist no diplomatic academies, no summer study groups are organized, no

---

[1] For a good discussion see: Zara S. Steiner, *The State Department and the Foreign Service*—The Wriston Report Four Years Later, Center of International Studies, Princeton University, 1958. This study, however, says little about science and almost nothing about the relations to the military and the need for acquaintance with weapons and weapons effects.

scientific advisory boards are created and constantly consulted, no effort is made to promote basic research on how to preserve peace, for example, by means of an "Office of State Department Research," no sufficient liaison exists (except on paper) with the Defense Department or the Atomic Energy Commission.

Foreign Service officers are trained in the traditional manner only and normally receive little formal education after their Bachelor's degree. A few study at the National War College or visit the Rand Corporation. The Foreign Service Institute makes a valiant effort to bring senior officers in touch with some university scholars. In quantity and intensity this cannot approach the similar efforts made by the military. The Office of Intelligence Research in the State Department is mostly concerned with current matters and does not deal with the fundamentals of political decision making, bargaining and arbitration. It is here where the theory of games of strategy enters; but so far efforts to apply it to international politics have all been made elsewhere, in universities and other institutions of learning. When will the State Department recognize the new possibilities and start spending at least one percent of its impressive budget for basic research in its own field?

The Department always seems to know all the answers and to have them instantly ready for the press. Answers to the world's problems come quickly to those who have prejudices, but we need answers that result from deep thinking.

The prevailing idea still seems to be that a reasonably well-educated lawyer is about the most skillful man ever needed in the Department. That—at a time when problems such as the human race has never encountered before are thrown into its lap. It is not surprising that the Department does not know what to do with them; it is profoundly disturbing that it does not seem to recognize what kind of world we live in, that our very existence hangs on a very thin thread indeed.

The arrogant attitude of the know-all is always unbecoming; it is blasphemous in the present situation. The country needs evidence of tough thinking as far as its political actions are concerned. It gets glimpses of such for the defense proper, but the defense effort has to be embedded in an intellectually and technically equivalent framework to be provided by the State Department. By "tough thinking" I do not mean, of course, harsh words used instantaneously in every crisis that occurs, but the hard, grim, persistent, exasperating thinking process involved in working out a difficult scientific problem. Tough thinking is characterized by intellectual effort—as distinguished from the casual (though unquestionably time-consuming) process of committee-group-thinking so customary in the social-political domain.

This applies to two fields essentially: *first* to dealing with the opponent, with the uncommitted and with our friends; and *second,* to generating the ideals we can live by, together with other nations, in the new age that is rushing toward us. It would be ludicrous here to say much about the latter, but one can hardly suppress the question of whether we possess a clear, convincing and comprehensive statement of our ideals, fitted to the conditions and needs of our age. It is a long time since the Declaration of Independence, the Bill of Rights and the Gettysburg Address were produced. What prevents men from coming forth with new, further expressions of the ideas formulated then so forcefully?

Negotiations with the Enemy

A fundamental principle that can be abstracted from the experiences of past wars is this:

Always talk with the enemy.

"Always" is to be taken literally: *even in war.* In fact, the hostilities themselves, the manner and speed with which they are executed, are a way of communicating with the other side. Sometimes it is the only effective way. There need be no narrow definition of negotiation in terms of formal diplomatic notes exchanged—a much wider conversation is always taking place no matter how difficult it may be to keep it going. The moment we are cut off from communication, we are deprived of opportunities to influence, to improve, to change or to stabilize. It is nearsighted to shut off the means of communicating voluntarily, no matter how tempting it sometimes may be to slam the door and be done with it.

Occasionally it is emotionally difficult or morally repulsive to sit down with some types of enemy. Yet emotions must be neglected in this game of survival. As for the moral difficulties we need only to look at history to see how quickly they are overcome, if it is convenient. In politics one sits down with murderers. They only need to be strong enough to get away with murder. Politics is that kind of activity. One also sits down with mass murderers, as if nothing had happened. Later on historians will glorify them anyway and poets will write epics about their "greatness." Alexander the Great, Caesar Augustus, Charlemagne, Cromwell, to name only a few at random, are now highly respected and honored names; one is even a saint. All of them killed wantonly, not only in battle, and were recognized as treacherous mass killers even by the different standards of their times. Will the historians of a hundred years hence perhaps lengthen the above list by such glorious names as those of Hitler and Stalin?

When in 1938 Chamberlain repeatedly met with Hitler, the latter had already committed the mass murders of 1934. There was no doubt about Stalin throughout the time one met at conferences with him and divided the world.

The point is that one negotiates no matter who the others are, either if one is forced to or if one can afford to do so. The only problem is how to make the bargain stick.

Negotiations are out only when one side has absolutely nothing to offer any more, when one of the opponents is utterly and completely finished. Such points arise only rarely in human history. At present the world is certainly not in this position.

No amount of hopelessness should ever stop the effort to negotiate. It does not matter whether negotiations are tedious, boring, frustrating. These reactions are only too natural with men of action; that is why military men make poor—that is, dangerous—negotiators. To negotiate is the task of diplomats. If sometimes a military leader was also a great negotiator, this quality merely attested to his exceptional greatness since he possessed skills rare even in the diplomatico-political field. One cannot reiterate often enough that political decisions are the ultimate decisions. They derive from the goals set by the political leaders; but they will make sense only within the framework of the militarily feasible.

Here is, therefore, a crucial point: How well do our political, and, in particular, our diplomatic, leaders know the technological facts? Are they thoroughly acquainted with weapons, their effects, the war plans, the target selections for all kinds of crises? Why do they talk only in crudest terms about "the" atom, "the" atomic bomb, etc., which makes one suspect that the knowledge of the whole spectrum of nuclear weapons has not been assimilated. Consider the vagueness with which the possible consequences of the possession of nuclear weapons by many countries is discussed. Quite different situations arise, depending on whether the other nations have megaton weapons and delivery capability, or only tactical nuclear weapons of a defensive character, such as Sweden and Switzerland might seek to obtain. It is most important to understand the influence of the possession of these various types of arms upon the probability and stability of coalitions and alliances. But these questions can hardly be approached as long as there are not enough distinctions made and models set up to study the implications for each.

The truth is that a fearful gap exists between the military realities and the technical level at which the political discussions proceed. There is no need for this gap to be as large as it is. As previously noted, *this* problem is simple to solve—which means that little will be done to get rid of it.

The State Department has access to the classified information of the Defense Department about weapons and other items relevant for its work. It knows perhaps less about Atomic Energy weapons design, and hardly will need technical details, although one could quickly think of borderline cases. But it would even make a great difference if the students of international affairs were to acquaint themselves thoroughly at least with the publicly available material. There would then no longer be the superficial talk about "the" bomb, etc. we still find so frequently.

The upshot of this is that neither those who determine policy nor the negotiators involved in its execution can any longer afford to have only a nodding acquaintance with the implications of the new weapons and of those still in the making. Just as the new weapons technology has overthrown standard military doctrine, it should have a formidable influence on political thinking and on the techniques for its execution. As an example, I refer back to the Oceanic System (Chapter 4) and its possible influence upon our system of overseas bases with their political implications for our alliances and the military and economic support we render. No valid political decisions can be made in this respect without that acquaintance with, and appreciation of, the modern military technology which many policy makers are sadly lacking.

Let us never forget the enormous disparity between the intellectual effort that went into the Manhattan Project and the making of the first few atomic bombs on the one hand, and that displayed in the few committee meetings where the use of the bomb was decided. The consequences of that decision were enormous. The minutes of these meetings were never made public; but it is known that Kyoto was suggested as a target until someone fortunately remembered that for the Japanese Kyoto is a kind of holy city like Rome for the Christians! The level of argumentation, education, effort to predict the consequences of the action, and the search for alternatives will not stand comparison with what goes on even in a routine scientific investigation.

Exactly the same and much worse happens now. The consequences may well be disastrous for this country and the world as a whole. This observation holds, obviously, also for the Kremlin, Downing Street and the Quai d'Orsay. Add to this Bonn, Peking and the capitals of the Middle East. Out of this stew a new, safe, stable world is to be born!

Negotiating during Nuclear Hostilities

It is possible that a large-scale thermonuclear exchange may last only a few days and the war may then stop because neither side has any power left to carry on or because there is nothing more to destroy. Both are the grossest prospects imaginable, but they are, unfortunately, not unattainable. The war may last longer, only gradually working itself toward its peak. Or, more likely, after the first violent disaster each side may try to gather strength in order to deliver the final blow. Even such hostilities have to be stopped somehow, and one side may find it advantageous to do so quickly. Can that be done technically? Can the enemy tell us that he is willing to surrender before both sides suffer still further, grievous damage? This is a problem of communication that has never existed before. Formerly there was always time and there was Switzerland, whose good offices were available to everyone. Switzerland, we hope, will survive, but can her services be used?

The bigger the additional damage that either party can inflict on the other, the more important it will become for either side to be able to say: stop! Yet with the modern weapons the speed with which additional damage can be inflicted has increased far in excess of the speed with which negotiations can be initiated, let alone be carried on. It is doubtful that there has been any increase in the latter. In earlier times these two speeds were more evenly matched: greater pressure on the opponent required time-consuming preparations, individual battles lasted days and weeks, time enough for the losing side to communicate. The end of the Japanese war already foreshadowed things to come in a fast nuclear war: The second atomic bomb was dropped on Nagasaki before the first one was "digested" politically by the Japanese and American governments.

A longer time interval would probably have produced the surrender before the second explosion. The American decision to use the second bomb so soon after the first was also an indication of a lack of understanding of the true situation and of the factors involved.

In a future war the problem of communication will be aggravated by factors of a thousand and more. Unless provisions are made before the outbreak of war there will be no chance whatever of stopping the holocaust even if *both* sides should wish to do so. Can there be a more peculiar illustration of the absurdity of our times than this? The United Nations, incidentally, would not offer the desired link, if only for the reason that they are located in New York and their glass palace would not survive. And how could they make preparations outside their normal scheme of activities and locale? Who else would take such steps? Would not that power immediately be suspected of planning a war?

The problem is complicated by another element that often has prolonged hostilities: If a government is overthrown, a new one always has difficulty in being recognized as the true spokesman for its people and in being accepted as capable of making an armistice. In a future war governments may simply disappear in a cloud of hot gas—unless they have time to go to their shelters.

Indeed, the enemy's government should be prevented from reaching their shelters. The proper conduct of a future large-scale war must be to destroy the enemy's government first of all. Since it is the government that makes the war, not the people, the government has to be destroyed physically as quickly and radically as possible. In view of the fact that the world has already sanctioned anew attacks on open cities and contemplates with varying degrees of horror, but nevertheless merely contemplates, the possible killing of millions of innocents, it is only reasonable to demand that the first effort should be made to eliminate the enemy's civilian and military leadership by whatever means, provided they are effective. In World War II the American government would not allow the deliberate killing of Hitler and his gang by assassins, calling it "murder," though it would have brought the war to an early end. There still seems to be some sort of professional, mutual loyalty among heads of government even when locked in deadly struggle. This is a residue from the God-King myths of the Middle Ages which is too costly to preserve. When governments understand that they will be the first killed, that they are no longer sacrosanct, but rather the prime targets, then we may see them pursuing dangerous policies with greater reluctance.

But once the government has disappeared and the futility of further conflict becomes apparent, who is to speak for a nation *and* be recognized by the other sides, or neutrals? Perhaps one should always keep shadow governments for different countries in reserve, safely tucked away for these purposes on some distant islands in the South Pacific Ocean! This is a nice problem for the United Nations to ponder.

Governments may have difficulty finding out that they are already beaten, that the destruction going on is purely, objectively, wasteful in the sense that no amount of effort can produce a favorable military decision, in other words that we have the situation described before. The more destructive a war, the heavier the weapons of the enemy in the sense that their continued use increases the destruction at an increasing rate, the more important it is for the beaten party to recognize this fact and to communicate it. Germany failed to do so in 1944 and even in the first part of 1945, with disastrous results to herself and at great cost for the victors. In any future war this situation will recur many times compounded.

Where are the new thoughts in diplomacy that would help to cope with such fearful developments? The frequent use of the words "nuclear," "atomic," missile," etc., occurring in the writings of authors on international relations is not a sure indication that they have come to grips with the reality behind those terms.

Techniques of the Political War

It was shown above, especially in connection with the discussion of limited war, how the stalemate in strategic capabilities pushes the conflict into the limited-war area and how, if we can hold our own there too, it is shifted still further to the economic and finally to the political area. It is always waged ideologically, but that area is beyond the scope set for present considerations.

Fifth column, subversion, infiltration are some of the techniques of warfare that have been revived in the twentieth century. Their peculiarity in the present struggle is that they are used only by the Communists (they were, of course, a favorite tool of Fascists and Nazis). The West has not used these devices. It has thereby deprived itself of a very powerful instrument. We have not instigated internal dissatisfaction in satellite countries, trying to pry them loose; we did not lift one finger when the great revolt occurred in Eastern Germany in 1953 or when Hungary tried forcefully to throw off the Russian yoke in 1956. The late American Secretary of State had only used big words, already in 1953, telling how we would "liberate" the Baltic States, intimating that this might even be done by force. This talk quickly subsided after having produced a great deal of trouble and even ridicule since nothing was done when the test came without our prompting and unexpectedly. Sometimes we have offered and given money, for example, to Yugoslavia and Poland. How original.

Russia, on the other hand, infiltrates and undermines—wherever possible. Communism, of course, feeds on the dissatisfaction that must exist among some groups in all countries. It uses at least the underdog, perhaps even broad masses, while we support the governing classes, the tax-evading rich, cruel dictatorial regimes, colonial masters. We work through "legal channels" and thereby stimulate about as much interest and appreciation among the people of other countries as a hearing of an antitrust case in an appellate court could generate with the general public in the United States.

We deem it "not cricket" to use more imaginative methods in the international political struggle. We almost always leave the initiative to the opponent, under conditions where having it often gives a substantial advantage. Instead of imposing a burden upon the adversary, we adjust as best we can to the lead he so frequently assumes. Yet it is clear that without a positive program we shall be pushed back more and more. There is mainly a fear for the physical standard of living, at best a defensive philosophy which can hardly inspire us, let alone gain the great masses in the uncommitted countries of the world. This contrasts with the militant, aggressive doctrine of a Communistic world revolution.

The passive nature of our present policy is of the same kind as that exhibited vis-à-vis Hitler until the fateful moment arrived. Up to then the Western powers did not even know what they did *not* want to happen. So Hitler had the initiative and could nibble away. The war was entered without any positive thought, merely in order to "stop" the Nazis. Now we are once more at the same point.

A good illustration of the technical changes in policy making is the transfer of "Polish" submarines to Egypt. Russia would clearly like to operate a fleet in the Mediterranean but cannot without bases. She wishes to destroy the effectiveness of the United States Sixth Fleet, which represents a major part of our deterrent capability. The appearance of "neutral" submarines in Mediterranean waters is an enormous complication for the Sixth Fleet. It is more: it is a threat. Suppose that their number increases to ten, to twenty-five? What is our answer? This is not a strictly military matter. Suppose some of these submarines follow our aircraft carriers, perhaps at the respectful distance of thirty to fifty miles. They have every right to do so. But will we, can we, tolerate this? Shall we protest? Shall we sink them? Shall we withdraw the Sixth Fleet? Shall we exert pressure on Egypt? What kind of pressure? Shall we attempt to dissuade "Poland" from "selling" any more submarines?

These moves and questions can be anticipated, but judging

from other occurrences there is no evidence that we have a positive policy. We do not even know what we should not tolerate. For example, could not countermoves be made, such as stationing an American submarine in the Baltic Sea for each one that appears in the Mediterranean? Or "selling" some to Turkey to be stationed in the Black Sea? There are many countermoves of a positive nature which would demonstrate the existence of flexibility and imagination in our policy techniques that are now not discernible.

Or consider the Caribbean, where similar troubles can arise. Will we not have to look upon that sea as if it were an American lake? Yet when some countries now try to extend the old three-mile limit of their sovereignty to a larger figure, we protest in the unthinking fashion of a lawyer who sees no farther than across the small print of a dusty piece of paper. That three-mile figure was related to the distance that could be reached by coastal artillery, and in the present missile age is about as relevant as how far you can shoot with a bow and arrow.

These are illustrations of a general principle that can be used two ways: It is a well-known device in science to "divide difficulties," i. e., to break a difficult problem into parts which can be solved separately in order to solve the entire problem. Thus the Russians are skillful in making many small issues out of a fundamental one, thereby hoping to gain the whole advantage which we would not let them have undivided.

There are countless other illustrations from the past, and many more can be imagined for the future. The awareness of future circumstances cannot be willed. It must come primarily from the State Department, but its staid, routine operations do not offer much scope. The Policy Planning Board, a small group of higher officials, picked for their intelligence and imagination, leads a shadow existence after originally having produced a few promising ideas. The recent lack of imagination was in part due to the concentration of all effort in the hands of a Secretary of State who consulted only with himself. But apart from this temporal, transitory circumstance there is the deeper reason for the old-fashioned make-up of the Department: its lack of contact with modern thinking and its negativistic relation to the world of the natural and social sciences.

It is reported that the Kremlin has set up a shadow American National Security Council, or Cabinet, in which the American reactions to each intended major Soviet policy move are debated from the American point of view as they might be debated in the real counterpart. This is not necessarily the best method for determining optimal policy but it is at least imaginative and may have given the Kremlin valuable clues. Do we have groups that are aware of the fact that dealing with the politicians of the Middle East is a very different proposition from dealing with those of Okinawa, Iceland or France?

An outstanding development in the policy area is the Russian tactic of suggesting negotiations of one kind and making threats of another kind elsewhere at the same time. So we have come to accept "technical" discussions on halting nuclear tests (during which we unwittingly may have given away valuable information about weapons), and discussions on surprise attacks, when by the very definition of "surprise" not even an enumeration of the different possible surprises can be made. Yet at the same time a near ultimatum is issued threatening us in Berlin, or the possession of functioning intercontinental missiles is used to exert pressure on visiting Senators. The fall-out debate proceeds, while Russia with complete unconcern explodes devices that produce more fall-out than any American test ever did. Has it occurred to us, then, to say that they have been deliberately producing dirty bombs (as they probably have been), i. e., bombs that rely for their effect more on fall-out than on blast? It has not. Instead we engage further in struggling with the genetic significance of minute changes in carbon 14. All very laudable but for the most part completely beside the (political) point.

American responses are usually naïve, traditional, predictable. It is difficult to foresee any change for the better. These are the consequences of the deadly conformism imposed upon our life and thought at the schools, the universities, by the business corporations and through advertising. One cannot demand that people in crucial positions should suddenly become original; but one might at least make provision to let imaginative men come to the fore. This would be a slow and uncertain process and unfortunately there is no time.

Negotiate we must; of this there can be no question. But the techniques are many. "Open covenants, openly arrived at" is one way of imagining it. This is what an average but idealistic professor of political science thought. Hardly any worth-while arrangement has ever been made in this manner. It is against all inherent properties of bargaining and negotiating processes. Secrecy of the proceedings, even secrecy of the very fact of a negotiation, is often unavoidable. Nor is it bad. Publicity commits; secrecy, like the ancient Chinese politeness, allows withdrawal from, and even failure of, conversations without necessarily bad consequences. Diplomats have understood this for millennia. But without confidence in the preservation of secrecy even that form of contact will fail. We do our best to destroy that confidence when former ambassadors and other high officials, after some important mission abroad, immediately break into print—sacrificing to the Great American God of Publicity —telling all about it without fail. Even their wives must rush into print about the peculiar habits of the diplomatic corps with which they came into contact, describing with arrogance due to ignorance the backwardness of dress, housing, food, etc., of the "natives." [2] All this publicity promptly destroys the precarious contacts. The successor has the greatest difficulties in repairing the damage done and will not easily convince the other side that with *him* secrets will be safe, confidences respected. The role of ambassadors has dwindled compared with former times be-

[2] This word is used freely among people in this country, let alone the various administrations such as the Army. But they are not aware of the insulting connotation it usually has. One would think that by now they would have learned of this fact at least from experience, though it should have been learned at school.

cause of modern communications and the travels of foreign ministers; but it is not necessary to destroy through ineptitude their remaining usefulness. Yet what should one expect of ambassadors who were picked for their jobs only because their contributions to the campaign fund reached or exceeded a certain figure?

Secret negotiations are obviously also dangerous. But the danger must not be exaggerated. The people have at any rate only a negligible direct influence upon the conduct of national affairs. As far as war is concerned it is always made by governments and only fought by the people.

Standard Illusions

There is an undercurrent of folklore running through our contacts with foreign countries, whether friendly or not, that has a deep influence upon our actions. When the results are quite different from our expectations we become unsure of ourselves, but usually with the consequence that the false principles upon which we built our actions are reiterated in the vain hope that they may thereby become true and practical.

Here are some of the worst of those beliefs:

(1) We are going to "win," because we are free, have a better, juster cause than the others, have always come out on top, and time will work for us.

(2) To the world we are the handsome, not the "ugly" Americans—to borrow a phrase from a current book. In other words, foreign people and nations like us.

(3) The Russians are dissatisfied with their regime; their political system will break down from within.

(4) A planned economy, such as Russia's, won't work. Our free economy is in every respect superior. Russia could not wage a prolonged war, particularly because her agriculture is so unproductive that food shortages would force her down.

(5) We make up in quality what we lack in quantity. Even though the Communists may have many more soldiers they are no match for ours, man for man. Our soldiers are better trained

and our weapons and machines are better made. Ultimately their greater quality will be decisive.

(6) The Russian satellite states will defect the moment there is some "real trouble" for Russia.

(7) The Russian scientific and technological advance is due only to spies and the capture of German scientists at the end of the last war.

(8) Our intentions are good, moral, peaceful, and if only we restate them often and loud enough they will ultimately be convincing to the world.

(9) We abide by the letter of agreements, cherish the United Nations, and *therefore* our actions are also just and sound. They will eventually be recognized as such by the world.

(10) If only more common people from different lands will come to know each other the nations will arrive at understandings. Therefore the exchange of students, professors, dancers, musicians and comedians will certainly promote peace.

I do not maintain that someone who holds one or the other of these views, in the above or somewhat different form, necessarily holds all of them. Nor do I exclude the possibility that there is a grain of truth in one or the other of these statements. But many of these are held simultaneously—and it is not impossible to do so since there is singularly little contradiction among these ideas. This lack of contradiction is rather noteworthy, considering how difficult it is in general not to get involved in conflicting attitudes regarding the world. The reason is, of course, that most of these beliefs have little to do with reality; they belong to a dream world.

The reader will have no difficulty in seeing the falseness of such views and I shall therefore not refute them one by one. If he accepts the tenor of the arguments so far presented in this book, he will agree that under the present circumstances it is exceedingly dangerous to adhere to such maxims even though some have a modicum of plausibility. This is particularly true if they become lodestars for official pronouncements and determine acts of national policy.

However, I cannot suppress a comment on the last point, because it expresses a very widespread belief. First of all, governments make political decisions, not the traveling students, professors, journalists and comedians. When government officials travel they are rarely the open-minded observers; they are instructed and committed. When they observe matters not fitting the current official line of thought—whatever its substance—they are not encouraged to insist on their different views. Even embassy and consular personnel are not always in a position to comment freely on their observations.

Next, let us consider the above free-lance travelers—not to mention ordinary tourists. Though they are bent on learning as much as possible about the other countries, and their opinions might have a good influence, there simply is not enough time for the slow process of forming opinions and conveying them into the stream of political decision making to become effective. The speed-up in making more dangerous and novel weapons systems, with which these travelers will hardly be acquainted, will have much more influence. Also travel from foreign countries to the United States may not always foster a friendly attitude; it may do the opposite: awaken envy, greed, lust for occupation. The Spaniards offer an example: They were drawn for these reasons to make war on Mexico and the Inca Empire. The gold treasure of our times is the power to produce for the benefit of the victor. We see before our eyes the inexorable, destabilizing influences arising from the ever-widening disparity of wealth among nations and the swiftly increasing awareness of this fact among the poor countries.

One basic difficulty with proclaiming peaceful intentions—which are undoubtedly true and sound convincing to ourselves—is that they are accompanied by acts which only we and our allies will interpret as peaceful. A clear example is offered by the construction of bases for the Strategic Air Command or the creation of missile sites in Europe and Africa. They are to serve for our protection, and since we do not plan to attack but only to deter, and to strengthen the deterrent power of allies, we hope the Russians will agree with us that there is no conflict between our avowed peaceful intentions and subsequent acts.

But Russia, like every other nation acting rationally, would be grossly at fault if she did not take into account our *capabilities* rather than our words. The words remain the same but the capabilities change. It was shown how discontinuous changes, in particular, generate tensions and sometimes produce critical conditions.

It is one thing to build bases and otherwise to strengthen one's power. It is another to produce at the same time a certain kind of verbiage and to expect that the latter will be considered on an equal footing with the former.

Yet there is no escape from words. The improvements in communications have made them cheaper than ever before. But for the direction of policy it is necessary to stick to the facts and be guided by them. Rarely only can words be counted among such facts. If the broad masses believe maxims of the kind listed above, it does not matter very much—though it would be better if they were less naïve. However, if the policy of the country is conducted with many such views guiding it, then we are indeed in great trouble. How can this soft thinking be overcome?

The End of the Struggle

As weapons become more effective, more horrible and all-encompassing, one will find plenty of good reasons why they should *not* be used: that is, against oneself! The case against using them against others appears to everyone unquestionably much weaker. There is an asymmetry here which rests in the very nature of war and its acceptance by men as a means for settling their disputes.

The time is with us when even a moderate edge gained by one side over the other, coupled with a will to exploit it ruthlessly, creates new possibilities of threats, ultimatums, blackmail: open and veiled. Then the hard and horrible question what can or should be given up in order to avoid destruction will be with the weaker side. The automatic reaction to the violation of formerly sharply drawn lines will not take place; the lines will become blurred. A desperate effort will be made to gain a pause for thought. This will be all to the good if it is filled with hard thinking about alternatives and not given to the kind of vague notions which were already being set into circulation, say, during the Berlin crisis of 1959.

The sharp lines will be deliberately destroyed: Russia may find it very much to her advantage to avoid producing clear alternatives; she may make the typical conflict situations quite ambiguous in order to make the reaction more difficult and to avoid our taking a clear stand on what is important, perhaps even vital, for our existence. Signs that this policy is being pursued are already before our eyes.

Consider the case of an ultimatum or blackmailing action by Russia against the West. No Western nation will resort to such a policy, first, because the time when it was profitable has passed, or rather, was allowed to slip by; second, because the shifts in balance are, if anything, going toward the other side since the United States is making a too small, and ineffective, effort to preserve the precarious stalemate.

Threats raise the question of the effectiveness of the deterrence which was discussed in earlier chapters. It is clear that if a threat in the form of an ultimatum is made at all this is in itself an expression of the lack of belief that an immediate countermove by force is to be expected. Threats are compatible with the mutual overall ability of the countries to destroy each other. If the threat is toward a minor position of the other country —minor compared with its survival, and that covers a rather large spectrum of possibilities!—*it is doubtful that all will be risked in order to gain nothing.* Nothing, that is, except the destruction of the enemy at the price of one's own annihilation. Such threats will therefore have a tendency to become effective, unless there exists a specific means by which the threatened party can counter the threatened limited operation in a similarly limited but effective manner. This means that we are back in the situation where limited wars become a possibility. In Chapter 6 we discussed the need for matching the enemy all along the scale where he might exert pressure—down to the economic and ideological spheres.

Assume, therefore, that Russia has a definite advantage in power, either strategic or for limited war, but the latter in a massive way, and that she now threatens the West under such conditions. The threat is directed toward an important position.

What does it mean to give in? We can lose the position in question, say Berlin, and yet survive. We can then lose West Germany, or the Middle East, and then Italy, and still the United States can go on: much reduced in position, influence, respect. We may have to pay higher prices for some raw materials, we may lose our overseas investments, our exports may shrink or, conversely, they may have to be made under very unfavorable conditions. But the economy of this country could at first absorb all this. Gradually there would be less expansion, the population pressure would become most unpleasant, unemployment would begin to appear, eventually political upheavals would ensue, great efforts would be made to come to terms with the enlarged, more powerful Communistic bloc. Such terms would certainly provide for reduction in the military power of the United States, unquestionably an immediate impounding of its nuclear material. From then on the downfall would be rapid.

We try to imagine sometimes, as well as we can, what the thermonuclear destruction would mean. But even writers of fiction have failed to give us a deep impression of the nature and extent of this catastrophe. Perhaps even they cannot truly visualize what it would mean to the survivors to see fifty, eighty, or a hundred million people killed within a few days or hours and tens of millions grievously ill, living without hope in hovels amidst poisonous radioactive debris. But still we have a notion of this kind of catastrophe; we may form the idea strongly enough to find it totally inacceptable ever to include such a disaster in the price we would be willing to pay for rejecting *any* demand made on us. Therefore, in our answer we need the power to impose the same kind of picture upon the enemy so that both will now and forever be deterred from considering the deliberate use of such power and will make every effort to prevent its accidental release. We also hope that means can be found for both gradually to climb down together from this peak of power, instead of raising it still further, as they must, so long as the antagonism continues and the technological progress persists. The antagonism shows no signs of disappearing and the technological progress, if anything, is intensified from year to year. Each new basic discovery in the weapons field nullifies even important moves toward reconciliation and disarmament.

But are we really always deterred? People have died for ideas and ideals for centuries. Some have fought for their physical standard of living. Sometimes whole nations have been wiped out. Why should not we be ready?

This question cannot be answered without considering the alternative of living according to the enemy's wishes and *dictat*.

No one can say reliably what the enemy would impose upon this country if it were to surrender without fighting. But some lines of this dismal picture can be drawn, and dismal it would be, indeed. The destruction of any vestige of military power would be imminent. Nothing would be easier to accomplish in this time when weapons are becoming smaller and more powerful, yet are concentrated in the hands of the few. The government would go over into the hands of Communist trustees; the well-trained, obedient underdog would take over. The inhabitants of our slums would move into the penthouses and those living there now would wind up in labor camps in Alaska and northern Canada. Motorcars would be produced, not for the United States but for Asia. Perhaps 100,000,000 or 200,000,-000 Chinese would be moved to this country, taking over the houses we inhabit now. According to their standards, even when crammed together with us, they would be better off than they are now. Our factories would produce "reparations" for the rest of the world while we would be put on a subsistence level, just good enough to secure the continuing services of the docile new slaves (easily kept docile by the administration of proper amounts of tranquilizers). Or perhaps the new masters would find it better to dismantle the factories and have them shipped to the underdeveloped countries of Asia and Africa in order to speed up their growth, while the remaining population in this country could be organized according to some new "Morgenthau plan" for food production only, the food to be shipped to the hungry billion people in Asia. It would then only be natural to put the inhabitants of the North American continent into "communes" or "komsomols," those mass groupings of people in which individuality and family is destroyed and the human being becomes nothing but a dumb number in a totalitarian state-machine.

There is no doubt that these and other much worse thoughts have gone through the minds of those who hope to bring the United States into the Communistic orbit and to rule the world from Moscow. We cannot shrug this off as implausible, fantastic or insane. Who would have believed, say in 1930, that the things would *ever* be done which Hitler did only ten or twelve years later—the systematic annihilation of millions of innocent men, women and children in factory-type establishments? It would be easy to think of more of this to come. Do not forget that technology steadily marches on and that it can easily be diverted to new forms of enslavement and destruction.

If such be our future should we relent and surrender piecemeal, there must be many who will feel that a point must exist where the price has to be paid to avoid this dismal destruction, no matter what the price.

Surrender does not merely mean that there would be a different government in Washington, that taxes would increase, that the newspapers would be censored and carry fewer, if any, advertisements, that the schools would be reorganized, that there would be no more stock market, perhaps a little more inflation and similar inconveniences, but that, for the rest, life would after all go on somewhat in the same fashion as before.

Nothing could be farther from the truth. Nor is there any chance that the "will of the people" could manifest itself when conditions become too unpleasant. There is no longer any need to occupy a country massively with foreign troops in order to impose a foreign will. The resistance by the European countries is not a counterexample to this statement: They survived against Communistic domination because the formidable power of the United States stood behind them. But if the United States goes, then all goes—in particular, the United States.

We are at present focusing attention on the physical holocaust that a large thermonuclear, atomic war would surely bring to the United States. We recoil from that picture of death and destruction, so unbelievably great. Our mind refuses to tell us that life after this war would be possible, or if possible, worth living. This may very well be so. But what about the other life, following a peaceful surrender with no immediate physical destruction and no immediate death for the masses (only the usual mass executions of present-day leaders and their hangers-on)? Though they will not die outright, the masses of the people will still perish, sinking from their present state of freedom and comfort to the subhuman existence of a mass animal.

Widespread death and destruction are a certainty if a large-scale war is our fate. But it would take a man with great power of illusion to see an acceptable alternative in surrender, and to see surrender in a better light than death.

Neither should happen. Somewhere between these end points lies peace and understanding. That is what we strive for. Imperfectly. Inadequately. But perhaps with some hope.

11 Epilogue

". . . human kind cannot bear very much reality."—T. S. ELIOT

The Conventional End

In books, papers, and speeches, in official statements and government releases dealing with the problem of defense of this country and the Western world one always finds a hopeful ending. No matter how grim the picture may be that has been painted, there is always a comforting note at the end. A little exhortation: "If only we do this and that," everything will be fine. In particular, a little more money spent will do the trick. Or, the traditional reference is made to previous struggles successfully won, to the underlying strength of the country, the fortitude of its people, its advanced technology, all of which should eventually assure a good outcome. Or, time will work in our favor and all will be well.

I see no justification for making such hopeful statements now. If the analysis in the preceding chapters has only a modicum of truth, then this country is at the most difficult point in its long and glorious history. It is approaching a peak of danger the like of which has never been experienced by a great nation.

The facts are still those from which we started and those which were uncovered during the course of the study: mortal peril from an avowed enemy who is constantly getting stronger; no shelters for anyone except for some leaders of government; capability of mutual annihilation; great possibility of surprise attack against our vulnerable deterrent retaliatory force; accidental war.

Why should the world look different at the end of a book than at its beginning? All a book can do is to influence the thinking of the reader. Even if this happens, as the author naturally hopes it will, what a long way from there to action, to the right action! In the meantime the tendencies we observed develop inexorably further.

The most frightening part of the picture is not the danger itself, but the fact that it is so little appreciated. Many a good effort has been made to tell the nation what the true conditions are. Numerous writers have endeavored to probe into the complexities of our defense establishment. No other serious study has had the wide distribution enjoyed by the Rockefeller Report of early 1958. No other event since Pearl Harbor has shaken the nation as much as Sputnik I of October 1957. Yet all these events, reports and studies vanish in short time. Their influence is momentary and disappears. Perhaps it would not matter so much that the masses of the people do not react in a more persistent, determined manner, but it is distressing that too few government leaders, most of them in Congress, give signs of continued hard thinking. This is a severe impediment to the great number of men in the services, the government laboratories and institutes, who are eating their hearts out seeing daily the dangers that threaten the nation and the world.

The Fascination of War

If we ask whether the ideological conflict between Communism and the Western world is a stronger force driving the world toward war than the instabilities due to the scientific-technological progress, the choice seems difficult indeed. Conflicts between ideologies have a habit of wearing thin after a while—even the ideologies themselves. There is hope in this fact. It is entirely conceivable that the contrast between the Communistic and non-Communistic conception of how to organize an economy and consequently a society will be lessened as time goes by, the former tending more toward the market and individual initiative, the latter imposing more and more regulations upon the exercise of free will in existing markets. This would largely be the consequence of the workings of the underlying technology, which forcefully pulls the economies of large countries into a very similar framework, provided they move at approximately the same technological level.

But as long as the conflict exists, one side aggressively striving for world domination, and the other side passively on the defensive, the changes in weapons technology alone exert a driving influence toward war. It is the stronger force by far.

So what pushes the war technology forward? It is not the basic discoveries themselves—they can always be used peacefully. It is rather that if people were motivated by peaceful purposes alone, many basic discoveries would not be made. The most interesting things in science at present are done only if they are related to war and war preparation.

"War is the father of all things" is once more true in a singularly perverted sense: war preparations are necessary in order to justify the deepest human desire for knowledge. Society will not support research and enormously expensive experimentation on other grounds. Society does not accept the desire for knowledge as legitimate unless it is somehow tied to war. Any other utilitarian end pales in comparison—whether it be the healing of the sick, the prevention of disease, the lengthening of life, the making of better mousetraps of all kinds. It is also the phenomenal complexity of modern war which itself has begun to pose scientific problems of the first magnitude—new problems moreover, problems that do not arise in the ordinary humdrum life.

In ancient times it was the adventures of the warrior, his wanderings through foreign lands, which pulled so many toward warfare. Now the same kind of fascination lies in the work the great experimental stations do all over the world—always connected with some potential or actual warlike application. So we get two things at once: we gradually discover more laws of the universe, and we have a spirit of another, though morbid, adventure thrown into the process.

The scientists working in those new, fabulous fields, fervently hope that their new weapons and devices will never be used, knowing too well the consequences. But the risk is taken: the weapons are being invented and eventually pass out of their hands into those of the policy makers, who have not developed comparable new methods to neutralize them, in particular, methods for working together with the enemy, who is subjected to the same influences and the same dangers. Safety will not be achieved by the conventional ideas and methods of disarmament and diplomacy, which are trivial and totally inadequate compared with the new elements of the situation. Fundamentally new ideas are necessary for organizing human society. Alas, they cannot be ordered.

The complex intermingling of war with a fast-developing science poses the greatest danger to humanity, certainly in the short run of the next few decades. If we survive this period, there is hope that the discoveries to be made during this time will truly make large-scale war impossible. We are near this moment even now, but we are not yet there.

War is, of course, not less absurd at this time than it will ever be in the future; but that does not mean that this absurdity is everywhere recognized and therefore becomes effective.

War has to become technologically impossible in order to be stopped.

There has to be absolute technical certainty of immediate self-destruction for those nations who start a war—not only a fair probability, as at present. When that point is reached the principal danger remaining is that maniacs may get control of

nations and that the increasing concentration of the most powerful weapons in the hands of a few people may completely upset
even existing patterns of political decision making.

I repeat: The impossibility of war has to be of a technological character. Moral or religious considerations have failed to
stop wars. Indeed, the greatest cruelties have been committed in
the name of lofty moral or religious ideas. It will take too long
for fresh moral values to develop which would make war impossible. It would take even more time for them to become effective enough to check the new destructive powers.

As it is, the probability of a large thermonuclear war occurring appears to be significantly larger than the probability of
its not occurring.

Will at least these probabilities be reversed?

Appendix:
A Note on the Literature

The literature on defense matters is immense, even if one considers only the problems dealt with in the preceding pages. The following few references may, however, be useful to the reader who wishes to enlarge upon one question or another.

A forthcoming book by Bernard A. Brodie should be mentioned in particular. This well-known author on military affairs will undoubtedly provide us with a thorough and authoritative discussion of the defense problems of the United States and the Western world. Henry A. Kissinger, in his deservedly widely read *Nuclear Weapons and Foreign Policy,* New York, 1957, has for the first time shown explicitly how the new weapons affect policy making in the international field.

The theory of games of strategy, mentioned in a few places, is expounded, at various levels of difficulty, in the following works: J. von Neumann and O. Morgenstern, *Theory of Games and Economic Behavior,* Princeton, 1944 (3rd Ed., 1953); J. McDonald: *Strategy in Poker, Business and War,* New York, 1950; J. D. Williams, *The Compleat Strategyst, Being a Primer on the Theory of Games of Strategy,* New York, 1954; R. Duncan Luce and Howard

Raiffa, *Games and Decisions, Introduction and Critical Survey,* New York, 1957.

The following books and papers, finally, deal with the topics their titles indicate and relate to corresponding sections of the present work:

M. Amrine: *The Great Decision, the Secret History of the Atomic Bomb,* New York, 1959.

A. Baldwin: *The Great Arms Race, A Comparison of the United States and Soviet Power Today,* New York, 1959.

R. Butow: *Japan's Decision to Surrender,* Stanford, 1954.

H. S. Dinerstein: *War and the Soviet Union. Nuclear Weapons and the Revolution in Soviet Military and Political Thinking,* New York, 1959.

K. F. Gantz (Edit.): *The USAF Report on the Ballistic Missile,* New York, 1958.

H. Kahn: "Civil Defense Is Possible," *Fortune,* December 1958.

M. Kaplan: *Some Problems in the Strategic Analysis of International Politics,* Princeton Center of International Studies, 1959.

W. W. Kaufmann (Edit.): *Military Policy and National Security,* Princeton, 1956.

P. Kecskemeti: *Strategic Surrender: The Politics of Victory and Defeat,* Stanford, 1958.

E. Kinkead: *In Every War But One,* New York, 1959.

K. Knorr: *Is the American Defense Effort Enough?,* Princeton Center of International Studies, 1957.

S. Melman (Edit.): *Inspection for Disarmament,* New York, 1958.

O. Morgenstern: *Some Thoughts Bearing on National Defense Policy,* Sandia Corporation Research Colloquium, 1958.

J. von Neumann: "Can We Survive Technology?" *Fortune,* June 1955.

Th. Rosebury: *Peace or Pestilence,* New York, 1949.

M. G. Saunders (Edit.): *The Soviet Navy,* London, 1958.

T. C. Schelling: "The Strategy of Conflict: Prospectus for a Reorientation of Game Theory," *The Journal of Conflict Resolution,* Vol. II., 1959.

A. Wohlstetter: "The Delicate Balance of Terror," *Foreign Affairs,* January 1959.

Index

Abyssinian war, 19
Africa, 83
Aggressor nations, as target, 63
Aircraft carriers, 40, 45
  for nuclear weapons, 84
Alarms, 56-63
Alaska, bases, 103
Aleutian Islands, ICBM bases, 103
Alexander the Great, 272
Annihilation, 106-107, 287
  mutual, 293
Anti-ICBM's, 25, 47
Anti-intellectualism, 183
Anti-submarine warfare, 93-94, 107-108
Anti-tank weapons, 22
Anti-weapons, 22
Assuan dam, 217
"Atlas" missile, 210
Atomic Energy Commission, 88, 170, 226, 227
  information on atomic tests, 257
  information policies, 245
  liaison with State Department, 270

and "scientific top secret" clearance, 255
  security system, 247
  weapons laboratories, 250-251
Attacks, 56-63
  identified and sub-critical, 59-63
  "ultra-", 58-59
  weight, 47-48
Attrition, 104-133 ff.
  and "force in being," 109
  in limited war, 109-110
  strategy, 106-109
Austria, 14, 136

Bacteriological warfare, 15 fn., 25, 80 fn.
Ballistic missiles, 36
  advance delivery, 162
  fleet, 91
  protection, 66
  underwater-fired, 24
  See also Missiles
Bases, early end of fixed, 87-91
  enemy, 59
  fixed, 44

Bases (*continued*)
  "hardening," 45, 46-51, 81
  missile, 67, 232
  movable, 45, 89
  oceanic, 45, 46
  variable, 44, 45
Basic research, costs, 174-177
  determined by Bureau of the
    Budget, 187-190
  weapons development, 171-177
Battleships, 105
Bazooka, nuclear, 149-150, 237
Berlin, 281
  blockade (1948-1949), 136
  crisis (1959), 287
Bogolyubov, Nikolay N., 180
Bombs, large-yield, 50
  small-yield, 147
Book production, 180-181
Budget, military, 202, 207-209
Bureau of the Budget, 187-190

Caesar Augustus, 272
"Calculated risk," 5, 6, 69, 193,
    203-204
Caribbean Sea, 52, 280
Central Intelligence Agency, 227,
    239-241
  personnel, 242-243
Chamberlain, Neville, 272
Charlemagne, 272
Chicago, evacuation, 121
  and megaton weapons, 55
  shelters, 111
China, 18, 75, 83, 96, 202, 214
Cities, deep shelters, 132
  defense, 87
  evacuation, 122
  fall-out shelters, 18
  linear strip, 125
  nuclear attack on American, 108
  nuclear attack on Russian, 67-68
  reliable alarms for, 57
  survival capacities, 54-56
Civil defense, 113, 122
  early warning, 53
  Russian, 114

Civil Defense Administration, 113,
    124
Clemenceau, Georges, 266
Communication, during nuclear
    hostilities, 275-277
  with submerged submarines, 95
Cost-of-living index, 199
Costs, attrition, 17
  basic research, 174-177
  of defense schemes, 81
  of fixed bases, 45
  "real," of attack, 17
  of shelters, 119-121
  of sub-economy, 127
  of weapons systems, 204
Counteraction, 62
Counterattack, 30, 76
Cromwell, Oliver, 272
Cuba, 29
Czechoslovakia, 136, 137

Decision making, 193, 224, 269,
    285
  economic, 198
Defense
  economic aspects, 191-223
  fundamental facts, 9-11
  minimum requirements, 193
  mixed system, 40-44
  objections of taxpayers, 200
  passive, 36, 106
  and percentage of national prod-
    uct, 200-201
  and retaliation, 32-35
  of retaliatory forces, 37-44
  See also Department of De-
    fense
Democracy, survival, 5
Denmark, 99
Department of Defense, 23, 43, 93,
    100, 157, 175
  and Bureau of the Budget, 189,
    204, 208
  information policies, 235, 245
  liaison with State Department,
    270
  1958 reform, 212
  research projects, 177-179

Deterrents, 27-79 ff.
  against expansion of limited war, 145
  direct, 29
  effective, 287
  entire military power as, 28-30
  imperfect, 120
  large weapons, 150-151
  national wealth as, 220
  Russian, 75-76
Dictatorships, and declaration of war, 70-71
Disarmament, 289
Dispersion, of nuclear weapons, 156
  systems of mobile, 91-98, 100-102
D(istant) E(arly) W(arning) line, 46
"Dual capability," of Army and Marine Corps, 155

Early warning, 52-54
Earth satellites, 7
Economic burden, of defense, 198-205
Economic power, American and Russian, 191-223 ff.
  indexes, 196-197
Economic warfare, 215-223
Effects of Atomic Weapons, The, 55
Egypt, submarines transferred to, 100, 279
  United States aid, 217
Einstein, Albert, 172
Eisenhower, Dwight D., 149
Eliot, T. S., 292
Errors, as cause of attack, 56-74
Evacuation, 121-123

Factories, dispersal, 125
"Fail-Safe" system, 71
Fall-out, radioactive, 15, 117, 167, 281
  See also Shelters
Finland, 137

Foreign policy, and need for a science of politics, 261-265
France, loss of United States bases, 99
  as nuclear weapon power, 10
  and Tunisia, 34
  United States aid to, 217
Fulbright, Sen. J. William, 191

Gaither Report (1957), 6
Galileo, 248
Games of strategy, mathematical theory, 61, 164, 192, 228, 265, 269
Gas warfare, 135, 167
Geneva Atoms for Peace Conference (1958), 231
Germany, 139, 277
  Nazi, 14
  recovery after World War II, 123
Goths, 33
Great Britain, current weapon power, 10
  steel production, 195
  United States aid to, 217
Greeks, 14

Hiroshima, 108, 112
Hitler, Adolf, 139, 185 fn., 231, 272, 277, 279, 290
Holland, 217

ICBM's, *see* Intercontinental Ballistic Missiles
Identification, preceding attack, 56
  in relation to vulnerable retaliatory force, 64-68
India, 214
Indochina, 217
Indonesia, 217
Inflation, 194
  and arms production, 199-200
  and unbalanced budget, 201-202
Information, and security, 224-260
  about classified personnel, 246
  giveaway, 232-237
  and interpretation of data, 244

Integrated economy, vulnerability, 212-215
Intelligence, 224-260
and early warning, 53
of enemy's capabilities, 13, 37
programing, 242-245
weapons, 168-172
Intercontinental Ballistic Missiles, American, 24-25, 40, 56, 210
bases, 47, 98
dispersion, 41
fixed land bases, 50
ground protection, 41
launching sites, 86
Russian, 7, 66, 67, 94, 96
See also Anti-ICBM's
Intermediate Range Ballistic Missiles, 40, 56, 92
bases, 98-99
Invulnerable force, 54, 80-103, 132
Italy, 217

Jackson, Sen. Henry M., 91
Japan, 84, 86, 236
United States aid, 217
Joint Chiefs of Staff, 43, 192, 225, 267
Joint Congressional Committee on Atomic Energy, 240

Khrushchev, Nikita, 9
Korea, 73, 135, 146-147
conventional weapons used in, 165
limited war, 218
Russian planes used in, 161
United States aid, 217
Kyoto, 274

Latin America, 83
Lead time, 209, 235
Lenin, Nikolai, 261
Libby, Willard F., 117
"Liberal education," 185
Logistics, 154-155, 215
London, German V$_2$ missiles, 56
Los Angeles, evacuation, 121, 176
Libya, 217

Machiavelli, Niccolò, 265
Manhattan Project, 176, 189, 236, 248, 274
Mathematics, 173, 269
McCarthy, Sen. Joseph, 177, 185 fn.
Meteors, mistaken for missiles, 67-68, 74
Mexico, 29
Middle East, 146
Military decision, 5, 6
Military force, readiness, 16
"Military worth," 203-205
Minneapolis, evacuation, 121
Minute Man installations, 87
Missiles, liquid-fuel, 72
solid-fuel, 64, 72, 90
"top secret," 232
Mobilization, 20, 151
Mongols, 14
"Morgenthau plan," 290
Morocco, 99
United States bases, 218
Mussolini, Benito, 19

Nagasaki, 111, 275
National Defense Research Council, 176
National Security Council, 93, 192, 239
NATO countries, attacks on, 65
bases, 92
early warning, 52 fn.
population, 146
steel production, 195
Navy, mission of, 85-86
"Need to know," 253-255
Negotiations, during nuclear hostilities, 275-277
with enemy, 271-275
Neumann, John von, 173
New York, bombproof shelters, 111
destruction, 130
evacuation, 121
megaton-weapon attack, 33, 55
Newton, Isaac, 7, 173, 248

North Atlantic Treaty Organization, *see* NATO countries
Nuclear parity, factors, 27-28, 61
  negotiations and diplomacy, 261-291
"Nuclear plenty," 28
Nuclear-propelled ships, 89, 90
Nuclear tests, 281
Nuclear weapons, 21, 27, 37, 73, 88, 167
  China, 202
  and declaration of war, 70
  high-precision, 147
  information on effects of, 235
  "miniaturization," 148
  propaganda against, 152-153
  small-yield, 147, 218
  spectrum, 148-154
  stockpile, 258-259
  storage, 47
  superiority, 161

Oceanic System, 80-103, 120, 197
  political consequences, 98-100
Office of Naval Research, 141, 175, 267
  funds, 208

Pearl Harbor, 20, 33, 226 fn.
Peterson, Val, 113
Philadelphia, 117
  shelters, 111
Philippines, 217
Planes, 85
  carrier-based, 85
  in-flight state, 61
  tanker, 78
Poison gas, 135, 167
Polaris project, 24, 91-97, 133, 162, 165
  budget, 208-209
  deployment of forces, 99
Policy Planning Board, 280
Population, expansion, 181, 222, 288
  ignorance of civil-defense precautions, 113-114
  potential protection, 115-117

Power, American and Russian, 191-198
  defensive, 21
  maximum, 60
  ready, 19
  superiority of offensive, 54-56
Probability theory, 269
Procurement, new budgeting procedures, 207
  strategic requirements, 205-209
  techniques, 206
Productivity, 209-212
Provocation, 19-22
  local, 144

Quantum mechanics, 180

Randomization, 88, 90
Reaction, imposed involuntary, 22-23
Reactors, small, 88
Recall, of bombers, 65
Recovery, after attack, 123-125
  by sub-economy, 128-129
Report of the Underseas Warfare Advisory Panel, 92 fn., 208 fn.
Retaliation, 30-32, 130, 220
  in colonial conflicts, 34
  versus counterattack, 33-35
Retaliatory forces, 27-79 ff., 87, 197
  defenses, 37-44
  hardened, 62
  invulnerable, 38-39, 61, 62, 74-77
  mixed, 40-44
  mobile, 88
  vulnerable, 39-40, 44-46, 49, 61, 105
  See also Oceanic System
Rockefeller Report (1958), 6, 293
Romans, 14
Russia
  bases, 51, 91, 279
  current weapon power, 10, 142
  defense, 55, 96, 106, 114
  early warning system, 66

Russia (*continued*)
economy, 144, 195-198, 202, 209-210, 215, 219-220
infiltration by, 278
information policy, 225, 230-232, 234-247, 250, 257
invulnerable retaliatory force, 74-77
"limited war," 28, 142
and nuclear parity, 27-28, 131
political war, techniques of, 278-283
propaganda, against atomic weapons, 153
submarines, 22, 94, 100, 279
science and technology, 161, 176, 180
threat to U. S., 17-23
weapons systems costs, 204
World War II, 107, 123
Russo-Finnish War, 231

Satellites, equipped with nuclear weapons, 101
Saudi Arabia, 99
Scientists, complete freedom for, 172
relation with military and diplomats, 265-271
and secrecy, 252-257
shortage, 170-171
Screening forces, 41
Sea power, new extent, 83-87
Seaplane, 86, 89
nuclear-propelled, 91, 95-97
Secrecy, 224-260
need for, 193
Security, 224-260
classification of data, 245-246
indiscretion and betrayal, 247-252
officers, 254-255
and secrecy, 245-247
Shelter time, 115-119
Shelters, 9, 21, 47, 110-121, 293
against blast, 111-112
construction as provocation, 129-133

costs, 119-121
against fall-out, 112-113, 115, 120, 126, 132, 197
Signal, preceding attack, 56
Smyth Report (1945), 236
Space, as system of mobile dispersal, 100-102
as weapons base, 44
Spain, 99
Spies, 257-258
Sputnik, 180, 186, 233, 244, 293
"Stability," of world situation, 11
Stalemate, 27-28
limited war and, 142-145
nuclear, 215
Stalin, Joseph, 230, 272
"Standard of living," 194
State Department, 43, 100, 141
foreign policy, 265, 280
Office of Intelligence Research, 270
relations with scientists, 268-270
weapons information, 273-274
State Department and the Foreign Service, The, 269 fn.
Steel production, 195
Stockpiling, 123-124
versus sub-economy, 128-129
Storage, active, 125-128
food, 124
fuel and nuclear weapons, 47
Strategic Air Command, 24-25, 29, 40, 61, 63
bases, 86, 94
budget, 202, 208-209
as distinguished from missile force, 64-65
as guard against accidental war, 71
overseas bases, 98-99, 285
and power to declare war, 70
protection of, 46-51, 54-55, 77-79
Strategic force, mobile dispersion, 91-98
Strategy, and technology, 159-190
"high," 250
optimal, 12, 74, 163-164

Strategy (*continued*)
See also Games of strategy, mathematical theory
Sub-economy, 125-128, 197, 215
Submarines, 40, 86
hostile, 93
nuclear, 108
Russian, 100
See also Polaris project
Subversion, 278
Surprise attacks, 38-39, 52, 76-77, 281, 293
Sweden, nuclear weapons, 273
shelters, 115
Switzerland, as communications center, 275
nuclear weapons, 273
technical superiority, 161
Syria, 100

Tanks, 22
Targets, nonmilitary civilian, 60
soft, 48
Technology, and strategy, 159-190
false beliefs about, 160-163
"Terminal guidance," 148
"Thermonuclear exchange," 17, 20, 103, 166
long-run prospects, 222-223
probability of, 296
Thermonuclear war, 9
all-out, 76
Thermonuclear weapons, 134
Threat, cost, 16-19
supreme, 13, 14-16
Torpedoes, 169, 253
range, 40
Transistor, 233-234

Unconditional surrender, 139
Underground installations, see Sub-economy
Union of Soviet Socialist Republics, see Russia
United Nations, 276, 277, 284
United States
civil defense, 55, 113-114, 122

current weapon power, 10, 26, 142
economy, 195-198, 214
versus enemy with invulnerable retaliatory force, 74-77
foreign aid, 216-218
foreign countries, illusions about, 283-286
information policy, 226, 227-230, 232-237
lack of scientists, 180
limited war, 28, 142
United States Sixth Fleet, 279
Universities, and basic research, 179, 187
intellectual leadership, 182-185

Vandals, 33

War, accidental large-scale, 61-74
chemical and biological, 167
duration of, 104-106
end of struggle, 286-291
fascination of, 293-296
limitation of, 134-158, 215
political aims, 140
political, techniques of, 278-286
technological, 159-190
War games, 156-157
Warheads, 36
megaton, 108
Warning time, 64
Washington (D.C.), destroyed, 118
megaton-weapon attack, 33, 55
Weapons, 9-10, 13, 35, 37
basic research, 171-177
concealment of true nature, 68
"conventional," 155-157
defensive, 24-26
dual-purpose, 94
high-yield, 36
and intelligence, 168-172
megaton, 36, 54, 71, 87, 122-123
offensive, 24-26
proper identification, 53
retaliatory, 36-37
small-yield, 36, 147, 218

Weapons (*continued*)
  specialization, 26
  technological change, 163-165
  See also Nuclear weapons
Weapons systems, for limited war,
    145-148
  mixed, 40-42
Wilson, Charles E., 96, 177, 179
World War II, artillery, 154
  destruction of industries, 107
  development   of   antagonism
    since, 10
  events leading to, 144
  as insufficient experience for nu-
    clear war, 57-58

procurement during, 205
recovery after, 123
weapons development since, 10

Yemen, 34
"Yield," 36
  See also Weapons

Zone of Interior, and fringe-war,
    158
  hardening, 81-83, 86
  mobile dispersal, 100-101
  See also Oceanic System; Po-
    laris project

A B O U T   T H E   A U T H O R

A native of Germany, Oskar Morgenstern came to the United States for the second time in 1938 and remained to become a citizen. He now lives in Princeton, New Jersey, where he is Professor of Political Economy on the Class of 1913 Foundation, Princeton University.

Dr. Morgenstern is a member of the advisory panel to the Military Applications Subcommittee of the Congressional Joint Committee on Atomic Energy; a member of the Board of Scientific Advisors to Convair; and a consultant to the Atomic Energy Commission.

He is best known as co-author, with John von Neumann, of *The Theory of Games and Economic Behavior.* Another book, *The Limits of Economics,* was published in London in 1937. He has written numerous articles for technical journals, and is co-editor of the *Naval Research Logistics Quarterly.*